W9-CHI-121

GETTING THE MOST

FOR YOUR

HOME

IN A DOWN

MARKET

GETTING THE MOST
FOR YOUR
HOME
IN A DOWN
MARKET

Dan Lieberman and Paul Hoffman

BOB ADAMS, INC.
PUBLISHERS
Holbrook, Massachusetts

ISBN: 1-55850-035-9

Published by Bob Adams, Inc.
260 Center Street
Holbrook, Massachusetts 02343

Manufactured in the United States of America.

A   B   C   D   E   F   G   H   I   J

This publication is designed to provide accurate and authoritative information with regard to the subject matter covered. It is sold with the understanding that the publisher is not engaged in rendering legal, accounting, or other professional advice. If legal advice or other expert assistance is required, the services of a competent professional person should be sought.
— From a *Declaration of Principles* jointly adopted by a Committee of the American Bar Association and a Committee of Publishers and Associations

Acknowledgments

Special thanks go to Barbara Leicht and Marlene Daniels who reviewed the initial manuscript and offered many useful suggestions. We would also like to acknowledge the many seminars, articles, books, and experiences that have contributed to the creation of this book. Finally, apologies and appreciation go to Miran and CindyLou who had to put up with us during the writing and revision process.

Contents

PART I: What Makes People Buy

PART II: Making Your Home the Best It Can Be

PART IV: The Financial Angles

Introduction

You've read the papers. Prices are flat or falling in your local housing market. You've felt the cut in tax breaks for homeowners, you want to sell your house and move, yet nothing seems to be working. Now, you think, is the time to act, before the housing market gets worse. But you're not sure where to start or what you're doing wrong.

Or you're upbeat about selling your house even though the market is down. You have a great house and live in a nice neighborhood, but you've noticed that other people in great houses in your nice neighborhood have had their houses on sale for months. You (correctly) assume that they are doing many things wrong, and you want to prevent yourself from doing those things when you sell your house. You know that, even in a down market, lots of homes still sell, and at reasonable and sometimes very good prices.

Welcome to the Nineties
Depressed real estate markets have taken hold in many parts of the country. Stiffer competition in the resale housing market has become a way of life for tens of millions of people. Cut throat competition among homebuilders seems to be the order of the day.

Yes, welcome to the nineties. Many newspaper stories and other articles would have you believe that everything can only go down, down, down. Yet even in this time of depressed markets and seller fears, over *one million* new housing units are being started this year alone! Obviously, many people are buying houses.

Many people do fine in down markets. Professionals such as builders, developers, and marketers are constantly devising techniques to help sell their inventories of unsold housing. Others have no problem in markets where homes don't sell because they have targeted the right niche and didn't aim at the mass market. Properly targeted developments sell out within days, even in a slow housing market where most people have been unable to sell their homes for months.

Obviously, even in bad markets there are many ideas, techniques, and strategies a property owner can use to sell his or her home without resorting to fire-sale prices. You know that it isn't all luck and that many people, not just a chosen few, are selling houses successfully even though the newspapers say that everyone is losing. This book is the reference guide and road map that will lead you to getting top dollar for your property in a down market.

Real Estate Is a Cyclical Business

If you're like most Americans, there was a time when you bought into the idea that the value of real estate could go only up, that buying your home was the best and safest investment you could make, and that owning a piece of the planet was a great investment: after all, they aren't making any more of it.

Well, if you lived in Texas, Oklahoma, or Louisiana in the early 1980s or Arizona, New England, or parts of California in the late 1980s and 1990, then you've seen that this is not always the case. By the time you read this book, there will probably be half a dozen other areas on the list, and there will certainly be more in the future before the real estate market gets better.

History shows that housing and real estate move in cycles, although the cycles are not always very obvious. The value of real estate is affected by the amount of money in the economy, how loose or tight banks are being with credit, and whether a home meets the needs and lifestyle expectations of today's buyers.

White-hot markets cool down. Forgotten markets heat up. It's part of a natural cycle of investment.

Business, too, moves in cycles. Bull markets become bear markets, then the bears become bulls. It is important to remember that the business and housing markets, while linked, do not generally cycle together. The need or lack of need for housing often goes against the expectations of those who look only at how the business economy is doing. Housing is a reusable commodity; in fact, the reason you are reading this book is probably that you have a house that you want someone to pay you for so they can reuse it.

Where Most People Make Mistakes

Even in the worst of real estate markets, people are buying homes right now. This is good news, but what is even better news to you is that people are *selling* homes right now, too. The key strategy that professionals use (and that few homeowners think of) is that you have to target your buyers and then market your home directly to those people: to their needs, their wants, and their values. Obviously, builders feel there will be at least one million buyers out there; for you to sell your home, "it takes only one."

It is easy to see where a lot of the current panic comes from. Newspaper headlines that tell of falling markets are self-fulfilling prophesies, as they tend to keep prospects who were on the fence about home buying away and waiting either for the day when prices have finished falling or for the day when they're definitely rising again. The job of a newspaper is to sell newspapers and advertising, and the job of a home seller is to sell his or her home. Don't get the two confused, since these are mutually exclusive goals.

Near the middle of 1990, the newspapers in San Francisco began running headlines warning of a crashing real estate market and telling how desperate sellers were waiting to take any offer. Yet this market was 63% higher than it had been three years earlier and was down less than 2% from the previous year. It is hardly a depression scenario to have your home worth 61% more than it had been worth three years ago.

If you fall for the newspaper's doom and gloom, you will likely sell your house for much less than it is worth. That doesn't hurt the newspaper at all, and it certainly should make your buyer happy (if he or she even noticed it). In fact, the newspaper will then use your house as "yet another example" of how bad the market is. You don't have to do this, of course, since you can be one of the many who are getting good prices for their homes. If the newspapers want to call you an "anomaly," great. You got what you wanted and your buyer is still getting a fair price.

It's not all the newspapers' fault. Many other people in your community who are selling their houses have let fear cause them to act foolishly, or are just plain lazy. You've probably talked to them at parties or at the office. "I don't know the first thing about selling." "A very nice buyer really wanted the house at our price, but he couldn't get a loan so it's back on the market." "I don't like my real estate agent, but I don't know anyone better." These people have heard that they are helpless, so they act helpless. With ten to twenty hours' of work, they each could have sold their houses and gotten good prices.

You don't have be arrogant or pushy to believe that you can sell your house in a down market. (In fact, you don't want to be, because no one wants to buy a house from an arrogant person.) You just have to know how people buy houses, how to make them want your house more than the many other houses available in your area, and how to help them buy your house.

Fighting the Down-Market Mentality

The first thing you need to do is get honest: admit that the drunken orgy of home buying because "prices could only go up" is over. It will certainly come back again, but that might not be for another ten or twenty years, or longer. You are in a down market right now, and that is the prevailing mentality out there. That honesty will naturally lead you to your next move: looking for the best way to sell your house.

Most owners won't admit that times are slower and thus don't adapt their thinking to the tough battle ahead. You are now in a tough fight, one to sell your home to people who feel either that renting is currently better than buying or that if they wait, prices will go down more. Strategy, planning, and knowing how to motivate buyers becomes the key. Keep remembering that there are lots of people out there today selling their houses; as long as you are one of them, you will be happy.

Selling your house starts with having a top product to sell that meets a market need and than getting the word out to the appropriate buyers and intermediaries. It then moves into how to give the buyer what he wants while getting what you want, and than into a successful sale.

Pepsi spends millions of dollars hiring entertainers like Michael Jackson, putting on commercials, and doing promotions to convince you to buy its product. Proctor and Gamble does extensive marketing studies on every nuance of their buyers and on the packaging, display, and quality of their products. When markets get slow, Detroit offers financing incentives, rebates, and specials to get buyers onto the showroom floor.

Yet the typical home seller thinks that by putting a For Sale sign out on the front lawn, he or she will get full price. When that doesn't happen in a few weeks, the seller panics and starts chopping the price.

Notice the difference?

The building profession has become very sophisticated in the last decade. The merchandising of houses has become a field in itself. The techniques used by many developers are designed to get a buyer to the home and to sell it to them. One of the first steps to selling your house is finding a good real estate agent who knows these same techniques. You must also help your agent by knowing the techniques yourself and implementing as many of them as you can.

The main purpose of this book is to change that for you. You are not selling your house as a hobby; you are doing it as a business activity. You are very much a professional at home selling, if only for a short time. Take on the strategies and tricks of other professionals, and you will do much better than those who assume that they are only amateurs.

Above All, Be Creative

Dwell on the positive. Instead of assuming it can't be done, focus on the question of "How can it be done?" Be solution oriented, not problem oriented. You can sell your home, and at a good price. People do it every day. The key is the match between what you have and what a buyer is willing to pay for.

Cultivate a probing mind. Look around you. What seems to be working for other people? What isn't? Talk to brokers, appraisers, builders. Get a feel for what it takes to sell a home for top dollar in a down market. Someone must be doing well. Find that person and ask questions.

Is it going to be easy? Probably not. The fact is, being success-ful and doing better than average means working smarter and harder and doing more than average. That's why you are reading this book. This book is a guide to marketing and selling your home successfully. It's meant to give you an advantage in a down market. Keep in mind that you are competing for buyers in a buyer's market. You have to be better, and you need to know what you are doing.

Is it going to take a long time? Probably not. Unless you are making a million dollars a year at your present job, spending time using the ideas you read in this book is almost guaranteed to be worth it.

Are you skeptical of that statement? Someone who makes $1 million a year earns about $500 an hour. If you spend ten hours intelligently working on selling your house with better market-ing and better advertising, making it more attractive to fence-sit-ting buyers, and helping a motivated buyer close the deal, you can certainly make your house $5,000 more valuable. That might be $5,000 more you can ask for in the selling price because you have made the house more attractive to a buyer—or $5,000 less that you have to lower your price for a quick sale. Ten hours for $5,000 is the same as what someone who earns $1 million a year makes. As you can see, it is certainly worth the effort.

There are people looking to buy a home these days, and homes must be sold. It's not going to be as it was in good times, but many people will still be successful. So, welcome to the 1990s, and to selling your home for a good price.

CHAPTER ONE

Strategies for Selling Your House

Times change. Where there was once a booming housing market with people overbidding every asking price, houses now sit waiting for an offer, any offer. New times require new strategies. Just as throwing a temper tantrum may have worked at age 5, it looks awfully silly at age 45. Trying to sell your home using strategies that were developed in a prosperous up market can be suicidal in a down market. You need to adjust to the reality of the times.

Learning from Others

You should learn the strategies of the successful professionals and then apply them until they are your own. Most of the people selling homes are really just amateurs. We have other jobs and other professions that occupy most of our time. When it comes to selling our biggest asset, we usually hand it over to the local real estate agent or try to sell it ourselves. Many have found that this is not working in a down market and are frustrated.

The quickest way to success is through "modeling." Modeling is observing how successful people work, think, and strategize and then doing the same thing in order to produce the same result without going through all the years of trial and error.

Many people out there will discourage you. They'll tell you it's a horrible market and no homes are selling. But that's not true. People need to buy homes, and homes are selling every day. But it takes some effort and the right plan. Excuses do not produce results. Successful people all around us are selling their homes in a bad market. Become one of them and move on with your life.

Many techniques and strategies have been developed by professional builders and developers in down markets all over the country. Many of these have helped them sell houses that had previously been sitting vacant, even while the competition went under. Many of these ideas are as applicable to the average homeowner as they are to professional builders.

It is these ideas, ideas proven by professionals, that you will find in this book. Of course, there is a difference between you and a professional builder. Large homebuilders take out full-page advertisements to sell their homes; you won't be doing that. What works for big companies may not work for the average homeowner, so this book gives you special strategies that relate specifically to people selling a house that they have lived in as their own.

The people looking at your house will be seeing many other homes when they look at yours. In a down market, a smart buyer will look at over a dozen homes before making a decision; someone who is not in a rush may see fifty. You will become just another one in the crowd unless you take the steps to make your home memorable and desirable.

Taking Control of the Process

You may currently have your home listed with a good real estate agent, but how much does he or she really understand what is going on? How much does he or she care about *your* house out of the many that are listed? Many real estate agents started selling in good markets and have never before seen a bad one. Other agents are great in both types of markets, but how do you know what type you have?

This is *your home* that is for sale. You must become the director. You must understand and take control of the process. Most homeowners are content to list their home with a local real estate agent and then wait for the offers to come in. Then, when things don't work out, they blame the market or the agent. It's time to stop placing blame on exterior circumstances and to take control. Your real estate agent is just that: an agent. If you house is not attractive or has faults that make it hard to sell, your agent can't correct them. But you can.

You don't need to be an expert in sales, architecture, construction, and law to be running the ship. You do need to be able to use your imagination and to realistically evaluate what is going on about you. You want to search for the opportunities that your community and the market give to you and then use them to your fullest advantage. People often get caught up in the little details and miss the big picture. As seller and director of your team, that is your job.

Learning the Rules

The rules in real estate are constantly changing. Along with a market of overpriced homes and underfunded buyers, more and more sellers are waking up to the fact that it takes a lot more than "a nice house" to sell a home. However, most sellers don't know where to look. They try hard. They place an ad in the paper, have a sign in front, hold several open houses, but still no success. And they start getting depressed and frustrated.

Not everyone gets hit equally in a down market. Some people actually are doing quite well in areas where the real estate market has been down for years. Sure, they would love it if homes were constantly being overbid like they were just a few years ago. Builders are constructing model homes that appeal to the buyer emotionally. They are hiring the best salespeople, putting together good financing packages, and using incentives like paying for closing costs or free upgrades.

We are entering a new age, one of image and identity positioning. The average person knows little about selling and marketing a home. For one thing, you've got to know who you're selling to before you can truly say that you are marketing your home effectively. If you have ever tried to give an appropriate gift to someone you've never met, you know it's hard. How much easier and more on the mark it is when the gift is for a close friend, or at least someone you know. You've got to know your buyer in order to package your house.

Selling a home in a down market takes a lot of time and energy. Unpredictable factors such as interest rates or changes in the economy will affect your sale. Builders and developers can't afford just to make a cursory examination of the market and then jump in: they would soon be bankrupt. You need to play this as hard as the professionals.

Taking Action Now

Many people feel that if they ignore what's happening about them it will somehow go away. These are the people who decide that the way to price their home is to calculate what they paid for it and then add $50,000 as a reasonable profit, even if they bought at the peak of the market and the market is now down. Markets change. Today is different from yesterday. Ignoring realities is a lot like procrastinating. It may feel better now than actually doing the work, but in the end it eats away valuable opportunities to do well.

This book is about taking action. It is about the actions you take to sell your home when most people are just sitting around frustrated. You are really interested in producing results, not just acquiring knowledge. Many people read a book and then just put it on the shelf. You need to take an idea and act on it. Disciplined effort eventually reaps rewards.

Realize right now that you are already producing results. However, they are probably not the results you want. You need to change how you act to change the results. Anthony Robbins says that people who have succeeded have followed a consistent path, which he labels the Ultimate Success Formula. It works as follows:

- Know your outcome.

- Take action so that desires don't just become dreams.

- Develop sensory acuity to see what is working and what isn't.

- If something is not working, change your behavior until it works: be flexible.

Effective Marketing

Times change. Usually you can evaluate who is moving into your neighborhood by looking around at who has bought nearby. This can help you determine the values of your ultimate potential buyer. Are young doctors and lawyers moving in and bringing values up, or is the neighborhood going the other way? In the 1960s, many people fled inner-city neighborhoods. Those that didn't notice the trend were left behind with declining property values. In 1973, when Americans were becoming fuel conscious and switching to economy cars, Detroit was still building large, gas-guzzling vehicles. Those cars sat in showrooms for months while the smaller cars sold out. In a slow market, those who aren't noticing the type of buyer looking in their neighborhood will not market accordingly and will be left with their house while others are selling theirs.

When a buyer is looking for a home, location is usually the first consideration. Buyers often make this choice before even looking and thus confine their housing search to areas where they perceive value. This can be either established value such as a "good neighborhood" or as bargain value in an up and coming area. You need to identify your home with the value as perceived in the marketplace.

Some major considerations in characterizing a neighborhood are

- Home values in an area
- The quality of the schools
- The demographics of the location
- Social acceptance of the area by peer groups
- Lifestyle opportunities
- Community activities and services
- Address value in contrast to other areas

If you have a home in a neighborhood that is perceived as desirable, you usually have built-in foot traffic. If you are located in a poor neighborhood, or one that is perceived by the locals as being on "the wrong side of the tracks," your best bet is to look for relocating out-of-towners, or trendsetting locals, rather than traditional natives looking for a new home.

Quality Is a Requirement

To do better than average in a down market requires three things: creativity, flexibility, and a quality product to offer. Even the best marketing in the world won't motivate an intelligent prospect to buy a poor product and be satisfied for long. And with our increasingly litigious society, it pays to make the buyer satisfied.

The first step in beating the market is to be aware. Just by being aware that there are other possibilities outside of the standard way of selling a home, you'll be ahead of 80% of the competition. As you become more aware, you'll become attuned to the many possibilities and ideas to help sell your home more effectively.

Outsmarting the Competition

David slew Goliath, but you have to beat only a bunch of other Davids in order to get what you want: a fair price and a fast sale. The key is simply to work smarter than the competition.

Don't compound the competition's mistakes with your own. If they are getting desperate and slitting their throats, don't immediately jump into that game. Analyze what is happening. Selling your home is a business decision as well as a personal one.

Commit yourself to using your time and money wisely. Rushing to put your house on the market and then waiting for it to get stale is a waste of time. Doing your homework, properly preparing the house, and devising a marketing plan will take little time compared to the many months your home would otherwise have sat on the market.

Most important, you must commit yourself to using all of your resources. Commitment allows us to go much farther than we normally would. Why can people finish marathons when they never ran 26 miles before? Because they've made a commitment to themselves or their friends that they will finish the race. Why does goal setting work? It is the commitment of writing it down and seeing the goals.

Why All This Work?

For many people, the house they own is the biggest investment they have, often larger than their whole retirement fund. Isn't it worth ten or twenty hours to merchandise your home professionally? The average homeowner will work forty hours a week all year for a paycheck of perhaps $35,000, yet these techniques and taking the time to employ them right can easily add $10,000 or more to the value of your home for very few hours expended.

You don't need to be a rocket scientist to figure out the payoffs there.

Donald Trump once said he could always tell a loser—the guy who didn't even bother to clean his car before he sold it. Don't be lazy. This is the time where every hour of effort can yield a maximum return.

Do You Need to Sell Now?

One of the biggest mistakes people make is selling when they don't have to or when it is not an appropriate time. Markets go up and down. Most people buy and sell at the wrong time. When home prices are rising higher and higher, people keep overbidding for the right to pay even more. When they are at the bottom, it seems that no one wants to buy. The professionals do it the other way. They buy when prices are low and sell when they are high. If you can wait it out, you can get a better price.

Even if you are moving, you might consider the possibility of NOT selling. Here are some things to look at before deciding whether to sell:

- Find out if the number of people moving into the area exceeds the capacity of new homes being built. If so, this shows a tightening market, and it is an OK time to sell. Also, things may get even better in the future.

- Determine where you are in the down-market cycle. Why take a bath now when in a few years your market may be recovering again?

- Do you have a large equity and small loan on your home? You could probably rent it out for a good cash flow until the market turns around. In some areas (particularly college towns), a down real estate market can actually be an up rental market.

- Do you feel you've done the most to create a property that will sell for a maximum price? If not, you should spend more to earn more before you sell the house.

Selling in a down market is always tricky. Seriously consider waiting out the down market and selling when things get better.

Selling At Or Above Market

What is market value? It's essentially the price a willing buyer will pay a seller given normal conditions. How do you sell above market? It comes down to economics.

You probably already know something about economics. It's called supply and demand. Within any given market there are many submarkets, or *niches*. Some of these submarkets will pay a premium because, although there is oversupply in the market in general, there is not enough supply in that niche. By target marketing, you can sell at a higher price than you would have to the general market, even when prices around you are dropping.

Some questions to ask yourself as you try to determine what market to target include these:

- Who is the market for my type of house?

- How deep is that market?

- How can I effectively reach that target market audience?

- Who should I work with to help me reach that group?

- What are the motivations of that group?

Just because the average three-bedroom, two-bath home is selling for $245,000 in your area doesn't mean yours has to. By a combination of appeal and marketing factors you should be able to get above average prices for your home.

How this Book Is Organized

This book has, essentially, four parts, which combine to help you create a marketable home and sell it quickly for a good price.

The first part explains what makes people buy, including how to get the word out that you have a desirable home for sale.

The second talks about how to make your home the best it can be. It shows how to find within your home the hidden potential for extra profit. Without a good product, you can't expect to get top dollar, especially in a down market.

The third part deals with the sale itself. You'll find out how to talk with buyers, show the home, and negotiate a deal. Even if you have hired a real estate agent, this section is must reading to understand what is being done right and what may be happening that is undesirable.

The fourth part explains how taxes and financing can impact your sale and be used to make your home more marketable and profitable.

Getting Started

Once you've assimilated the knowledge in this book, you must be honest with yourself in assessing the worth and potential of your home. You will be able to see what its potential is and who your best market will consist of.

One thing to keep in mind is that you are competing with other people for the buyer's attention. You will have the advantage of a system of strategies to help you outmaneuver most of the competition, since only a few other sellers will be taking the steps you are. In a down market, more people may be working to make their house sellable, but you can still easily beat the majority who are sitting back and relying on their real estate agents, half of whom are below average.

Here are six simple items you can do to get started. All are explained further later on:

- Go to open houses in your neighborhood. This will allow you to check out the pluses and minuses of other homes and give you a good sense of the market. It also allows you to observe real estate agents in action and notice what they do well and what they do poorly. You might even find your future agent this way.

- Get your house inspected by a professional inspector now. Your buyer is going to do this sooner or later, so you might as well know what problems there are in your home, whether they're serious, and how they can be downplayed before the buyer finds them out.

- Develop a fact sheet detailing your home's pluses and minuses.

- Figure out in advance how you'll react to getting an offer. You need to know how to deal with the inevitable low offers that come in a down market.

- Look into the tax consequences of selling your home. You don't want to get top dollar and then lose a lot of it to the government. You may find that selling for all cash is not the best way to go.

- Start evaluating your house unbiasedly, or bring in some agents or friends. Explore what you can do to make your home irresistible to a buyer.

Keep in mind that understanding the problem is the first step in creating a solution. If you understand why your home isn't selling now, you will, after reading this book, be able to create some effective strategies. So relax, and know that you are gaining an advantage on your competitors right now by reading this book.

Some Simple Truths to Remember When Reading This Book

- The market is constantly changing. You must watch it all the time, not just when you start selling your house.

- Marketing gives you an advantage over competitors who don't market.

- Marketing is easy and inexpensive, and it will always be noticed by the buyer.

- Being a pro will help sell your home. Most home sellers are amateurs, and a buyer feels more comfortable with someone who is active and confident.

- Everyone is tempted at some time to sell their houses themselves. Do this only if you are sure that you are better than every agent in your area, which is unlikely.

- The best way to excel is to commit yourself to working only with pros. Whomever you work with should be a top professional. The real estate market runs on the 80/20 rule: 80% of the people make only 20% of the sales and the top 20% of the people make 80% of the sales. Commit yourself to only working with those top 20%.

- You can't do everything. If you act on only one idea from this book, you will benefit, but you will benefit more from acting on more. If you feel overwhelmed, take the 20 ideas that most apply to you and your house and start there.

PART I

What Makes People Buy

CHAPTER TWO

Entrepreneurial Marketing

In the fall of 1990, Detroit was feeling the pinch. Throughout the country, gas prices were high, people were spending less for fear of recession, and car dealerships were offering incentives just to get buyers to walk in the door. Car sales were down dramatically. Yet, in this same market, the Honda NSX was selling for 50% over list price and had a waiting list 18 months long at dealerships in northern California. Why the difference? Honda had a good product and knew how to market it.

Now look at the typical home sale. In many cases, a seller will use the same method that his neighbors have used for years. He or she will either call a real estate agent and list the property or look around at open houses, get a sense of the market and try to sell it himself (called a For Sale By Owner, or FSBO). This might work fine in a normal market, but in a down market, a seller could be committing economic suicide. His home might sit on the market for months without a single offer. Panic, concern, or depression might set in. He'd be forced to lower his price if he needed to move or really wanted to sell.

How different it might be if the seller knew about the market and knew how to take advantage of that knowledge. He or she should have known that a large company was relocating its employees to his town soon, or been aware of some change in demographics in his area. He would have seen that it was mostly young couples that were looking in his neighborhood and that his dark, dreary house was a turn-off at the price he was asking. Perhaps if the seller had made the down payment low enough and carried some of the financing, one of these young couples could have afforded the house that was currently out of their reach.

In a down market, the psychology of buyers changes. While only a year before, people might have been talking about homes as investments, now you will find people talking about a home they will stay in for awhile. This changes the emphasis in what they are looking for. The quality of the schools, the number of bedrooms in the home, and the location play a much more important role in down markets than in hot markets. People aren't as interested in moving into "up and coming" neighborhoods. All of a sudden, those neighborhoods are just "marginal."

But this doesn't mean you can't sell your home. Americans get bored easily by their old patterns of living. Our attention span is as short as the next television commercial. Many people will move because they're tired of where they are and want something different. To cater to these people, you have to find out where your potential buyers are coming from and show how your house is different in a positive fashion.

The bottom line is this: properly marketing your home could make the difference between a sale and no sale and will get you a better price.

Tip 1: You must view the sale of your home as a marketing director views his company's sales and look for a way to maximize your profit.

Every year companies spend millions of dollars to gain market share and try to beat the competition. Market surveys are conducted, psychologists are hired, the best advertising men are brought into the fold, and jobs are gained and lost over how to convince a buyer to look at one brand over another.

As a seller of real estate, you have a job, too. You are now the marketing director of your own home sales company, and you have only one product to sell. How you go about it will determine whether you are successful or whether you lose out to a smarter and harder-working competitor.

> **Tip 2: Do market research that other home sellers rarely think about.**

If you were a builder planning on building a home, you would want to consider many factors. You'd want to know what other projects were planned, when they would be completed, and the local government's attitude toward even more construction. You'd also want to check some economic conditions. Are companies laying off employees or is there an anticipated expansion by some corporations (whether announced or unannounced). Is a moratorium on new construction coming along? How about interest rates? Will they rise or fall?

In other words, there are many factors you'd consider before you planned your construction. The bottom line would be to determine whether or not you could sell a house for more than it would cost you to build it. These are the same determinations you need to make when deciding to place your home on the market during a slow time.

Your research may uncover that good times are not too far away, or that there is no new supply coming on line and demand has been increasing. Many real estate agents and appraisers are reactive: they view today's market based on yesterday. That's why, just weeks before a market crashes, they'll be telling you how housing prices can only go up. You need to become proactive: to see where trends are going in your area. Armed with this information, you can determine a realistic asking price, perhaps much better than the "pros" can.

Analyzing your market means more than just looking at comparable houses. It means looking at those priced above yours and those below it. In other words, it means looking at *all* the houses in the market. You're in a market where you are vying for the consumer's discretionary income.

Once you've analyzed the competition, step back and compare your house on pricing, financing, options and amenities, style, and so on. Now the key is to figure out a way to differentiate yourself.

You must constantly check the details that the average sellers leave behind. If you have some dead grass or a dead bush, remove and replace it. Throw in some special touches a prospect will appreciate, like dimmer switches on the lights or new appliances.

Tip 3: See if a need is not being addressed.

Ideas appearing in new-home communities often totally escape the resale market. These ideas would help a home sell more quickly but most real estate agents specialize in either one or the other and so tend not to put two and two together. Look to see if a desire is not being addressed in your area.

Also, few homeowners take the time to do what you are doing. Perhaps you see that empty nesters want to buy in your area. You can address this trend by working on safety-oriented projects such as increased outdoor lighting to address this need, as perhaps   none of your neighbors is doing. It might just close the sale.

Tip 4: Know your product well, since the buyer will expect you to.

To be an effective marketer, you must know your product. Most of us have not studied architecture or building, but a little knowledge will go a long way in properly marketing your home. By knowing the product, you can point out advantages which will compensate for the inevitable deficiencies buyers will find in a house.

For instance, a buyer might ask you how your house compares to the other houses in the neighborhood. Of course, you are not expected to tell the buyer about the nicer houses that are for sale. However, you can impress him or her by showing that you have studied the rest of the neighborhood to arrive at the price on your house. Or you might tell the buyer about the amenities in your house that are in few of the other houses. Your real estate agent is expected to know all this, but buyers probably may not want to speak much with a seller's agent. If you know these things, you can make a personal contact with the potential buyer that can make all the difference in the sale.

Tip 5: Select your team carefully.

Other people provide a wealth of experience and skills that it would take you several lifetimes to develop. Use the leverage of other people's minds to get the best talent you can find. You are the director, and it is time to select your team. While we believe that many of the functions of marketing your home effectively in a down market can be performed by the homeowner, there are many times when specialists are necessary.

The team usually consists of one or more of the following specialists:

Real estate agent

This person is responsible for knowing the market and market values. A sharp agent will notice trends and price barriers and will have a wealth of knowledge on competitive properties. The agent is also your salesperson and must be easy to get along with and good with people. You need someone with a proven level of performance and the highest levels of integrity, someone who is creative in marketing and sales. It is important to the buyer that your real estate agent be enthusiastic and experienced, especially in knowing what it takes to close a deal. You can go without a real estate agent, but you should choose yourself only if you are sure that you can do as well as the best agent you can find (not likely).

Real estate lawyer

You don't want a general practice attorney, you want one with plenty of real estate experience to help guide you in your sale. These attorneys often work in larger firms, which means you have access to experts on tax planning and estate planning, too. A good lawyer's focus is to negotiate a win-win deal. Start looking around now, before you sign a sales contract. Ask your friends and associates or call up some successful real estate agents or developers and see whom they use. Although a good attorney will cost a lot, a bad one will cost you a lot more.

Architect

Use architects when doing major renovations and additions. A good architect knows costs and has a good sense of value. An architect can often help you create a very special place out of an ordinary home for a lot less than you might imagine.

Interior Merchandiser

This person might be an interior designer but there is a large difference between design and merchandising. Interior design highlights the personality (or ego) of the designer or the client, but merchandising makes a home desirable to others. It appeals to the emotions of your prospects, not yours. Few individual homeowners can afford a merchandiser, but everyone can see what merchandisers do by looking in new home developments.

CPA or tax planner

You need to know the tax consequences before you ever put your home up for sale. There's not much point in working hard marketing and renovating your home only to give a third of it away in taxes. There are many tax incentives for home sellers which you should know about.

Contractor

If you are planning any significant renovations, you are going to need a reputable contractor. Quality, reliability, licensing, experience, and cost are all important considerations in choosing the contractor. He or she can also make suggestions about low-cost renovations which can add selling appeal to your home.

Tip 6: Locate the best talent for the team that you can find.

Finding the best talent for the job is a universal management challenge. Yet for such an important task as marketing what is probably your largest asset, you don't want to go second rate. The key to using your money wisely is to spend more money on people who can either get you an even larger return or save you more than they cost.

It's not hard to find the best: just look around you. Who is winning sales awards consistently at their real estate firms? Who has been designing or doing work on the houses that are selling for top dollar in your community?

Tip 7: Gather data from the professionals.

When you are contemplating putting your home up for sale, you need to judge the status of the marketplace. Don't rely on the real estate section of the paper, which is usually behind the times. Talking with the right professionals is a good way to get started.

One of the first places to start is talking to real estate brokers. This is their business, the buying and selling of homes. Call up a few whose names you've seen in the newspaper for some award or whose names seems to appear on most of the for sale signs in your neighborhood. These are the people who will probably be most up to date on the realities of the market. Ask your friends for referrals to good agents.

Talk to lenders. Loan officers who specialize in home mortgages have a different point of view than do real estate agents. Banks also usually have good data on what's happening in various areas. Larger banks have research departments, and many smaller ones buy this research. It shows employment data, forecasts trends, and gives you a better sense of the bigger picture.

CHAPTER THREE

Why People Buy

Going through the traditional school system in this country, few of us were taught the proper way to persuade and sell. We were taught the logic of debate and how to convince people rationally. All too often, many of us have seen people getting into arguments, trying to convince each other by logic. We all know this doesn't work.

Even in sales, until recently, the focus was on rational, conscious selling. Most salespeople still think selling is persuading buyers consciously and then hitting them with a hard close. Traditional sales advice said to find needs and fill them. The key to untraditional sales is to create needs through emotional, unconscious persuasion.

> **Tip 8: People buy for emotional reasons and justify their decision with logic.**

When they buy houses, people buy wants instead of needs. Most successful salespeople know that you don't sell products, you sell benefits. The key is to make the buyer's wants real enough that they become needs in the buyer's mind. Persuasion is the key, but it is not a hard closing argument that sells a prospect; it is a soft building of motivation within the prospect himself of herself.

If someone falls in love with a home, it is very hard for anyone else, even a spouse, to logically convince that person not to buy it if it costs only a few thousand dollars more than had been budgeted. The choice becomes, "buy the house or damage the marriage."

Emotions are much stronger than logic, even when someone is spending hundreds of thousands of dollars on a house. It's like the iceberg. Imagine the tip as logical reasons—the reasons we see, that we talk about, and that we justify our purchases with. But 90% of the iceberg is what we don't see. These are the emotional reasons to buy. And these are what successful salespeople and marketers tap into. Your buyer may be strong and hard like the Titanic and may be able to avoid the logical reasons to buy, but if you get him with the emotional reasons beneath the surface, he's sunk.

Tip 9: It is unconscious persuasion, not a hard close, that really sells people.

Many salespeople feel that the way to sell is to try to logically convince a person to buy. Such a salesperson tells prospects all the good reasons to buy but never gets them to really feel the positive consequences of the decision. The salesperson keeps adding logical reasons, or asking why the prospects won't buy. Pretty soon the prospect gets the feeling that someone is doing a hard sell.

People communicate values and desires much more strongly through the nonverbal sensory system than through words. People tend to react more strongly to, and remember more of, what they experience than what they are told. Professionals know you need to appeal to the buyer's emotions and unspoken needs first, before you try to add that little bit of logic that lets buyers justify the purchase to themselves.

Ever hear of something called "buyer's remorse"? It happens when someone buys something in the heat of the moment and then realizes that he or she didn't really want or need it. To reduce potential buyer's remorse, you need to sell people on the benefits of what they are buying. Have them visualize themselves in the future and imagine how much they'll be enjoying their new home next year. Get them to imagine all the wonderful times they'll have in it.

We operate on many levels that we are not even aware of. Most of the decisions we make don't really have any logical basis, but rather are caused by deep emotional programming that comes from our previous experiences. There are many ways this programming can be used to help in sales. For example, studies have shown that referrals are over ten times more effective than cold calls. Ten times! Why? It's called "social proof." Because someone you know referred a salesperson, then the service must be good. It may be no better than the service the guy who just cold called you a few minutes earlier provides. There's nothing logical in that; it is how we've been socialized—it's unconscious.

In the same way, using the rules of socialization to help in your sales and marketing is much more effective than trying to convince someone logically to buy your house. By appealing to their dreams, goals, and social programming, we are forcing a sale.

Tip 10: By linking your product to values and beliefs, you are letting the buyer's own years of associations sell for you.

In the world of advertising, product linkage, or associations, are very common. In fact, that's most of what advertising is. The old generations of commercials used to try to sell you on why one product was better. The method is called "USP," or "unique selling proposition." Later, as advertising became more sophisticated, image was important. Advertising guru David Ogilvy was the leader of this school in his ads for Rolls Royce and Schwepps. Every commercial was a small part of creating an overall image for the product. Lifestyle started being sold through products.

Today, sophisticated advertising works with associations. That's why actors are paid huge sums of money to do endorsements. If we trust the actor in some role on TV, and then he pushes a product, we associate our trust with that product. It's why Bill Cosby sells Jello and why Michael Jackson sells Pepsi. We see Michael dancing, feeling good, and we then see images of

Pepsi on the screen. Logically, it makes no sense, especially when you doubt that Michael Jackson likes or even drinks Pepsi. But subconsciously we link the good feelings we have for Michael Jackson to Pepsi. Since Pepsi started using those commercials, its sales have gone up.

Tip 11: There is nothing wrong with targeting emotions in home buyers.

New home builders are starting to target the emotions with sophisticated marketing and merchandising techniques. Few homeowners and only a minority of real estate agents are even aware of what is going on about them. The key is to link basic positive values to the home for sale. Through the proper merchandising of your home, you can create motivation. Create the internal pressure to buy. Link the sale to higher needs, dreams, and aspirations.

Sophisticated builders know that a model home can stir up the emotions inside the buyer. To make owning the home real, you must tap into a buyer's beliefs and values through the way you merchandise your home. You must link owning your home to the buyers' needs and desires for security, status, and the like.

Tip 12: Find the emotional appeal of your home.

Every home has some emotional appeal or ties to people's wants and needs. Look at your house from the front. Step back and squint your eyes. Ask yourself, "What is the emotional appeal here?" What is the romance value—or how can you create some. Practice on other homes. Look at them and evaluate their emotional appeal from the street.

Once inside, look for that warm fireplace, the sunny breakfast nook, or the private deck off of the master bedroom. Think about how you would describe this home to someone. What do you like best? Now look at your own home. Where are those special places in your home, the ones you go to on a sunny morning or a cold, rainy night? These are the areas that sell a home.

Tapping into a Buyer's Hierarchy of Needs

Noted psychologist Abraham Maslow showed that a person's focus depends on which of his needs have already been fulfilled. One moves vertically up the pyramid from more basic to higher needs. People seek satisfaction of the higher needs only when the lower ones are satisfied. Conversely, if some crisis hits below, people will go back down and focus on the lower need until it is satisfied again.

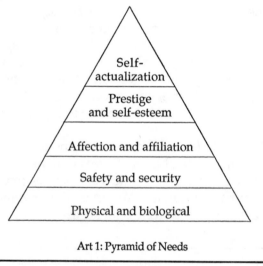

Art 1: Pyramid of Needs

In a country as affluent as ours, most of the basic necessities of life have been taken care of and our focus tends to be above the lowest level. However, a home can tap into many different levels of a buyer's consciousness, and none should be ignored.

Physical and Biological

These needs are the desire for increased comfort and convenience. Seeing the latest in push-button living makes many people feel they are currently living a life of drudgery in the Dark Ages. Contrast always helps create desire. People want physical comforts. If you offer them and your competition doesn't, you will certainly win some people over.

Many houses also have aspects of biological needs that are often overlooked. While some people think of two-story houses as being more luxurious, older couples realize that there is a time when they won't want to trudge up and down the stairs. You can sell a single-level house because of its physical advantage for older people.

Safety and Security

Physical security is very important. Because of people's perceptions of an increasingly dangerous society, the house and neighborhood must feel safe. Your house for sale must bespeak security and safety without feeling like a prison. Use electronic security systems rather than bars; let the look of the exterior and landscaping with privacy screens and walls all contribute to the feel of security without bringing up the fear of danger.

One of the most common reasons couples move from the city to the suburbs is that they are looking for a good place for their children to grow up. Although many suburban areas lack the cultural amenities and other blessings that can help a child develop, the perceived need for safety and security, realistic or not, overrules such considerations. It is sometimes tricky to emphasize security without bringing up negatives like crime, but it can and should be done.

Selling "community" is a way of emphasizing safety without connotations of danger. People move to smaller towns because they want the feeling that everybody knows everyone else. People may not know each other any more than they do in the city, but that is the feeling of security many buyers are looking for.

Another need people have that relates to security is the need for privacy. Fences, properly screened views, and separation from noise and other nuisances are all strong selling points. The more the world intrudes on their daily lives, the more people associate privacy with security.

When you think of security, do not overlook financial security. One would expect some rational decision making when buying a home. We need logical reasons to justify our emotional investment. Financial security helps fulfill that need. Realtor associations, banks, and the media have helped to portray home buying as a safe investment, a forced savings plan for the average American. And most wealth in America is now invested in real estate. "Why pay rent to a greedy landlord when you can make similar payments and own your own home" has been the call to the first-time home buyer for years.

Love and Affiliation

Neighborhood values are important to people who grew up in a small neighborhood, but it is also important to those who grew up in big cities but longed for the neighborhoods they see only on TV. People buy products to fill a need for belonging. AT&T increases its sales with the "Reach out and touch someone" campaign. A house that exemplifies "belonging" in its marketing will sell. Most Americans want to belong to a better social or economic group than the one they are actually in. Sell "belonging" to a status level just above what the economics of the typical buyer might justify and you can usually generate a stronger sale.

Don't overlook the desire to conform. Although Americans like to think of themselves as strong individuals, most share a desire to feel that they are "in the swim of things." They want to emulate their social betters and catch the trends they don't realize are trends at all, but think are just "better taste."

People do not rationally admit they are conforming. They use phrases like "it's the smart thing to do" or "I love that, I saw something like it in a designer magazine" or "We need to have a Jacuzzi in the bath" (notice how just a few years ago, almost no one had any of these, but now they are "necessities"). Play up to people's desires for the latest in home design.

Prestige and Self Esteem

Notice that you never sell your home as a "used home," it is always for "resale." That appeals to our needs for status. Even when buying a small home, it must be treated as if it were a castle to the man or woman purchasing it.

The desire for independence and the feeling of the average American that a successful person must own a nice home can be fed in the marketing of your home. A neighborhood connotes social status. When you are successful, you want something to show for it. Either a large house or a prestigious address will help do this.

Sometimes price connotes status. Many people in the gourmet food business know that by packaging a product properly and raising the price, they can actually increase sales. Price cutting is the worst strategy one can use in that business, where low prices imply lower quality. Your house can be clothed in a similar package, where your price doesn't work against you.

Certain types of rooms suggest status. People associate a wine cellar, a billiard room, or a library with a more luxurious home.

Values, Demographics, and Lifestyle

A value is anything that we feel is extremely important to our lives. Values are learned entities. As we grew up, we learned to believe that certain things are more important than others. School, the home, the media, and society all pushed their values on us; we absorbed or rejected each of them.

A person who puts a strong value on success will search for achievement because this means happiness, love, power, and much else desirable to that person. He or she will also seek at all costs to avoid failure, since it would bring the ultimate pain.

Anthony Robbins defines two sets of values: means values and ends values. Means values are cars, money, a nice home, and so on. You don't really want means values for their own sake; what you want is ends values, such as: success, security, and happiness. Ends values are the feelings you want to get from owning things like cars, homes, and so on.

In selling, it is important to elicit a person's ends values. This allows you to align and link the home with the prospect.

Tip 13: Understand the types of values your buyers might have.

The Values and Lifestyle (VALS) typology became popular in the early 1980s. VALS was a new way of organizing selling based on common beliefs and values throughout the culture. Before VALS, most selling was done demographically by age, income, or educational level. VALS took the multitude of values, drives, beliefs, needs, and dreams of our culture and found nine distinct lifestyles which they categorized:

Survivors
The lowest level of the model. These people are poor, and their lives are dictated by need rather than choice.

Sustainers
Similar to survivors, but they haven't given up yet. These are the working poor.

Belongers
This is the largest category in the VALS model. They are traditional, hard-working people. They long for the "good old days" and don't really like high-tech things. They are sold on family values.

Emulators
These people want to be successful. They are striving. They desperately want the lifestyle of the more affluent achievers.

Achievers
These people have "made it." They are self-reliant and hard working. They account for nearly a quarter of the population. They are managers, doctors, executives, accomplished artists, entertainers, and professors.

I-am-me's
Mostly young people rejecting traditional values. They are not a significant home-buying group.

Experientials
Experientials quest for direct personal experience. They take great satisfaction in a sense of growth and personal accomplishment. They take little notice what others do or would like them to do.

Societally Conscious
These are successful people who value that we should all live in harmony with nature. They value the nonmaterial aspects of life such as community and believe that each person should contribute rather than take. They are high-

ly educated, with over half in technical or professional occupations.

Integrateds
These people are at the highest level of the Maslow hierarchy. They are pursuing self-actualization and self-fulfillment. They often hold positions of fundamental responsibility within the community.

Each lifestyle reflects the values and needs of the people that generally fit into them.

The survivors and sustainers rarely are of interest to home sellers since people with these values have little money and are rarely in the market for new housing. It is important to know the differences between the remaining lifestyle types when marketing your home. For example, an achiever seeks success, power, and recognition. Thus, a home in a prestigious neighborhood, or with grand architecture, would be ideal for this person. When advertising the home, you would talk about status and prestige, not about family togetherness. If you were marketing to belongers, you would point out that the dining room is the perfect size for family get-togethers, not how their friends would envy their new home.

Certain products are more value-expressive in nature than others. The brand of food you buy is usually less important to your image than the type of car or home you have. But even food can be value driven; for instance, many people buy "health food" just so they can feel they are being "healthy," even if they never exercise and lead stressful lives. But most people assume that others rate them on the type of house they own and are thus much more conscious of how a house will affect their image.

Tip 14: Target your house to the values of the potential buyers, not your own.

You must pick up on the buyers' orientation, their values. Do they go with the crowd (Belongers) or against it (Experientials)? Look at the type of products they buy, such as the cars they drive. This will help you come up with logical and emotional reasons that are appealing to the prospect.

Appeal to larger image. An efficient kitchen might appeal to a busy executive, a gourmet kitchen to someone with family values. All elements can have their appeal oriented to a particular type of buyer. The location of a home can appeal to social mobility. If it is in a very desired location, you can appeal to the desire to move up, even if the price is high.

Many buyers have some fears and insecurities when it comes to purchasing a home. After all, it is the largest purchase the average person makes. Homes cannot be sold on fear. The buyer must be reassured that he is making a sound and wise decision.

Tip 15: Watch for demographics and life stages.

Attitudes, lifestyles, and what appeals to people from one life-cycle group to another differ greatly and yet consistently. Although it is easy to understand why someone in his or her twenties might be concerned with diapers while a sixty-year-old is not, it is a little less obvious to see what in a home appeals to someone in his or her twenties versus someone who's older.

When developers market homes to young couples, they know that these people "want it all" even if they don't have much money. They have dreams and hopes for the future. So developers decorate the home to paint a picture of a lifestyle filled with consumer goods aimed at a young household. When marketing to older residents, they know that spending patterns have shifted from material goods to recreational interests such as golf, tennis, reading, and relaxing with friends, so they decorate their models accordingly.

When you are setting up for the sale of your home, it is wise to do some research on the demographic makeup of your community and on who is moving in. Your home might be ideally suited for more than one possible use. This information will show you which is the best group to target.

**Tip 16: Focus on changing demographics,
nationally and locally.**

Changes in the size, composition, and lifestyles of the population have significant implications for real estate because demographic factors are an integral component of demand. Focusing on national demographic trends is important because they give us a sense of the values Madison Avenue will be pushing to the American public. When the baby-boom generation was in its twenties, advertising was aimed at the large youth market. This helped set the tone for values and what was considered important in the media. As the baby boomers reached thirty, Yuppies became popular subjects in the press.

The two fastest-growing demographic groups in the 1990s are The Aging Baby Boomers and the Maturity Market.

Age of head of household

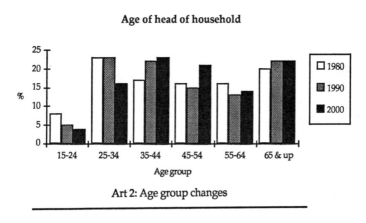

Art 2: Age group changes

Local demographic trends are more important than national ones. The contrast between the two helps you to spot local trends. The reason it is good to look at both is that most builders are so busy following national demographic trends that they may miss local anomalies. For example, national trends may indicate a decline in first-time home purchasers. Thus most builders who read national publications may shift their home building to larger homes for the move-up market. However, local data might show that employers are attracting many young workers into the area, thus increasing the numbers in the younger age group.

CHAPTER FOUR

How to Market

Always give the home buyer a strong purchase motive. This motive does not need to have anything to do with your home's real value, only with the value in the mind of the purchaser. The buyer of a big flashy car can think that it is an acceptable purchase because "it's a good investment" or because "it's safer for the family." If the prestige of being a member of the local country club will lead to business contacts, then it becomes acceptable.

Marketing is linking your home to values and benefits that are important to the buyer. Phrases such as "you owe it to yourself," "you deserve it," and "you need it" link items to security or popularity needs. Good marketing will find an acceptable motive that does not need to have anything to do with the real one.

Tip 17: Most buyers are much less price-conscious than they think they are.

Many home buyers like to think they are economically oriented. They think they want the best price. In reality, however, you will often find that prestige, status, and other needs are more important to many of your prospective buyers. Sales books for real estate agents often instruct them to question their buyers when they hear an emotional price ceiling. For instance:

Agent: What is the most you want to spend on a house?

Buyers: $175,000 is all we can afford.

Agent: If I found you the perfect home, the one with the Jacuzzi and the gourmet kitchen that you want, and that is in the XYZ school district, but it cost $180,000, do you think you could scrape the money together, or should I not even bother showing it to you?

Buyers: Well, we probably could borrow some money from Uncle Joe.

It is rare that a buyer is totally price oriented. The emotions are stronger, and by appealing to wants and needs you can overcome price objections.

Tip 18: What buyers see is only what they think they see.

People are always working from their sensory perceptions and the associations they have to them. That's why the new traditionalism in architecture is hot. New-traditional houses are new houses that look like traditional homes but are upgraded for modern tastes. Builders are creating homes that harken back to a time that never was.

Advertisers are working with similar fantasies. The Mazda Miata was a hot seller among baby boomers who were reminded of their old red MGs. Yet it isn't really anything like the MG. New houses now have details that look Victorian but really aren't. Baby boomers are buying new homes that speak of nurturing and security. They have large front porches, brass faucets, fancy moldings, and lots of wood. When asked why, they say that this reminds them of childhood. Yet most of these people grew up in 1950s tract housing! However, they spent years of their time watching TV shows that showed happy families living in Victorian houses. People make decisions on the basis of associations, and the key to effective marketing is to link your home with those good associations.

Remember the Coke versus Pepsi taste tests back in the early 1980s? The Pepsi challenge was showing the public that when people didn't know which was which, they would tend to choose Pepsi (which they felt tasted better) instead of Coke (which had the name and marketing appeal). If people knew which was which, they would choose Coke. Why? Because Coke had built up an image of quality and of being what people wanted.

You can package your home to tie in with the wants and needs of Americans. They can associate your home with quality, value, and other elements if it is packaged appropriately. That image is important for the look of the house, the advertising, and how you present yourself during home tours. Of these, the look of the house is the most important.

Even words suggest certain values. "Diet" beer would not go over as well with beer-drinking Americans as "lite" beer. The home you are selling will mean different things to different people. How you display it, how you market it, and how you link it to the values of your buyers will make a large difference in whether you are a frustrated seller in a down market or a successful marketer of your home. For instance, the word "home" appeals to the emotions of the buyer more than the word "house."

Tip 19: Perform a market analysis before you start selling your house.

From the largest corporations to single-person businesses, a market analysis is a necessary tool to determine how to proceed with a new product. Your house is certainly a product and you certainly want to market it as best you can. The following steps show you how you should be thinking before you start to sell your house.

Step One: Define the problem
Who is your customer? This is where surveys and trend studies come in. What do these people want? What is not being offered? What are the needs of my buyers?

Step Two: Clarify what you wish to obtain

You want to make the home desirable to your ideal buyer. How do you do that? How will you market it?

Step Three: Study

Consolidate your information. Brainstorm for ideas. Ask yourself questions like "What can I do to make the buyer's life easier," "How can I attract buyers and real estate agents to my home," "How can I make the sale simple," and "What unique things do I have to offer?"

Step Four: Implement your research strategy

Market analysis:

- What are the current trends? What do buyers want today?
- What are the demographics?
- What is the projected growth for the region, the town, local industries, and so on?
- How many new building permits are being issued?

Competitive analysis:

- Which homes are selling well, and why?
- Which neighborhoods are hot, and why?
- What are your competitors doing?
- What do they have to offer?

Product analysis:

- What do I offer that is unique?
- In what ways am I vulnerable?
- Why should someone *not* buy this house?
- What objections do I normally hear from prospective buyers?
- Why do I lose prospective buyers?

Prospect analysis:

- What conditions prevail in the prospect's mind?
- What has the media been telling him or her?

- What are buyers looking for?
- Who is the key decision maker?

Remember, value is in the eye of the beholder. What may be valuable to you may not be valuable to your customer and vice versa. If you want to charge more than the competition, you need to create a greater perceived value.

Tip 20: Use the market analysis to determine your strategy.

You're looking for the group of buyers that your home will appeal to. The market analysis will show you who your most likely buyer is, the price and style of home that will sell best, and what amenities are most appealing to this buyer.

When successful developers build a home, they build for the market. That is, they take such market data as population growth, age segmentation, employment statistics, family income and education levels, and existing and planned inventory, and then they design a home for a need that is underaddressed in the market. Unsuccessful developers build a house that looks like all the others, playing follow the leader, and then wonder why there is an oversupply of their type of home with not enough buyers.

After performing your analysis, you will have a sense of what market segments are moving into your area. Take a look at a map of your neighborhood and note where homes are for sale or have sold recently. Determine the sales prices of these homes, their square footage, their room breakdown, and any special features they offered. Compare what has been selling to your market analysis. Is there a need that has not been addressed that your home would be ideal for? Perhaps you can target a certain age group.

A good example of how market segmentation works is that all groups want a kitchen, but some want a large gourmet kitchen while others want only an efficiency kitchen. What constitutes the proper size is different for each market segment. Determining your most appropriate segments will help you in renovating your home and accelerating a sale.

For example, a consumer profile of the marriage and family status of homebuyers might look like:

Singles	10%
Professional couples without children	17%
Traditional couples without children	38%
Professional couples with children	12%
Traditional couples with children	18%
Empty nesters	5%

In looking at a study such as this, one sees mostly young couples either with or without children. Many of those without are likely to have some soon. Thus targeting them with small efficiency kitchens would be a bad mistake, since most households will consist of growing families desiring a larger family environment. Remember, successful marketers are always asking the question, "How does my product meet the consumer's needs better than the competition."

Appealing to Buyers' Physical Senses

We all have five physical senses and these senses have a large impact on what we like and don't like. No matter how rational we think we are, the only way we experience the world is through our physical senses. Everyone has positive and negative associations with various sights, sounds, touches, tastes, and smells. Your job when selling your house is to emphasize the positive images in all five categories and avoid the negative ones.

As a simple example, imagine hearing about a fair-priced house in a good neighborhood. As you walk up the driveway, you are impressed by the gardening and the maintenance. As you step inside, you are overpowered with the smell of freshly-cooked Brussels sprouts, a vegetable you have hated since childhood. Are you really going to spend much time in the house? Remember, this is a down market and you have already viewed a few other houses today that were also fairly priced. You might take a look around and, if nothing extraordinary pops up in the first few seconds, leave.

You have just made a significant financial decision based on a simple, temporary odor. All your talk about looking for the best home value went out the window because of a small sensory defect that you know has nothing to do with how the house will be when you own it.

(Methods for implementing the changes in this chapter are covered in more depth in the chapters on renovations.)

Tip 21: Most people think about houses in visual images, so you must cater to the positive images.

Color affects our mood and our perceptions of objects around us. Decorators will tell you that whites with a hint of yellow will tend to warm up a room and are more effective than pure white.

A recent flop in the world of marketing was Smurfs cereal. The Smurfs were very popular, and the cereal should have done well with children, as have many others based on cartoon characters. Yet it flopped miserably. Why? The Smurfs cereal died because it was blue. Blue is not an appetizing color.

Homes are expected to look a certain way. If you have Day-Glo orange walls, your home has lost value because buyers will assume that you were not a serious owner who took proper care of the house and that there must be other problems with the property. Color also affects how we react. Fast-food chains used to use bright reds, oranges, and yellows to get us to eat more quickly. These colors actually have a physical effect on the body. If the same environments had been green, customers would have eaten more slowly and the restaurants would have been more crowded.

Color can also be used to affect our perception of room dimensions, to even out uneven areas, and to make a home feel worth more. Be careful and discriminating in the use of color in your home. It's easy to become accustomed over time to dull, outdated, or simply inappropriate colors in a home.

Tip 22: Sounds are more often negative than positive.

Sound also plays a role in the perception of a home and of its value. A negative example of this is noise. Expensive cars are expected to have a dull thud as the sound of a door closing as contrasted to a tinnier sound in cheaper cars. Manufacturers will go to great lengths to give their car doors that thud sound even though it is of no acoustical, structural, or functional value. It is simply that the public perceives that sound as a sound of quality. Similarly, a house that transmits sound from room to room is perceived as cheap. Similarly, you want to exclude street noise and other exterior sounds from the home for the same reasons.

Sounds that connote "work," such as the dishwasher running or the lawn mower in the yard are poor sounds to have going as a buyer tours a house. These sounds remind them of the realities of running a home rather than the dream and fantasy of owning one.

Most sophisticated marketers of homes use calming instrumental music when showing homes. Music has a strong effect on the body at the subconscious level. That's the main reason many stores subscribe to Muzak: it has been shown to increase sales.

Tip 23: Touch is the best subliminal way to leave a positive impression about your house.

The sense of touch can be a valuable marketing tool. If you've ever walked into a china shop with a child, you know that the urge to touch is very strong in people. One of the best ways to make the home memorable to buyers is through touch. A house that is only "seen" is harder to recall than one the buyer experiences with many senses. And if buyers can't remember your house, they certainly won't buy it.

Many builders are becoming keenly aware of the value of touch, especially in creating a good first impression. That's why they often use solid brass hardware on the front door, even if they use less expensive hardware on the interior. Quality hardware is one of the attributes of expensive kitchen cabinets: they feel more valuable if they open smoothly.

Weight plays a factor. A heavy door that swings solidly on hinges is perceived as more valuable than a light, hollow-core door. Although the cost difference between a heavy and a light door may be only $40, the difference in the perceived value of the house can be much greater.

Tip 24: Smells are surprisingly important to first impressions of your home.

Although a dog can distinguish thousands of different scents, humans can consciously distinguish only a few. Yet unconsciously, smell can have one of the most direct and powerful effects on the brain.

There are good smells and bad smells to have in a home, and both create strong impressions. Examples of smells that mean bad news are musty smells, pet odors, and anything that smells like wood rot. Many homes sell for thousands of dollars under their real value just because potential buyers couldn't stand some odor in the house which the owner had become accustomed to.

Smells of strong ethnic cooking make a buyer feel ill at ease. Remember, you want them to feel as if this home were theirs, and if they don't usually cook curried chicken, the odors will only point out more that it isn't. If, however, you are appealing to one particular ethnic group, the smells may remind them of home-cooked meals and make them comfortable in your home.

Just as bad smells can quickly send buyers running to the competition, certain smells can greatly enhance the value of your home. Smells of a barbecue on the back porch or of bread or pies baking in the oven, or just the smell of new paint can add positive associations to the quality of the home.

Certain cooking smells seem to work in your favor. The smell of bread baking in the oven or putting a little vanilla smell in the air have become cliches. But olfactory sense impressions are strong and go directly to the brain. Be attentive to smells.

Tip 25: Eliminate strong smells that take away from that "new home" smell.

Just as the smell of new cars helps in selling them, the smell of a new home helps to sell it, too. Certain smells detract strongly from the appeal of your home and subconsciously supply the buyer with information about its quality. Getting rid of these smells requires almost no money but will add many dollars to your pocket.

Smoke
You can get rid of smoke smells by putting a plate of vinegar in the room and letting it sit for a few days. Than discard it. Another way is to use an electronic ionizer to help eliminate odors.

Pets
Some people love pets, others are allergic to them. Give the house a thorough cleaning and make sure the pet is not around when showing the house.

Mildew
Clean and scrub away any visible signs of mold or mildew from surfaces. Having the carpets cleaned and deodorized professionally will take care of any mildewy smells in the carpet and other odors lodged there that you may have become accustomed to.

Pesticides
Stay away from spraying pesticides. It is a danger signal to buyers. If you must,   do it at least a week before you show the house for the first time to give adequate time for the smell to dissipate.

Tip 26: Make the olfactory sense work for you.

Because the sense of smell is so powerful, it can be used to put buyers into positive mental states. Certain smells just seem to bring positive associations to them.

If you have a lawn, you have a silent sales partner. Freshly cut grass smells wonderful. Once you've set the date for your open house, let the grass grow a bit, then cut it the morning of the showing.

An old trick is to have vanilla wafting through the kitchen. Put a pot of boiling water on the stovetop, pour a teaspoon of vanilla in it, and then add some cinnamon and cloves. The kitchen smells will sell your house. Alternately, bake bread in the oven the day of the open house. Everyone loves the smell of freshly baked bread, and of course you can offer it to people who visit your house.

Some people spray cologne in the air just before a showing to add sparkle. You can also use a lemon-based furniture polish on the wood to help give a pleasing scent to the home.

Tip 27: Recreate the smell of a model home.

Just as the smell of a new car makes you associate it to good maintenance, little wear and tear, and a long remaining life, the smell of a new or refurbished home gives buyers subliminal associations about the quality and value of the home. Unfortunately, there isn't a product that you can just spray on the home but there are several things you can do to make smell work in your favor.

Polyurethane is an ideal product for making a room smell "new." It is commonly used on wood areas after they have been sanded to provide a beautiful and durable finish. Just a little will provide the smell you want, so you don't need to redo your whole house. A set of cabinets or a couple of wooden doorknobs will do the trick.

New paint will give rooms a new smell, but you must air it out. You don't want to overpower prospects with paint fumes.

Tip 28: Don't ignore taste since, like touch, it forms an important subliminal memory.

Although the sense of taste is not applicable directly to the selling of houses, it can have an effect on the overall impression a buyer has of your home. Quality food can make help with the impression of your home. One common sales technique is to put chocolates near the entry. It helps put people in a good state of mind because of their associations to chocolate. It also affects the brain chemically and helps put people in good moods.

Another common use of taste is to offer food at open houses. Serving expensive foods that people usually get only at classier affairs or on special occasions helps raise the perceived value of the home in the brain of the buyer through associations and linkages to past memories.

Don't dismiss the influence of the senses. There are many subtle differences that can change a buyer's "just looking" into a more receptive "wouldn't this be a great place to live."

Niche Marketing and Market Segmentation

Years ago, builders recognized the concept of market segmentation. Buyers were categorized as move-ups, starters, or empty nesters. These are the definitions most real estate agents are still using. However, this method of segmenting the population has been rendered obsolete in favor of a psychographic division of the population, basing sales on common psychological tendencies and desires. Now in addition to the VALS system, there are definitions such as Tigers, Winners with a Heart, and the Environmentally Aware.

Although it is new to the building industry, advertisers have been using psychographic techniques for almost a decade. While still under the old thinking in advertising, Merrill Lynch commercials used to show a herd of bulls. But the typical successful investors did not like to think of himself or herself as one of the herd. Later, Merrill Lynch switched to a single bull with the subtitle "a breed apart" to appeal to successful people with money who felt themselves to be individuals. The firm's market share increased dramatically.

Now that there are fewer hot markets where everything sells, builders are starting to use these sophisticated market segmentations. Housing builders have become niche builders. Procter and Gamble knows much more about the buyer of a 59-cent bar of soap than most home sellers know about the buyer of a $150,000 house. Builders have started doing detailed research about what excites and motivates the buyers of their homes.

Psychological motivations are the key. Regional or neighborhood values also play a part. These "psychographic" or "geodemographic" profiles are used as reference points in architecture and interior design. For example, vast entries, portico columns, and circular driveways appeal to the "achiever." In builder ads, these same symbols dominate the advertising.

The traditional mass marketing that most real estate agents have used for thirty years is a thing of the past. With fragmentation in people's tastes and lifestyles, the successful seller targets a specific buyer. You can use the same type of marketing for selling your house that major builders use to sell new houses.

Tip 29: Position your home in a defined niche so that a buyer will remember it better.

Positioning means determining exactly what niche you intend to fill. Most large, successful companies position themselves strongly. Rolex and Timex aim at two different markets with the same product. Many advertising professionals claim that positioning is the most important aspect in a successful marketing campaign.

We live in a world of information overload. The conscious mind can hold only so much information before it stops letting more in. Positioning is a way to make your product unique, so it can fit into the prospect's overcrowded mind by relating your home to ideas already there.

Tip 30: In a down market, home buyers look in many neighborhoods, so you have to position your house competitively against other houses.

Whenever a company releases a product, it tries to target a group and then position its product against the competition. Seven-Up, the "uncola," is a clear example of this. The key difference is that rather than selling your product on its merits, you sell it in the prospect's own mind by making it become something he or she already relates to.

For example, you can position your home as being on the next level higher than it really is. By relating your home to a better class of homes, you bring the value of yours up. In essence, you become the least expensive home in the higher category. Getting your home included in a certain school district or neighborhood is a clear example of this, but you can also do it by less formal means.

Some apartment complexes on "the wrong side of the tracks" have linked themselves to the better part of town by using the same decor as the "better" complexes next to them. Thus, they create a continuation of the "better" neighborhood into the complex.

Buyers are less inclined to go into "up and coming" areas as they get more conservative in their buying. They are also likely to take much longer to buy a home. All of a sudden, there is an emphasis on established locations.

What image do you want your house to project? How can you position your home against all the noise and the competition? The key is to show the similarities to the image you'd like to have and the difference from the one you don't.

For example, you can position yourself against the big guy. Fight the new home developer. Don't have a used home, have a home that was built with quality unlike the cheap new construction at that new development down the block.

Give your home an identity. In the San Francisco Bay Area, there is a city called Piedmont, full of mansions and very expensive homes. There is also a city called Oakland, which doesn't have nearly the reputation. So where do you think Piedmont Avenue, a main commercial street is located? That's right, in Oakland, *next to Piedmont*. Not surprisingly, the street is well to do, and has become a favorite shopping street.

What position do you want to own? Who must you beat? Is there a unique angle you can find that will raise your home above the crowd in the eyes of the real estate or home buying community? That's what positioning is all about.

Tip 31: Look for pricing niches (price breaks) when setting a price on your home.

Ever see those ads for a product at only $9.95 instead of $10.00? Well, advertisers are aware of psychological price breaks for buyers. Marketing a home is no different. But it isn't always as simple as pricing your home at $295,000 instead of $300,000. There are often unseen price breaks within a target group.

Price breaks are related to income, expectations, and competition. Three-bedroom homes have a different set of price breaks than do two-bedroom homes. Ask real estate agents for acceptable price ranges. Also ask if they have noticed a particular floor or ceiling for prices for particular types or sizes of homes. The key is to tap the top of the appropriate niche without going over an acceptable price.

A similar issue came up with some rental units in the San Francisco area recently. For over a month, there were six vacant apartments in a 32-unit complex asking a rent of $710 to $725 per month. The apartments were loaded with amenities and strongly advertised and marketed. Yet the owners received few responses. They lowered the rent to $695 (breaking the $700 barrier), and rented all of the apartments in under two weeks. It wasn't a matter of money, since there were many apartments nearby renting for $850: it was that the group that could afford over $700 went into the nicer apartments, while the group that would have loved to be in those particular apartments never even considered looking at a place with a rent of over $700.

CHAPTER FIVE

Pricing and Value

A house priced at the market will sell. The goal of this book is to raise your market value. "Market value" is defined as the price a house should sell for if there is a willing buyer, a willing seller, and a reasonable exposure to the market. A house priced "over market" might also sell, but it needs to have something special for this to happen. By adding that special ingredient, you can either make more money when selling your house or sell your house faster at the market value.

To get over market, you absolutely need to have a motivated buyer or an higher-than-average exposure to the market. In other words, you need to do your homework, properly prepare the house, outwork the competition, and excite the buyer when he sees your product.

The right way to start in pricing your home involves using professionals. Call a few brokers who are familiar with your neighborhood to get a sense of the value, or hire an appraiser. If you are using a real estate agent, he or she should be able to price your home for you as part of the selling fee. If you have doubts, feel free to ask for a second professional opinion.

Tip 32: Avoid setting the highest or lowest price in a market.

One simple rule is to try not to have the highest priced property in a neighborhood. In a down market, people tend to become much more price-sensitive. The people who can afford your price won't be visiting your neighborhood if yours is the highest-priced property. They'll be looking in better neighborhoods. Hopefully there are bigger or better homes than yours in the neighborhood. Then you can slide your price up to the top of your bracket. Just be sure not to be at the top of all the brackets.

Similarly, you don't want yours to be the lowest-price house in your bracket because either buyers will wonder what's wrong, or you are probably leaving some money on the table that you could make through improvements or better marketing.

Tip 33: Be honest about the value of your house when you set the price.

It is easy to overprice a house even if you are not a greedy person (it's even easier if you *are* greedy). There are four major reasons why people tend to overprice their houses:

Ego
Some people feel the need to get more for their home than the neighbors do. Maybe they want to be able to brag down at the local bar or country club about how much they got for their house. The problem here is that, in a down market, these people are slitting their own throats. Unless they can truly add value to the home, buyers will go elsewhere.

Imperfect markets
Sellers don't really know the market. Unlike the stocks they own, they can't read the paper and see what the value of their home is today. Real estate is an imperfect market. This means that, because the value is set by negotiation, prices can vary widely for similar houses.

Note that, in some down markets, banks and other lenders sometimes pressure their appraisers to give lower appraisals.

Emotions

Although you may have slaved for nine weekends to put the false stone front on your house and it actually lowered your property's value, you can't admit that to yourself. The amount of emotion invested is worth too much. Likewise, fond memories of your family growing up in the home since the early 1950s may blind you to the fact that what was once a good neighborhood has now declined significantly and few people want to move there unless a house is priced right (that is, low).

Pride

People can't admit they made a mistake in real estate. Many people just can't admit they made a bad purchase on their home. So, even thought the market dictates a lower price than what they bought it at, their egos won't let them see the reality.

The key is to get an objective look at value and then work from there to increase it. This is like the Alcoholics Anonymous philosophy. You need to see the reality before you can make improvements. And finally, don't regret anything that was done or any mistakes you made. Just because the house was "worth $300,000" a year ago and market value is $275,000, don't think you've lost $25,000. Bear in mind that if you sold last year and then bought another house, it probably would have cost an additional $25,000 too. Stop carrying that emotional baggage around.

Tip 34: Overpricing in a down market is much more dangerous than in a normal market.

Although this book gives you many ways to create value and get a higher price, beware of listing a house too high and then lowering its price by tiny increments. Nothing turns real estate agents off more. By the time your house is at the right price, it is a tired, dead listing. Don't be tempted to "try out" a higher price than you expect to get with the idea that it can later be lowered if no offers appear.

In a down market that keeps getting worse, you may have only one shot at the best buyers. If your house is obviously over-priced, they may not come back to see it at a lower price if there are dozens of comparable houses on the market.

Tip 35: Determine if you really are in a down market.

Relity and public perception are seldom the same. Usually, while you are entering a down market, the public thinks the market is still hot. And usually the converse is true. Your area may be pull-ing out of a down market just as everyone thinks you're in one. You need to watch the trends. Have houses been selling more quickly lately? And closer to their asking prices? These are the signs to watch.

Tip 36: Don't look at averages.

There are lies, damn lies, and statistics. Don't just look at average sales prices; look at the ones in your neighborhood for houses the size of yours. In California, as average prices fell there were really two things going on. Lower-priced homes in outlying areas were rapidly increasing in price while the more expensive middle-class homes were falling 10, 15, or 20% in value. If you had a smaller, lower-priced home, reading about a down market was irrelevant in this case because you actually had a hot property for the market.

Tip 37: Don't get caught in a spiral of lowering the price of your house.

The way *not* to price in a down market is to take the price your neighbors got for their house in a good market last year and than raise the price a little because you know your home is better than theirs.

Having too low a price is seldom the problem with home sellers. Yet, before you think about cutting your price as the only alternative, examine another alternative: adding value. A house is worth only what the market values it at. This book is about adding value rather than cutting your price.

The effects of cutting price versus adding value are easy to see with a few examples. Assume that you have a house that you want to sell for $300,000. Of this, you have $121,000 in equity and $179,000 in mortgages and liens.

A Normal-Market Scenario

If everything goes as hoped, your house will sell something like this:

House Price	$300,000
Mortgages and Liens	$179,000
Equity	$121,000
Sale Costs	$24,000
Profit (Equity – Sales)	$97,000

As you can see, if everything went well and this was a normal market, you could reap $97,000 in profit on the sale of your house.

If your house doesn't sell at $300,000, you have to do something. The most common assumptions is that you have to cut the price. A second, often better assumption, is that you have to raise the value.

Lowering the Price
When you cut price you lose profit quickly. Because your profit is the final slice of the pie, the amount left over after everyone else is satisfied, reducing your price by a sum as small as 10% could cut your profit dramatically. Assume you had to cut the price by 10%:

House Price	$270,000
Mortgages and Liens	$179,000
Equity	$91,000
Sale Costs	$21,600
Profit (Equity − Sales)	$69,400

In other words, a 10% price reduction lowered your profit by 28%, almost three times as much. What seemed like a reasonable reduction was a major loss to you.

Raising the Value
Instead of cutting price, you can add some physical value to the house and leave the price the same. For instance, assume that you performed $12,000 worth of valuable renovation, enough to get a buyer interested.

House Price	$300,000
Mortgages and Liens	$179,000
Fix-up & Marketing Costs	$12,000
Equity	$109,000
Sale Costs	$24,000
Profit (Equity − Sales)	$85,000

You've hardly lost anything. And, depending on what your house needed, you might have even been able to ask a higher price than your original $300,000 estimate.

People are more price-sensitive for the necessities of life than for the luxuries. For many people, the difference between buying a house for $270,000 or $300,000 is only a matter of desire. They can borrow the additional money from a relative or take a loan that will allow for lower payments so they can qualify. Remember, people buy wants, not needs. You have to make them want your house badly enough that they will pay the extra money to buy it.

People love to think they are very price-sensitive, especially during lean times. That's one of the reasons you have to show them the value for their money. But emotions go a lot farther in selling a home than any amount of logic will do. Compare magazine ads from the 1920s and 1930s and you will see that the values being sold did not change much at all. Similarly, in a down market, buyers want the same things they wanted in an up market. Help them think they are being price-conscious, but emphasize the values that make them want your house.

Tip 38: Consider the impact of financing when you price your home.

Many items affect the price of real estate. Of all of these, financing plays a key role (see the chapter on financing, below). A 2% difference in the interest rates between two houses translates into thousands of dollars per year.

Sometimes people will actually be saving money if they buy a more expensive home but at a lower interest rate. Your job is to explain that to buyers. Sometimes you can offer them different prices for different financing alternatives.

Tip 39: Leave some bargaining room in the price.

When pricing your home for sale, always leave a little room for negotiations. In a down market, it is very rare for a buyer to pay the full asking price. It's not because the value isn't there; it is just the psychology of buyers: they like to feel they are good negotiators and are getting a bargain.

It's best to determine the minimum price you will take ahead of time, as well as what you feel is a fair market price.

Appraisal and the Art of Valuing a House

Many economic conditions affect the prices of homes—everything from job formation in your area through supply and demand for homes to the functional obsolescence or style obsolescence of your home, its location, general market psychology, and so on. In order to get a true handle on the local picture, there are a few simple things to investigate.

Tip 40: Know the important market indicators for your area.

% Difference between asking and selling prices

This percentage indicates how much in demand houses are in your area. A large percentage difference between asking price and selling price indicates a low demand: prices fell significantly before a deal was struck. Houses selling near their asking prices indicates the opposite: that many buyers feel those homes are a good value. Sometimes selling prices are higher than asking prices, but not in down markets.

Time on the market

Another key economic indicator is the length of time it takes to sell a house. When demand is high, houses sell in under three months. If it takes longer than six months, you are in a down market. This is when you need the extra strategies of this book

Timing

Note that there tend to be seasonal variations in demand in most parts of the country. A house that is new on the market gets the most attention. March through September tend to be better months than the Christmas season. Find out when are the best months to time a sale in your area. Sometimes prices in areas change dramatically and quickly. If your area's popularity is rising, than it might be best to hold off for a little while.

Ask local real estate brokers about when the best selling season is. Often, it coincides with the school year, especially if you live in an academic community. Remember that you need to have your home up for sale during the early part of the peak selling season. If you wait until the end, you will have lost many buyers who have already signed purchase agreements.

Trends

Statistics are not static; they are constantly changing. Also be aware of averages: they rarely apply to your home, although they do give you a good sense of buyer sentiment.

Through the 1970s and 1980s, demographics were clearly on housing's side. House-hungry baby boomers pushed construction (and prices) to astronomical levels. These baby boomers are still house hungry, but now for bigger and better houses. If you have a large house or one that can be enhanced through remodeling, you may be able to tap into this trend. If you have a smaller home, another group that is growing is the move-down market: seniors and retirees.

Tip 41: Always check your house against the "fourfold path to value."

Appraiser Wallace Kaufman, in his book *Finding Hidden Values in Your Home*, describes the fourfold path to value as desire, utility, scarcity, and purchasing power. When statistics and analysis get too confusing, the key is to go back to the basics:

- Is your house desirable? Desire is a fickle thing. What makes a neighborhood hot, a home special, or a garden attractive? These are the questions you should be asking yourself on a consistent basis. Why will people pay more for a Rolls Royce, Chivas Regal, or certain perfumes? Understanding what is desired and how to create desire can have a great impact on your home's value.

- Utility. Does your home have a floor plan that works for today's buyer? If you have only one bathroom in your house, you are at a distinct disadvantage compared to the homes with two. Bathrooms are more important to buyers than they were thirty years ago.

- Scarcity. Another element that adds value is scarcity. In many apartment markets today there are waiting lists for three- and four-bedroom apartments while studios and one-bedrooms sit idle. Because of supply and demand, a premium can be charged now on the larger apartments. Every home has something unique. Whether it is a view, a special front porch or some other desirable item, if you market what is scarce, you can get a higher price for your home.

- Purchasing power. If people can't afford to buy your home, they won't, no matter how much they would like to. The availability of money in our society will affect the value of your home. If interest rates are high, purchasing power drops. Having financing alternatives is a key way to raise the purchasing power of the public for your home.

By following careful appraisal guidelines and staying with the basic principals, you can gain value and make your home more desirable than others which have the same basic characteristics.

Tip 42: Value is subjective.

Many types of value can be ascribed to real estate. There is replacement cost value, assessed value, insurable value, and salvage value. But the true definition of value is what a willing and able buyer will pay for the house. Note that value is not the same as cost or price!

Many factors come into play in determining value. Any one of these can make your home more desirable in relation to others in the same area. When marketing the home, play up the appropriate factors that will impact value positively with a particular buyer.

Value factors include the following:

- Proximity to employment

- Quality of schools

- Recreational and amusement facilities

- City services

- Distance to facilities (how far your home is from schools, churches, major shopping centers, other cultural and religious institutions)

Market the factors that will raise the value in your target group's eyes.

CHAPTER SIX

Homebuying Trends

Who Might Buy Your House

As you look at how much you want to ask for your house, you should consider what type of people would want to buy it. Do these people have a high or low need? Lots of or little money to spend? All of these issues are studied in great detail by demographers and economists. You can usually get access to their conclusions simply by looking in the newspapers.

Tip 43: Know what types of people will be buying homes this year.

Between 1990 and 2000, baby boomers will account for 54 percent of all households. This will cause a bulge in move-up buyers, those seeking larger houses with more amenities, assuming that they can afford to move from their current houses or apartments.

The "baby bust" will cut entry-level demand. The baby bust will probably do to housing what it did to school systems in the 1970s: cause some painful shrinkage after several boom years. What could offset this in boom areas are migrating job workers who will settle for a smaller house. Another possible offset is that of first-time buyers' ages moving up. Many people put off home purchases through the 1980s and rented. Now they can finally afford to buy. On a more positive note, low home-ownership rates in the 1980s mean millions of hungry first-time buyers at the peak of their earning power.

Tip 44: Look for secondary trends that may add value to your house.

Demographics also suggest that second homes will be hot in the 1990s. For one thing, the number of householders of age 54 to 65 should increase from 12.3 million to 14.1 million. These buyers are likely to be the wealthiest generation on record. If your home is in a vacation area, this may be a good way to market it.

The steady growth of small, nontraditional households and single-parent families will keep specialized markets for condominiums, townhouses, and similar products active.

The evolution of the "yuppie" is accelerating. As boomers start having children and spending more time at home, they want amenities that connote traditional values and make their lives easier. They will look for products that will give them status and prestige still, but now geared for the home. These would include a bathroom spa or a wine-storage refrigerator.

Tip 45: Know how many people are looking and what their ages are.

Slower population growth will be the general rule for the 1990s. By the late 1990s, household formation will have dropped 25% to about 1.1 million a year from about 1.4 million a year in the 1980s. When you combine this with the demographic fact that there are fewer people in the first-time buyer range, you get a huge drag on housing in the 1990s. The age groups expected to swell in the 1990s are the older baby boomers and the 65+ age group. The 45–54 group will increase 46% by 2000.

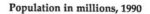

Population in millions, 1990

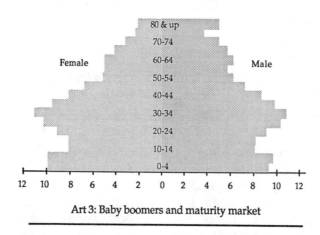

Art 3: Baby boomers and maturity market

On a positive note, the numbers can be misleading. Just because there are fewer younger people doesn't mean there will be fewer first-time buyers. The first-time buyer has now become someone from the mid-twenties all the way up to the mid-forties. But it is agreed that because of rising prices in the 1980s and because of fewer households at the bottom end in the 1990s. It will take more target marketing and a cleverer approach to house selling to move a home and get top dollar.

Trends in Housing

Every few years, new trends in houses pop up. They are often spurred on by building magazines and the home sections of newspapers, which are always eager to write about the next big thing. Some trends, such as those toward more energy efficiency, can last for decades; others, like hot tubs, can come and go in a few short years.

It is important for you to know what the trends in houses are, so that you can price your house accordingly. If you have none of the latest ideas incorporated in your house, you can't ask for as much. If you have many, especially the enduring ones, you can ask for more. Your buyers may be very tuned into the trends if they have been reading the home magazines before deciding to buy a house.

Tip 46: Understand how your home stacks up against new houses and other houses on the market.

Property developers are building homes bigger and better these days. Baby boomers are fueling the rage to move up to better homes. The following statistics, easily obtained from the Department of Commerce, are very revealing. The typical house is bigger than it used to be, and has all sorts of amenities that it didn't have before:

	1980	1989
Central air conditioning	63%	88%
At least 2½ baths	25%	44%
Four bedrooms or more	20%	28%
One fireplace or more	56%	65%
Garage for two or more cars	56%	70%
Two stories or more	31%	49%
2,400 square feet or more	15%	26%

The baby boomers make up a full 25% of the population and their needs have driven this culture for the past 30 or 40 years.

Tip 47: Read some builders' magazine to catch the trends.

Keeping up on the latest trends and desires of home buyers is easier when you get a copy delivered to your home each month. Many home building publications are available to the general public at a small cost of $20 to $45 for a year's subscription. If you don't want to spend the money to get the magazine for a whole year, many local and university libraries carry copies of builder magazines. You can also often find them in larger building supply stores.

Tip 48: Make your home a "model home."

Throughout the 1980s, builders fine-tuned the concept of the model home as a marketing tool. It wasn't long ago that many builders actually sold homes from plans. That practice is happening less and less as markets become buyers' markets rather than sellers' markets.

In recent surveys among builders, a resoundingly common response was the need to pay attention to the growing number of specialty markets. These include single parents, foreign buyers, and empty nesters, to name a few.

Quality was the buzz word of the 1980s. Merchandising that can capture the many cultures and lifestyles of today's buyers, or "colorization," is becoming the word of the 1990s. When builders design the furnishings of a home, they target a market. Although it would make no sense for you to toss all your furniture away and start all over just to appeal to some buyer, there are a number of things you can do.

For example, recently a builder wanted to appeal to affluent buyers, so it furnished a fifth bedroom of a house to look like an *au pair*'s and register in the buyer's eye the type of use for that room that was highest and best for their market.

Tip 49: Consider showing part of your house as a home office.

Homework isn't just for children anymore. Home offices are hot these days. There are seminars and books on how to work out of the home, builder magazines are pushing their clients to build home offices, and telecommunications keeps getting more and more advanced. This, coupled with families wanting to be together and people getting tired of traffic and commutes, is fueling the trend to work at home, at least part-time.

There are now more than thirty million people working at home, with over half using home offices as their primary work space. Over 50 million are projected to work out of their homes by the year 2000. More than half of home workers have college degrees, and the group's average income is around $42,000, a full $10,000 above the national average. More money in these people's pockets means a buyer more likely able to spend a lot on your home.

There's a real need for home offices. Many women are tired of sending the kids to day care while they work at jobs outside the home. They prefer being able to handle career and motherhood with the reduced stress working at home brings.

There are many ways to create a home office in an existing home; these are covered in the renovations section of this book. Some ideas include:

- Convert an extra bedroom downstairs into a home office. If you have a three- or four-bedroom house, especially with a room downstairs, your home will be in demand if approached correctly.

- Create a separate entrance to the home office to allow for client visits. This is a must in many home based businesses.

Tip 50: Adding an in-law apartment can increase your home's value and make it more salable to a larger segment of the market.

Adding an apartment to the home will make the home more salable in many areas for several reasons:

- The increased income will help buyers make mortgage payments which they might otherwise have to stretch for.

- There are an increased number of elderly occupants and others who want to live in nice neighborhoods and will pay high rent to do so.

People are also returning in many cases to intergenerational living. This is especially true of many immigrant families. Providing a separate apartment for an elderly family member or a cousin increases the marketing appeal of the home.

Be sure to check with the city and county offices about ordinances and permits. Some areas are much more restrictive than others.

Tip 51: Consider turning your house into a duplex.

Duplexes were big at the turn of the century and at many times when markets were softer. The positive aspects of a duplex are similar to those of a granny flat: income, tax benefits, and so forth. However, if you can legally convert your house to two units and architecturally make it work, this could be a good profit opportunity for you.

You do not need to perform the duplex separation yourself to add value to your home. If the buyer is looking for a house to convert themselves, you can show that you have anticipated their needs by going to the local zoning board and getting all the relevant information. This frees the buyer from having to do it, and it also shows that you and the buyer have something in common.

Tip 52: Transportation from home to work has become very important.

As freeways get more and more congested and with infrastructure construction far behind growth in many parts of the country, it is expected that public transportation will be a growth area in the 1990s.

As the suburbs grew after World War II and people fled the cities, the idea of a large home on a large lot, separated from the city, was an ideal. Now, however, as traffic becomes a major issue, people don't want to be so far away from work these days. Areas which used to be a twenty-minute commute are now a forty-minute commute. Also, the allure of driving your own automobile is losing some of its luster in the environmentally aware boomer 1990s. If your home is near a commuter rail line, or transportation hub, that can be a major selling point and a hot button in the 1990s.

Infill building (building in the city) has become popular among builders and developers. Previously passed-over sites are becoming appealing because they lack the impact fees and transportation issues that less expensive land further out may bring. You are already at an advantage with a built house.

Bedroom communities far removed from jobs, shopping, and leisure activities are now a thing of the past. The neighborhood of the 1990s, like those before 1940, will have these services nearby. And if they don't, they still want them there. Use your home's location as a marketing advantage to tap into today's desires.

Traffic has become public enemy number one in many neighborhoods. The town of today will not separate jobs from home from shopping. Homeowners may not be able to walk everywhere, but they won't have to take the freeway there, either. If your home has some of these features you can tap into the needs of today's homebuyer and they'll beat a path to your door.

Tip 53: Emphasize the low maintenance aspects of your house.

With the continuance of two-income households and the decline of the traditional American family, where the wife can clean all day, low-maintenance houses will appeal more and more to buyers, especially in the move-up market. Many people who have previously owned a home know how long it takes to mow the lawn or deal with cleaning an oven that is not self-cleaning. Swimming pools, flower beds, and other high-maintenance items, while beautiful, lose some of their luster when a sophisticated buyer comes through. Low-maintenance houses featuring easy-care surfaces and time-saving appliances will continue to gain in popularity.

Tip 54: Be very aware of toxic substances in your house.

First it was asbestos, then radon, now formaldehyde; next, who knows what. Toxics have become a concern in real estate. Although few people envision Love Canals when they look at a typical home, there are many chemicals and other components used in house construction through the 1980s that are potentially toxic. If you are doing some remodeling, or if your home is relatively new, a "healthy house" will be a real selling point. The question is whether you can convert your home into a healthy house inexpensively. This is covered later in the renovations chapters.

Some products will probably be banned in the 1990s, and their impact on the value of your home could be significant.

Tip 55: Consider selling your house as a second home or vacation house.

Higher incomes for an aging population, two-income households entering their higher-income years, and an expected increase in foreign tourism into the United States suggest a favorable future for vacation housing in the 1990s. If you have a property in a vacation area, this is a market to look at.

Because tax reforms have eliminated many benefits of single ownership, partial-interest properties are an alternative form of ownership. The more you know about these issues, the better prepared you will be to help a potential buyer who is interested in them. Remember, you are probably competing with dozens of other similar homes, but it is unlikely that any of them can be as helpful on technical issues such as these.

Tip 56: Adjust your house for an ethnic market.

As more and more ethnic cultures make up a greater proportion of our nation's population, gearing your home toward the traditional white, middle-class family has the potential of alienating what might be a strong ethnic market in your area. What might be fine to you might actually mean bad luck to someone from another culture. We tend to view what we do as correct, as the "natural" way to do things.

To make your house more attractive to more people, you must be open to and aware of ethnic trends in housing. This is equally true for non-ethnic people selling to ethnic buyers and ethnic people selling to non-ethnic buyers. Each buyer is different and may have few desires in common with the other people of his or her ethnic background, but you should be aware of general patterns so that you can cater to them in the same way you cater to the other desires discussed in this book.

For example, one will note that in Feng Shui, the Chinese art of designing a harmonious environment, there are special rules and traditions for landscaping, the site, the home, and the workplace. In other parts of Asia, the emphasis is on shared spaces with only small rooms for privacy. Families from the Indian subcontinent have other desires, such as more emphasis on beauty added, usually in the form of art and sculpture. For many Hispanic buyers, a private kitchen with a little pass-through window may be preferred to a kitchen completely open to the dining room.

Buyers from different ethnic groups have different needs. Many have several generations living together and want a separate living area downstairs for an elder family member. Although this is common in most other parts of the world, few builders create new houses with such spaces. Along with a full bedroom, there should be a full bath downstairs.

If your house fits an ethnic desire well, you should consider advertising in local ethnic newspapers. Be sure your real estate agent mentions the relevant features to buyer's agents in communities where the people you wish to attract live.

Tip 57: Note whether your buyers are looking for the latest in technology.

There was a time when many houses did not have indoor plumbing. Those that did had a market advantage. Today, home builders are starting to put high-technology features into homes. Although many of these features must be installed when the house is built (or significantly remodeled), these features will become more and more common in the next few years, and a home properly equipped will be at a significant marketing advantage.

For example, people who work at home on a computer often need to communicate with the office over a second phone line. If you have a second line already installed, be sure to emphasize it in your marketing. Likewise, if you have speakers in many rooms, your house has an advantage with some buyers since this lets them avoid a tedious task.

> **Tip 58: The master bedroom is an icon of a modern house.**

After 1945, the master bedroom became a selling point in suburban home developments. What made a master bedroom master was its size and the fact that it had an attached bathroom. Over time, more amenities were added to the master. First there were walk-in closets, then his and hers closets, and then sitting areas. This has now evolved into the master suite. A master suite is a retreat within the home. Soaking tubs, fireplace, reading area and luxurious surroundings are all part of this latest trend. Your buyer is looking out for himself or herself and the focus is on the bedroom. This is fully covered later in the renovations chapters.

> **Tip 59: If your town exemplifies what the buyers want, you can sometimes charge extra.**

This trend toward traditional American values is also turning up in the types of towns many people are choosing to live in. If your town fits this description, it could be a strong selling point to those wishing to escape the city or suburbs.

Note that this is a tricky issue. If someone is looking in your town or area, it is likely that that person is looking only around there. Thus, the additional value will already be reflected in the prices of the houses with which you are competing. Don't inflate the price of your house just because the community is great, but keep it in mind when you total up the value that your house reflects.

Tip 60: Be sure to disclose as much as possible, since buyers are now exercising their rights more often.

The days of "let the buyer beware" are long gone. Not too long ago, if you covered up some dry rot and painted over it, it might be several years before a buyer discovered the problem, and the new owner would have to cover the costs of fixing it. Consumer protection laws have sprung up to cover buyers in real estate transactions. If anything, the law has now swung strongly to the buyers' side. Developers are being sued for negligence if the house has noisy pipes. Home sellers are being sued if they didn't disclose that some teenagers hang out at night at the park down the block.

In selling a home today, disclosure is extremely important. But knowing that, you can disclose negatives without them becoming so overwhelming to the buyer that it scares him away. Talk with your agent about what the disclosure form should say before filling it out.

CHAPTER SEVEN

Advertising

The key to good advertising is to get prospective buyers to your home. You've probably heard radio spots for new housing developments, seen large display ads in the paper advertising homes for sale by brokerages and builders, and probably even seen an occasional TV spot. Obviously these ads must work or they wouldn't be used again and again. Just remember that most of these techniques do not apply to the sale of a single home: they are just too expensive. When you see large ads in the paper, they are usually promoting the real estate brokerage more than any particular property. A homeseller must focus on smaller ads. The key is to make those small-budget ads pay big dividends.

Tip 61: Standard advertising is not the only way.

At the other extreme from the groups that spend thousands of dollars on advertising are the ones that spend almost nothing in either time or energy. Too many real estate agents and sellers have gotten used to placing a classified ad in a newspaper or a real estate weekly and leaving it at that. Some just place a sign in front of the home. In a down market this just won't work. Advertising must not be viewed as a substitute for other marketing and sales techniques; it is only the beginning.

You don't have a $5,000 advertising budget to attract buyers. You are working in the land of guerilla advertising. The key is to use your imagination and resources in the most effective manner. You need to modify what works and apply it to your situation. Sellers of new home developments often hold a grand opening party or sponsor an event such as a race that ends at the development itself. Sometimes these creative ideas can get buyers to you.

Before going into some of the more creative endeavors, start with getting the basics right. If you do these few things properly, they could double the number of prospects who walk through the door.

Tip 62: Classified ads are the format by which real estate gets sold.

More than display advertising, TV, radio, or any other medium, classified ads are the medium of choice among real estate professionals. Yet most homesellers and many agents haven't really thought about how to write a truly effective ad for selling and positioning a home. Think about the times you've looked at the classifieds. Very rarely did it excite you. Creating an ad that pops out from that crowd shouldn't be hard, although it will require a little thought and energy.

Classified advertising is a unique medium. Classified ads are short, but they can be powerful. Lacking any illustrations and full of abbreviations, they can be a bigger challenge than creating a display ad. The keys to think about in classified advertising are Whom am I trying to attract? Where am I placing the ad? Why am I running it there? Why am I choosing these words? How much will it cost? and When should I run it?

Some ads are better appearing each day, but sometimes Sunday only is the best. Your goal is to reach the largest qualified audience most cost effectively. This often means running some slightly different ads in a variety of local papers, using each only on specific target days. In my community, home advertising and rental advertising are typically looked at in the Sunday paper. However, on an apartment complex we owned in another town, the home emphasis was on Saturday. Running ads on Sunday without investigating cost both lost money and time. Choose the right day.

Tip 63: Decide where to advertise so you don't throw away money.

Before you write a good ad, you need to know where to place it. You could write the best ad in the world, but if it doesn't reach your target market, you've wasted both your money and your energy. Different publications are read by different people.

Whom are you trying to appeal to? Are they executives or first time buyers? What papers do they read? Are they likely to pick up one of those HOMES magazines? or just look through the classified ads in the major papers?

Most people simply put their ad in the paper with the largest circulation. This is the simple solution, but it could be both foolish and expensive. A five-line ad in the Sunday *San Francisco Chronicle* costs around $60. And when there are two newspapers in town, cross-readership tends to be low, so advertising in both is probably necessary.

You can't always know in advance which paper will attract your target buyer, but you can be alert to studying which ads in which papers seem to work. When advertising in multiple papers, evaluate the response you get to each ad. That way you can judge where your money is going farthest. Take a guess at which papers seem most likely to work. Talk to successful real estate agents and see which papers they recommend. That's usually a good start. Just don't discount the others right away.

Many communities also have neighborhood papers. These can have the advantage of being targeted directly to the people who want to live in the neighborhood. Because rates are cheaper, your ad can be larger, if you want. Sometimes a foreign-language newspaper is a good bet, especially if you are targeting a specific ethnic group to buy your home. Make sure your ad is translated correctly.

Sometimes special magazines or throw-away papers are appropriate. There are magazines that are given away free which advertise only homes. These also allow for a picture of the property. Since your home will show well after doing the work described in this book, this can be an excellent medium to display your home. The people looking through these magazines are usually specifically looking for a home, although some might be just lining their bird cages. Pay attention to what works.

Tip 64: The section of the newspaper that your ad appears in can be as important as the choice of newspaper.

Most newspapers regularly publish special sections or additions such as the "spring buyer's home guide." If these issues are likely to reach your target market, they are probably more effective than the general classified section. There are often special sections such as the "open house guide" which are an extremely effective tool to grab prospects. Buyers often cut out only these lists and then drive around all afternoon looking at the houses. Failure to be on these lists means your house is passed over. These special real estate sections will work for you because the most interested and motivated buyers are looking through them.

In the classifieds, make sure your ad is located in the appropriate section. Sometimes homes are broken down by neighborhood. Your home may be right next to a better neighborhood and you might want to attract those buyers. Place the ad in the "wrong" section, or maybe both sections.

Professional management firms renting apartments often place ads in the "condominiums for rent" section instead of the apartment section if their apartments are condominium quality but the rents were significantly lower than those of nearby condominiums. Potential renters don't mind that they aren't legally condos: they are just looking to rent a place to live, anyway. What they want is a nice place, which is why they avoided the "apartment for rent" section.

Tip 65: Sunday ads are sufficient for most homes.

Although classified advertising costs little compared to other media, the cost can ad up to a significant amount over time. Many newspapers recognize this and offer lower rates for extended runs. Usually there are one-day, three-day, one-week, ten-day, and 30-day rates or some similar combinations. A three-line ad which might be $30 for a one-day run might be $22 per day for a 30-day run. This is usually false economy, though. People who are seriously looking at the ads and they see the same ad day after day, they start wondering why the house isn't selling. You get the "tired listing" syndrome in miniature, and the effectiveness of your ad is lost. Also, paying for four Sundays ($30 x 4 insertions = $120) only versus one full month at the lower monthly rate ($22 x 30 times = $660) may be just as effective for a fifth of the price.

Timing can help. Many brokerages reduce their ads during the holidays because business is slow and most brokers want to be at home. This thinner classified section could make your ad stick out more, and you will reach the serious prospects who need to buy now.

Tip 66: Evaluate which ads get more response and cut out ads that don't generate potential buyers.

You should evaluate which of your ads get the most response in order to use your budget most appropriately. If you are selling your house yourself, use the checklist on the following page to rate your response. If you have an agent, he or she should be doing this themselves.

Date	Time	Weather	Source Of Call					Name and Phone # of Caller	Appointment Made to Show Home	Rating/Notes
			Tribune ad	Times ad	Sign	Referral	Other			

Art 4: Sample daily call sheet

You and your agent should be continually revising your ads to gain better response. Try rewriting the ad with different ideas emphasized. Perhaps emphasize the financing in the headline one week, the location the next time. Try bold print one week, normal print another. Sometimes increasing the number of lines will draw more people; sometimes a more compact ad works.

By varying your ad and the wording of it, you will soon see what works and what doesn't. Be flexible. Alter it. Adjust the size. Adjust the type face. But most importantly, always keep your goal in mind: to create interest in the property so that you can sell it.

Writing a Good Classified Ad

The goals of your ad are to catch the interest of your target buyers and to motivate them to call or come by and see your house. To do this, your ad must be visible: it must be worded in such a way that it contrasts with other ads in the same section.

Tip 67: Make your ad stand out so the buyer will notice it.

Although classified ads don't contain photographs, many graphic techniques can typically be applied. Most sellers and brokers ignore these. Many newspapers offer standard characters such as stars or bullets (★ •) which can be used to make your ad pop out from the crowd. You might also be able to have a darker border or to shade your ad to make it pop out.

Variation in type size can also be used. A large catchy headline draws the eye. Some papers will even allow your ad to straddle two columns, making it easily visible. Contrasting the use of CAPITAL LETTERS ONLY with a more standard mix of upper and lower case can also make your ad graphically more interesting. Don't overdo it, but use graphics to your advantage. No one ever said your ad had to be visually dull and boring to be allowed in the classified section.

> **Tip 68: If you list features other ads don't, you will get more people to come and look.**

Focus on the features that appeal to your target group. If you are going after young families, than talk about the playroom or the fenced yard for the kids. If it is a move-up market, talk about the luxurious bath or the showplace dining area. You've already decided who are the people most likely to buy your home, so why advertise for everyone: go after your niche.

Say "attractive yard for children" rather than "yard" if you are appealing to young families. If you are targeting retired couples, than state "low maintenance, ideal retired couple's home". Remember, appeal to the emotions of the buyers; don't just state the physical characteristics of the house.

> **Tip 69: Don't be wordy, but use words that make people want to come by and see the house.**

Be efficient in your writing. Your goal is to get your point across effectively, not necessarily have a contest to use the fewest words. If you need to use a few more words, it's usually worth the money. Not everything can be said minimally. "Fabulous view of the bay" is stronger than "view."

In creating your ad, use some of the basic rules of advertising. Have a catchy headline, keep your ad short (but not at the expense of effectiveness), use adjectives to enhance the ad, and emphasize the features most likely to appeal to your eventual buyer. Most importantly, make sure buyers can understand the ad.

Certain facts are necessary to make the ad satisfactory to buyers. Surveys have shown that prospects responded best to ads that included definite information on the following:

- location of the home
- number of rooms
- price and terms
- age of house or design of house

- present condition of house

Many people use abbreviations in order to save space and money. But if the buyer doesn't know what a "4 bd Col, AEEIK" is, he's not going to get excited by the ad. How much better to describe the "4-bedroom colonial with a modern, all-electric, eat-in kitchen." That might be what the buyer wants. Use abbreviations sparingly in your ads.

Using English instead of "want ad talk" can be much more effective. When creating a classified ad, think first in terms of clarity, then in terms of reader interest. You must catch the reader's attention, as you have only an instant to do it before readers move on to the next ad.

Here are examples of poorly worded ads:

4 bd, 2 ba brick home. New Kitch &
W/W, LR, DR, Pvt. entr., wlk to RR.
C/A/C$129,000. By owner 555-5555

Upper Claremont. $238,000 4 bd, 3 ba
frml din & family rm. Great
opportunity to decorate. Near freeway.
Call agt. 555-5555

Art 5: Examples of bad ads

_____

Notice how much more enticing the following ad is. It gets you to want to call:

New listing! Charming, gracious 3500
sq. ft. Victorian. Only $129,000. Orig.
moldings and wood floors. Dramatic
view. Fireplace. All executive
amenities, must see. 555-5555

Art 6: Example of a good ad

_____

Here's another poorly written ad and a rewritten version of it. Notice the difference in the appeal the two ads create.

Bright home w/lge. LR & entry.
Formal D/R w/French doors. Fam.
rm. 4 lge BR & Snrm w/pano ocean &
south views. Lge. bath w/Kohler sinks
& fixtures. 2-car. Finished x-wide bk
yd. w/fountain.
$235,000.   555-5555
Open Sunday 1-4. 2027 Elm St.

OPEN SUNDAY 1-4

Elegant Mediterranean in prestigious
Elmwood Heights. Sweeping city and
ocean view. Grandeur and
architectural integrity are the
hallmarks of this home. 4 bd, 2 ba,
formal dining and fam. rm. Beautiful
grounds w/ fountain. $235K
2027 Elm St.   **555-5555**

Art 7: Transforming a bad to a good ad

Don't state everything in the ad. Ads that tell the buyers everything they need to know are both expensive and counterproduc-
tive. Pique the reader's interest, but have enough information to
qualify prospects so that you don't get people looking for a six-
bedroom luxury home calling on your two-bedroom starter.

**Tip 70: Structure your ad so that the reader will
want to read the whole ad.**

The ways to create ads are infinite. The following breakdown
may help you understand the anatomy of an ad a little better.

1. Write a hot headline. You want to get attention
   and draw the reader's eye to your ad. It
   promises a quality which will appeal to your
   targeted buyer.

2. The body. The goals here are to maintain the momentum the headline created while giving the facts of the house.

3. The closing. This is the call to action. It can be as simple as a phone number or contain a little more motivation. Examples include:

Won't be around long at $xxx,000

Best value in the neighborhood at $xxx,000

The key is to create both the desire to buy and the desire to know more. Don't get bogged down with unnecessary facts or words. The Gettysburg address is one of the most memorable of human documents yet it contains only a couple of hundred words, few of which are of more than one syllable. Be strong, be powerful, and be concise.

Tip 71: Take the best from the good ads you see in your paper and use it in your own ads.

Study the ads in your local newspaper and see which ones excite you. Start cutting them out now! You will find that every week, a new interesting one seems to appear. Make a collection and then start applying the knowledge you gain to the creation of your own ad.

One word of caution: Don't write your ads like the real estate agents. Their ads are designed to get reader to call the brokerage, not necessarily to sell the property advertised. You don't have the luxury of steering buyers to other properties, so make your ad work for your home.

And remember, you can do better than the "pros." Real estate agents and brokerages spend millions each year on classified advertising, yet most of those dollars are wasted because many of these same people don't understand how to write a truly effective ad. The resulting glut of ineffective, marginal ads will allow yours (and those of good agents) to pop out and strike a chord with your prospective purchaser.

> ### Tip 72: Don't reveal your personal problems to anyone.

How many times have you seen people advertising houses with lines like "divorce—must sell now" or "owner transferred—will take any offer." Unless you want to put the call out to the bargain hunters, there is no reason to reveal this information. The people who want a home will never give you top dollar if they think you are in a forced-sale position. Be careful about whom you're attracting by how you word the ad. You want people who will pay a premium, not those who want a discount.

> ### Tip 73: The followup phone call is almost as important as the ad itself.

Many people have become good at writing ads only to have no skills answering the telephone. You want to be available when you expect people to see your ad. If it runs on a Sunday, be around the house that day to answer calls. If you won't be around on Monday, because you go to work, then you should state the appropriate times to call in the ad. How you answer the phone will go a long way to getting buyers to your home.

Never forget that classified ads do not sell homes: people do. The ad is there to pique someone's interest, to get someone to call or drive by. It makes the reader want to get more information and gets the excitement going. But unless your product or your personality can take the ad from there, you will not be as successful as you could be.

Don't run the ad until the home is ready. A premature drive-by could lose the prospect who just might have become your buyer. First impressions last a long time.

CHAPTER EIGHT

Showing Your Home

No one buys a house from an ad in the newspaper. The most important moment is when the prospective buyer comes to your house for the first time. That moment will make or break the vast majority of sales.

Many home sellers assume that the house sells itself. They figure that as long as everything is clean and neat a buyer will understand how wonderful the house is. This mentality in other home sellers works to your benefit, since you will go to much greater lengths to impress people as they come into your house. Remember, all people want to be pampered. They certainly don't expect it, especially if they have just seen some uninviting houses, but they really want it. Cater to them and you can turn a slow market into a fast one even if your house is similar to others on the market.

Tip 74: Be prepared at all times for visitors.

Real estate agents tell horror stories of showing properties for sale where tenants have answered the door naked, where they have walked into bedrooms where couples were in bed together, and other homes where the owners were in the middle of cooking dinner with the relatives. Although you can't totally alter your life to sell a home, you must realize that some of this activity might turn off prospective buyers.

In a down market, you are lucky when you get someone to come by and look. Likewise, people looking will do so at their leisure and on their own terms. They may say that they can come only after 9p.m. or during the middle of the day. Keep this in mind. If you need time when no one will come so that you can just relax in what is still your own home, be sure your agent knows that and never breaks the rule. At worst, he or she can call you if there is a hot prospect who can only come during your "down time."

Tip 75: Use your sign to its greatest advantage.

The sign is one of the most important marketing tools for a home seller. Signs catch the attention of people looking in that specific neighborhood even if those people haven't looked in the newspaper. In a down market, buyers often avoid the newspaper because there are just too many ads. They'll find an area they like (or one that has been recommended by a friend) and cruise around. In many cases, they'll actually walk the streets with a map and mark where they see the "for sale" signs.

Obviously the sign should be easy to read. Red on a white background reads well. Keep the sign simple and don't try to clutter it by listing amenities or price and terms.

Many real estate agents will lend you a sign with their name on it. In fact, most will insist you use theirs. If you have a choice, consider whether you want to use theirs (of which there may be dozens in your neighborhood) or your own. If you use theirs, be aware of making the sign friendly. For example, many agents' signs say "DO NOT DISTURB OCCUPANTS" or "BY APPOINTMENT ONLY." You can guess which of the two of these is more intriguing and gives your home an exclusive feeling, and which is an unfriendly turnoff.

Use separate signs for open houses. You don't need your signs to go everywhere, just to lead prospects to your home. If there are four other open house signs at a main intersection, putting up a fifth one won't do much good. The key is to divert those shoppers. Follow the lead of those signs and then at key points or intersections along the way, place your sign, so that it might divert some drivers to your house. Using a separate open-house sign also tells a buyer who can't come to the open house but who drives by that he or she may be able to see the house at some other time.

Most signs can be purchased at a sign shop. Look in the yellow pages under "signs." There are many prefabricated signs, or you can have them custom made. Open-house signs can be stock. The sign in front of your house should have some attention paid to it and might best be custom-made depending on cost.

If your "for sale" sign looks like all the rest, your house won't stand out. A way to gain extra attention from your sign is to add a little strip hanging from the bottom with an enticing line such as "Low Down Payment" or "Ocean View." This additional strip separates your sign from the rest and induces purchasers to call.

As an addition to the sign, you could put sales flyers in a plexiglass bin so that prospects can get more information and so that you can entice them to enter your home at your next open house. This should not be your information sheet. This must be sales oriented. You want prospects to enter your home, not write it off before they've ever seen it. Remember to put the date and time of the next open house on the flyer so people will feel welcome.

Tip 76: Always use word of mouth to tell people your home is for sale.

You overhear two people at a Sunday brunch. One says to the other, "what a beautiful home and a great view! I'd love to live up here." The other says, "Well, Joe Smith just put his house up for sale down the block. They've got an even better view. I'll call now and we'll check it out."

That's how houses are sometimes sold, just through word of mouth. Just running an ad isn't enough. If you want to sell your home quickly and for top dollar, it is time for "guerilla marketing."

Talk to people you know and ask them if anyone in their company is thinking of moving. A common mistake is to tell all your friends after you sell the house that you are moving. If you tell them before you start to sell the house and they find someone who might be interested, your friend has done both of you a favor. Talk to your doctor, your lawyer, your neighbors, and anyone in your social clubs.

If someone you talk to shows any interest, send them your fact sheet. This may seem very forward, but it is the best way for them to know just how good your house is. Why wait for them to come by when they might never get around to it?

Tip 77: In a down market, many buyers are very detail-oriented. A clear, complete fact sheet will impress them.

A fact sheet is a sales tool for your home just as a resume is for a job applicant. In a world where buyers see five houses in a day or 15 to 20 before buying, your fact sheet triggers memories of your home in their minds, especially if they are picky. Fact sheets contain a lot of information and answer some basic buyer questions such as square footage and number of rooms. Here are some tips for writing a good fact sheet:

- Look at other fact sheets for houses in the neighborhood. Note the ones that excite you and the ones that turn you off.

- Be creative. If you have a computer that can print out fancy (but readable) text, use it for your fact sheet.

- Print the fact sheet on bond paper. Use a cream or colored paper to make it stand out from other papers people might find in their mailboxes or put on their desk.

- Sell the virtues of your house. You may need to re-aquaint yourself with your house. Try to use as many positive words as you can.

- Don't confine the fact sheet to the house itself. Talk about the neighborhood, access to shopping, the great school district, and so forth.

- Get accurate data for your fact sheet. What are your property taxes? How much did it cost to heat your home last winter? To cool it last summer? What is the average water bill?

- Put together an accurate renovation and maintenance history, with such items as these:

  1986: painted exterior of house

  1987: added new roof

- If you have additional information that would make your home more exciting, put that together on a separate sheet. This is a good example of how to make your home memorable. Maybe it has historical significance, or perhaps there is something that might point to the quality of the construction that a buyer could take home and read. If the owners before you were famous, certainly include that.

- Be accurate. In most states, the fact sheet is a legal document when you sell your house. Don't gloss over negative aspects, as for example if you have been told that the chimney needs work or you know that rain can seep in under a particular door.

SINCE 1887

THOMPSON-ADAMS

REAL ESTATE INC.

260 SUMMER STREET
OAKLAND, CA 94609

Delightful sunny victorian era cottage with lovely yard, bright and airy throughout. Great convenient location to Oakland, Berkeley and San Francisco! Affordable! Seller will provide termite clearance.

- Gorgeous new kitchen!
- Three bedrooms, two baths!
- Wonderful enclosed yard!
- Lower Rockridge location!

- New bathrooms!
- Seller may participate in 80/10/10
- Vacant and on lock box!
- Move-in Condition!

$249,500

Peter Doyle off. 555-1212 res. 555-2121

Thompson-Adams Real Estate Inc. believes all material to be correct but assumes no legal responsibility for its accuracy. Offering is subject to prior sale, change or withdrawal without notice.

Art 8: Example of a good fact sheet

FOR SALE BY
OWNER

CURB APPEAL

* 2 BEDROOMS

* 1 BATH

* REMODELED KITCHEN

* FORMAL LIVING ROOM WITH WOOD BURNING FIREPLACE

* SUNNY FORMAL DINING ROOM

* BONUS ROOM

* BASEMENT

* PRICE INCLUDES REFRIGERATOR, WASHER AND DRYER

* OFF STREET PARKING FOR THREE VEHICLES

8981 DUBOCE STREET, WALLACETOWN

LISTED AT $229.500

OWNERS NO. 555-5555

Art 9: Example of a bad fact sheet

Tip 78: Give your potential buyers a floor plan.

Most new-home subdivisions contain floor plans of the home as a standard part of their marketing brochures. It gives the buyers something to take home with and look at to picture how their furniture will be arranged. What better way to keep the picture of your home in the buyer's mind than to provide the actual floor plan for them. You can draw them up yourself or hire an architecture student from a local college.

The size of the floorplan affects the value perception of the buyers. A large floor plan makes your home seem more valuable. Color and shading to highlight rooms, patios, landscaping, and features add more excitement and impact to your floor plans.

Color graphics help make the floor plan come to life and sell the home.

In a down market, your potential buyers will have seen many homes in your neighborhood. It is your job to make yours memorable. If you have a memorable home layout, reinforce it by giving the buyer something to look at after he or she has gone.

Tip 79: Take a good photo of your house or have an artist sketch it.

Images sell homes. When people see your fact sheet, they should conjure up an image of what the home looks like. Why not help them out by presenting your home in the best light? There are two popular mediums, photographs and pen-and-ink drawings.

Black and white mode rather than color photographs are usually used. This is because black and white reproduces better on copy machines. Sellers of exclusive homes and expensive commercial properties usually use color. They then print up the flyer and glue a color photo to each one. This is not economical for the typical home but might work for a limited run in presenting your home to a target group that you feel is likely to buy.

The purpose of this photo is to sell your home. So don't be cheap and take only one or two shots. Act like a professional and use the whole roll, taking pictures from a variety of angles and at various times of the day in order to get the best light. Wait for a clear, sunny day, and don't forget to remove any distracting elements that might interfere with the image of the home such as cars or signs. Also, trim and prepare the exterior as if you were having an open house tomorrow. If you know someone who is a good photographer, you might want to ask him or her to take the pictures. Even a good amateur photographer (someone who has taken a few photography courses at a community college, for instance) is far preferable to a rank amateur. Spend your money wisely. Shooting and developing a whole roll compared to one or two pictures only costs a few dollars compared to the thousands at stake if you fail to appeal to people's emotions because of a poor shot.

Pen-and-ink drawings are also used quite a bit in the industry. These usually cost $50 to $200 to produce. However, they have the advantage of the artist's eye. Flaws can be deleted in the drawing and view and perspectives not possible with a photograph (perhaps because another building or a telephone pole is in the way) can be created that show your home in its best possible light. Also, pen and ink reproduces much cleaner than photographs on copy machines and gives your fact sheet a clean, crisp image.

Tip 80: Distribute the fact sheet broadly.

In addition to giving your fact sheet out to your neighbors, try taking it to some large employers in the area. Many larger companies and organizations such as universities and hospitals have their own housing offices. They will probably post your flyer on one of their bulletin boards.

In addition to the fact sheet, you can promise a referral fee. Perhaps this could be a few hundred dollars or an item such as a new VCR. Cultivating people who will push your house for you is one of the oldest tricks of professionals. Why not have the people at the housing offices pushing extra hard for you because of the referral fee they stand to gain?

Tip 81: Dogs can turn off some people faster than almost anything else.

If your dog is large or frisky, barks a lot, or is overly friendly, be sure to leave it tied up outside when people come over. If they don't like dogs, this will keep them happy since the last thing they want to deal with is a strange dog. Many people are afraid of dogs, even small ones, and you do not want them coming away from your house with a sense of fear.

Of course, the people who look at the house might be dog lovers. If so, they will certainly notice your dog and probably give it a pat. Engage them in conversation about dogs. Tell them what you have done to make the house dog-friendly. Be sure to tell them if you have a vet who you like and about any city services that dog owners would be interested in. This is a great way to make a memorable bond with a potential buyer.

Tip 82: Use a lockbox so that agents can show the house when you are not at home.

It's possible someone will walk in on you, but putting your home on lockbox will allow agents to show your home when you are not there. Just leave instructions that they call first. If you are home or if you don't want entry at that moment, leave a note on the lockbox.

Tip 83: Be wary of strangers, but don't automatically say no.

If someone just rings the bell without an appointment and says he or she wants to see your house, be wary. It could be a burglar wanting to case the property. However, many times buyers will be out driving, looking at other houses, and just accidentally stumble upon yours. They are curious and right now very excited to see and possibly buy your house.

If they are with a real estate agent, get the agent's business card and consider letting them in. A high percentage of these incidents turn into sales, so it is certainly to your advantage to cooperate. Remember, many of these people are psychologically set to buy your house. The curb appeal has emotionally excited them, and if their real estate agent knows what he or she is doing, the agent can convert this excitement into a sale.

Tip 84: Investigate how others are promoting their homes in your market.

It is perfectly normal to look at the other houses for sale in the neighborhood. You can be better prepared for buyers if you know what the other houses that they have looked at are like.

How did you learn of a neighbor's house for sale? How effective was their promotion? Can you use similar techniques?

How easy was the showing of their home? Did they pay attention to you or ignore you? Did the seller hover too close? Did you leave dissatisfied? How can you change your approach to be more attractive to potential buyers?

What information would you have wanted to know that the seller did not provide? Are you sure that that information is clear in your own fact sheet?

The Open House

Some buyers insist on private showings, but other, more timid buyers are comfortable viewing a house only during an open house. In a down market, an open house can sometimes be a depressing event for the seller if only one or two people come by. Don't let it be: those people are just as valuable as those that come by appointment. You should stay cheery and helpful without hovering.

Miracles are rarely performed at open houses. Almost all sales that start at an open house are made after a second, usually private viewing. If you are lucky enough to have a crowded open house, be sure to meet everyone and offer to answer questions. That way, if they think of questions later, buyers will feel free to ask you directly. Note that some agents prefer not to have the sellers at an open house so that the agent can handle all queries professionally. Be sure you know how your agent wants to handle this ahead of time.

When you put up your "for sale" sign in the front yard, have information flyers ready, along with the invitation to the first open house and drop them into all your neighbors' mailboxes. Make your first event a popular one.

Tip 85: Enthusiasm at an open house will get you everywhere.

Be enthusiastic about your home. Mention one or two big benefits of your home to all who walk through. These can be physical benefits, like the great back yard, or locational benefits, or sales benefits, like "we'll carry back the entire loan for 15 years."

If you hear a negative comment like "the bedroom's too small," agree and respond with another benefit like "This home has a fantastic view." Never argue with a buyer. Remember, the customer is always right. If you think that the buyer is a do-it-yourself type, you can respond to criticisms with a line like "We thought so, too, but we never got around to a simple renovation like expanding the bedroom more." This helps turn a negative view into a possible positive one.

Make the open house like a party. You can have an open house to which you also invited all your friends. There should be crowds milling around, food everywhere, and a great atmosphere. Be sure to focus on selling the house during the entire party; the prospects will leave feeling, "that was a wonderful house."

You can do the same and get a double benefit by inviting your neighbors to the first open house. In many neighborhoods, word of mouth within the area often sells more houses than the professional real estate agents. It is almost as if the insiders had people in their pockets they'd love to place in your home. Use this tendency in human nature since it is only to your benefit.

Even if you're not going to throw an event, welcome all prospects as if they were guests in your home. Show enthusiasm for them as people, not just as potential buyers. Feel free to ask them about themselves so that you can extol neighborhood advantages to them (like easy transportation to their places of work or groups of interest).

Ask people how they heard about your home. Remember what is drawing the crowds and what is not working. Then focus on the former and lessen or drop the latter. This is a good way to judge how well your advertising is doing.

It helps to have a friend or your agent help at the open house. By having two people, you can focus better on several buyers. One can keep greeting people and getting things off to a good start while the other shows prospective purchasers around the home and answers questions.

Some agents don't want you at your own open house because they worry that you are going to "give the store away" in conversations with potential buyers. Reassure your agent that you have read this book and are prepared to turn buyers over to them, but that you want to help out in any way possible, such as being a good host or hostess.

Focus on what is important to particular buyers. Some will focus on the yard, others on the kitchen, others on the school district. Have the sensory acuity to focus in on what is important to your prospect.

Tip 86: Make it easy for people to come to your open house.

You want to make your home easy to buy. That means making it easy to see, setting it up right, and making the buyer feel right at home. If agents look at your house, you're giving favorable impressions that will be passed along by word of mouth.

Schedule two open houses—perhaps one on the usual day and time (Sundays, 2–4) when most people are out looking, but also one mid-week, such as on a Thursday night. That way when buyers call, you can just say "drop in Thursday night between 7 and 9" and they won't feel pressured. You might also catch someone before he or she ever makes it to the Sunday open houses.

By knowing in advance when your home will be available, you can always show it in its best light. Put out fresh flowers, set the table, put on the proper lighting and music. If you have these "events" often enough, buyers never need know that the house was set up for them this way.

If you have a church or synagogue near your house, or some other place with a regular meeting, time one of your open houses to correspond to when the people break from their meeting. Offering refreshments at that time is sure to catch some interest. You just may find a buyer or someone who knows one.

If you have a regular open-house schedule, it is easy to suggest to people when they should drop by next. You could easily bump into someone and say, "Oh, come by Thursday, we're going to have the house open anyway." Thus you take the pressure off the prospect to feel he'll be getting a one-on-one sales pitch.

Tip 87: Don't dismiss the influence of the senses.

The senses play a key role in all showings, as mentioned earlier, including open houses. Don't be afraid to play up to people's subliminal memories.

Have coffee available at your showings. It is rarely declined and helps set a friendly and informal atmosphere. It also usually requires the prospect to spend more time in your home and not just run in and out. Even people who don't drink coffee usually like the smell.

Maybe have some very light background music on the stereo. New age music is very popular (although almost cliche), and classical piano or operetta gives the house a nice upbeat feeling.

Tip 88: Have visitors sign a guest register so you can contact them later.

An open house can be a successful sales event only if you can get the prospect to come back and make an offer. People often sit at home on the fence and need a push to make a decision. By having all visitors sign a guest register as they enter, you can have a source of names and phone numbers to contact those who seemed most interested again. You must take the initiative. You have nothing to lose in contacting these people.

The guest register is also an excellent marketing tool. You can contact people who didn't like your home to find out what turned them off. Was it the kitchen, the yard, the neighborhood, the price, you? Try to not be defensive, so you can get objective answers. Tell them that your goal is to make your house more marketable and that you would like their suggestions.

When talking to people who didn't like your house for some reason, be sure to tell them that you are still looking for a buyer and to tell their real estate agent and their friends about the house. If there was just one big reason for them disliking it, other people they know might be interested.

Tip 89: Be alert as to the scheduling of the open house.

Timing is everything in life. Make sure you don't schedule your open house to conflict with a major holiday, a major sporting even, or the day the local team is playing. You will only end up wasting your time and your advertising money if no one shows up. Be aware that weather can also have a strong effect on open houses, so if a huge storm falls during your open house, don't expect many people to show up.

CHAPTER NINE

Just Before You Sell

Below are listed some items to check before putting your house on the market. Most of these can be dealt with in the two weeks before the first time you show the house. You may want to do these things even before you show the house to your real estate agent, so he or she will know how good the house looks and can make other small improvements.

Entry
> Check that the area is warm and inviting. Use memory anchors such as a rocking chair on the front porch and a welcome mat to trigger good feelings.
> Make sure the doorbell works, that the doorknob is firm, and that the front door is clean and looks new.

Kitchen
> Wash cabinet fronts.
> Clean all appliances, focusing especially on the refrigerator and stove.
> If you have a tile counter, check the grout. Clean it or regrout it.

Make sure the ventilation system is working. Clean any dirty screens or filters.

Rearrange the pantry and cupboards to create a neat and orderly appearance.

Remove all garbage from garbage cans.

Make the room bright by putting in higher wattage bulbs.

Replace or polish cabinet hardware.

Bathrooms

Remove personal items from sight in the bathroom.

Put in a copy of a designer magazine like *Metropolitan Home*, and some flowers.

Add higher-wattage bulbs to the bathroom to make it brighter.

Caulk and grout the tile joints.

Remove all grime, water stains, and mildew.

Repair any leaky faucets or shower heads.

Put out fresh towels, including a guest towel.

Replace the shower curtain with a new one.

Check the strength and condition of towel racks or install new towel racks.

Living Room

Rearrange the furniture to enlarge the room and enhance its appearance.

Rearrange bookshelves, personal items, and pictures to enhance the room's overall impression. If you have just finished reading a best seller, put it face out on the bookshelf.

Remove all spent ashes from the fireplace.

Restock the fireplace with wood.

Dining Room

Set the dining room table. Stimulate the buyer's imagination of what the home could be like.

Clean light fixtures and glass on china cabinets. Remove excess clutter from china cabinet.

Bedrooms

Rearrange furniture to improve perceived size and to enhance overall impression.

Put on new bed coverings.

Remove personal items such as nightgowns and religious items.

Closets

Install lights where needed.

Remove all clutter.

Rearrange clothing to create an orderly and roomy impression.

Repaint inside surfaces if needed, to make closets as bright as possible.

Install shelving units in smaller closets to increase storage space.

Garage

Remove all clutter and storage.

Clean floors to remove oil stains and dirt.

Clear workshop area and arrange tools for a neat appearance.

Make sure the garage door works easily and properly.

General Interior

Repaint any walls or ceilings that are in poor condition or whose paint is faded or too dark. Keep the surfaces neutral. Use brighter colors on accessories.

Clean all moldings, doors, and dirty walls.

Wash all windows so that they glisten. Replace any cracked or broken glass.

Check windows for ease of operation. Repair any that stick or don't function properly.

Lower all shades to an equal level within the room.

Have carpets professionally cleaned.

Put out fresh flowers, candy, and other items to put people in a good mood.

Seal and spot prime any ceiling stains.

Open the curtains to make the house warm and sunny.

Remove excess pictures and posters to allow for more open expanses of wall.

Lawns and Plantings

Rake the lawn to keep it clear of grass, trimmings, and leaves.

Remove garden tools, toys, bicycles, and hoses from the front yard.

Trim your lawn edges where they meet walkways and driveways for a neat look.

Set out lawn chairs, grills, and other items to help the buyer visualize themselves entertaining friends and enjoying themselves.

Terraces and Decks

After your garbage is hauled away, hide the trash cans or arrange them neatly in an appropriate area.

General Exterior

Clean dirt off surfaces, especially around the front entry.

Check that the house numbers are clearly visible. Buy new ones if your current ones are small or old-fashioned.

Clean the windows.

PART II

Making Your Home the
Best It Can Be

CHAPTER TEN

Renovating for Profit

Your marketing system and sales techniques may be excellent, but ultimately it is the home itself that you are selling. The house has the capacity to be attractive and desirable, or mundane. The next chapters describe how to add value to your house: how you can gain $2–$4 for every dollar you invest.

Tip 90: Renovating is important both to increase profit and to make your house stand out from competing houses in the crowded market.

There are two reasons for doing some market-oriented renovations on your home. One is to maximize your profit and earn additional dollars on the work you do, just as a car dealer increases his margin by selling air conditioning and other options on the car. The second is to sell a home that might otherwise sit on the market for a long period of time by turning it into a product that hits the hot buttons of your buyers. All economics work off of supply and demand. You want to create a greater demand for your home than there is now so that you can sell it for a higher price, or faster, or both.

Renovating is especially important in a down market where the potential buyer has many more houses to choose from. This is particularly true in an area where the houses have many of the same features. You have to make your house stand out and be memorable. The most common way sellers do this is by lowering the price so much that they stand out as fools. A much better way to attack the problem of getting attention is to add big items and small memorable touches to your home so that, when the buyer goes home after a long day of house hunting, yours stands out from the rest.

You don't need to be a building contractor to perform most of these renovations. In fact, for most you don't even need to know which end of the hammer to hold. Adding lights, repainting areas, or installing a new kitchen counter are activities most homeowners can do or easily hire out.

Finding Hidden Potential

There is gold in your home, hidden potential waiting to be mined. Few homes cannot be made more attractive, marketable, and valuable with some simple changes and alterations. You are adding value to the home by uncovering the features buyers want, meeting buyers' needs, and appealing to their senses.

→ **Tip 91: Ask your real estate agent what he or she thinks you can do for your house to help it sell.**

Sound obvious? You would be surprized how few people spend more than an hour or so with their agent getting ready to sell a house. Sure, it may take hours to go over the paperwork, but that is only part of the agent's job. He or she is supposed to help you find ways to squeeze out extra thousands of dollars in price or, as is often the case in a slow market, help prevent you house from sitting unsold for months. Remember, most agents make their money by commission; the longer it takes to sell your house, the longer it is until they see their money. Be sure your agent knows you want him or her to help but that, at the same time, you expect your agent to be active.

In a down market, experienced agents can be great assets. From their conversations with people they have sold houses to, they know what kind of things have helped sell houses in the past. For example, you might be concerned about the poor condition of your hardwood floors. An experienced agent will probably have sold a house with floors in the same condition. Ask whether it was a big detriment to the sale.

Have your agent take a long walk through the house, noting things that he or she sees that might prevent the house from selling quickly. Take copious notes, being sure to write down your agent's feelings on how serious a liability each item is. After the tour, reorder the list from most serious to least serious. Then put an estimate for the cost on each of the items. Don't worry if the sum is astronomical: you aren't going to fix everything. You must fix the most important things first, then decide about the others.

Tip 92: Don't trust your own biases. Always think in terms of what a buyer would want to see in a house.

When you think about renovating a house, remember that you live there and probably have already done many of the things on your own "to-do" list. Forget that list as soon as possible. You are not trying to sell the house to yourself.

The best way to forget your own assumptions is to openly accept criticism from as many other people as you can. As described above, an experienced real estate agent is a great person to start with. Maybe have a few friends who do not live in your neighborhood come by and pretend to be buyers. Never disagree with them; just take notes. If your friends are too close to you, ask if they have other friends whom you don't know who might want to come over and help you out. Many people would find this type of exercise interesting for a few hours one evening.

The best designers and architects don't really design the homes they work on; they merely act as conduits letting the owner design each home, using their skills and knowledge to create the ideal environment for the owner. In the same way, you are renovating your home for the market. The best renovators don't put their ego into the design; they act as conduits, tapping the needs and desires of the marketplace to create the ideal environment for the buyer.

Remember who your target buyer is and work toward that. Obviously, retirees will want some different items than will a young couple with children or a status-oriented young professional. You are marketing your home by altering its physical structure. Know your market.

Tip 93: Someone who has just bought a home has lots of ideas about what your house should be like.

If you have followed our advice about checking your neighborhood for other houses for sale, you have also probably come across at least a few that sold recently. (You can also get this information from your real estate agent.) You may find it a bit brash, but introduce yourself to the new owners and ask them to do you a favor. Invite them over to your house and ask them to pretend that they are buying again. Keep careful notes, since this is as close as you will get to a real homebuyer.

People who have just bought a house have wonderful insights about how to appeal to homebuyers. Ask them what their biggest turnoffs were when looking around your neighborhood. Did they have another house that they "almost bought?" If it is still for sale, definitely go check it out. Even if your house is very different from what they were looking for (too few rooms, too much yard, and so on), press them for details about the good and bad parts of your house.

If these people have lived in their new house for a month or so, their views about what features are important may have shifted with the new realities. Try to keep them thinking in terms of being a homebuyer, not a new homeowner.

Tip 94: Professional home inspectors can help find structural problems that you haven't seen but careful buyers would.

Home inspectors are good advisors for determining if there is anything basically wrong with your house. They don't look at the cosmetics; instead, they check for things like foundation work that needs to be done, bad wiring, exposed asbestos, and so on. In a slow market, you should assume that potential buyers have lots of time to do their homework and will know to look for these things. A thorough inspection before you put your house on the market can help alert you to these things and let you fix them before they are discovered by a buyer.

Home inspectors come in many varieties, and you may want to use more than one. Often, they are general contractors who have worked on houses long enough to know what is good and what is bad. Many home inspectors are architects who have designed renovation plans for houses and thus know what might go wrong. Since few states require licensing for home inspectors, you should get one recommended to you. Your real estate agent might have some suggestions, as might friends who recently bought or sold a house.

A good inspection will cost you between $200 and $400. If you are going to spend this much, it behooves you to get the most out of the inspection that you can. Take copious notes and feel free to ask about things that weren't covered. Remember that your main effort is to make your home as attractive to buyers as possible, especially relative to other houses on the market. If your home inspector has performed many inspections in the past few months, ask him or her to compare your house to others on the market.

Tip 95: Avoid the common mistakes of amateur renovators.

The most important rule in adding value to your home is, *don't overimprove*. Overimprovement is putting in too much house for your area. Your goal is to meet neighborhood needs and to bring your home up to the median value in the area. Homes don't vary too much in price in any given location. Improving your home too much means that the people who can afford your price are looking at homes in a better neighborhood, not yours.

Profitable renovating does not have to cost much. It depends more on attitude, on looking at the home with the eye of a true merchandiser and seeing what can be done to increase its value. Sometimes this can be as simple as repainting and adding a few light fixtures. I've even seen rooms that had a dramatic change in their feel after some burned out light bulbs were replaced! But sometimes getting the best value for your house requires some structural changes. These can be as small as adding a few skylights to brighten the place up or as large as actually adding rooms.

Tip 96: Don't confuse repairs with improvements.

There's a big difference between performing repairs on your house and doing profitable renovations, renovations designed to maximize the value and merchandising appeal of your home. Repairs involve broken items you must fix to keep the house working such as patching the roof or replacing old plumbing. Repairs might add value to your house, but they usually don't.

Renovations are value-added improvements. These include painting the bathroom an appealing color, opening up a dark kitchen to the back yard, or getting new landscaping in the front. Sometimes there is a fine line between improvements and repairs. Knowing the difference between the two can make you thousands of dollars and is crucial to your success.

What is the fine line?

Tip 97: Renovate for your target audience or keep it neutral.

Don't make the home too personal. Remember, you are selling to someone who isn't you. You may like to paint your walls deep purple, burn incense all day, and listen to Jimi Hendrix at high volumes, but the young couple with the four-year-old daughter probably doesn't. Better to paint the walls a neutral color and keep the home full of fresh air.

There is one exception to this rule, though. If you have a target market, you want the home to be somewhat personalized, but you want it to be aimed at their personality, not yours. Decorating the extra bedroom as a children's room will do more to attract the young couple than "keeping it neutral." Building that entry gate and lining the long drive with trees will do more to attract the status seeking individual than "keeping it neutral." Target your market and keep your personality out of it, unless you're selling the home to you.

Tip 98: Designer magazines have lots of ideas for low-cost renovations.

You can find them in practically every supermarket: home and decorating publications. These can be an excellent source of ideas for your own home. The people that write the features are professionals who know how to make a home look appealing. When you find something you like, analyze it. What makes the room inviting? How does the room achieve balance? How can I apply this to my house?

You don't need to be *Metropolitan Home* or *Progressive Architecture*. You just need to make your home marketable to your target audience.

Tip 99: If you think you need some help, by all means get it!

An hour of a designer or architect's time does not cost much compared to the money you will be investing or earning. Professionals are skilled in the use of color and form and have probably dealt with a house similar to yours in the past. Proper improvements, although they do not have to cost much, can add thousands of dollars to your sales price and move a home in a short time that might otherwise languish on the market for months.

Don't worry about these people being offended by a small job. In a down market, these people have less work anyhow. They know that if they give you good advice at a low cost, it will probably turn into more work for them in the future.

Tip 100: Plan before you build.

There is an old saying among carpenters. Measure twice, cut once. Planning on paper, although it may be time consuming, is infinitely less expensive than physically moving walls which were not planned well. If you intend to do any sizable renovation, go through your plan thoroughly.

Planning is not necessary just for large remodeling jobs; it is also required for maximum effectiveness and impact. Rooms do not exist in and of themselves, separated from the house as a whole. Walk through your home in your own mind, visualizing your self going from room to room. Look for the places where you could add a little drama or for underutilized areas that could be made appealing to a buyer.

Even if your home is well maintained, many renovations must be done over time. Although fertilizing the lawn takes only a few hours, it may take two or three weeks for the effects to show. A complete paint job on the house may take three or four weeks. And any large remodeling job, such as redoing the kitchen, can take a month or two. Some items are sequential. You can't paint before you do the wallboard repair. So plan early and give yourself the time.

Tip 101: Imagination and a positive attitude are the most important ingredients.

Planning a marketable renovation can be frustrating. Keeping a positive attitude and using your imagination are the keys to success. Sometimes you know a room isn't right but you are not sure how to change it. Don't give up. Ask friends or designers for their opinions, look at magazines, and keep thinking about the problem. Eventually you will find a solution.

Make this fun and profitable! While everyone else is in the doom-and-gloom mode, you will be creating value in your home.

CHAPTER ELEVEN

Create the Illusion of Spaciousness

Buyers are looking for the most home for their money. All things being equal, buyers will pay more for a 2200-square-foot house than for a 2000-square-foot house. But people don't actually buy square footage, they buy perceived space. Your house should *feel* as big as possible. Carefully placed sightlines, volume spaces, and open plans will all help enhance the experienced size of the home. If you have a small home, you must make up in excitement what the house lacks in size.

Tip 102: Use color to expand a room and make the house flow.

The key to using color effectively is to understand how it works. Light colors reflect light, making them seem to recede from the field of vision. Painting a wall or ceiling a light color visually pushes them away from you, making the room seem bigger.

You can also use color to alter the shape of a room. Just as light colors expand a room, dark colors absorb light and seem to advance toward you. Painting a distant wall dark can help give a room more pleasing proportions than it had before.

Color is great at masking flaws. Paint out awkwardly placed moldings or doorways to match the walls, and you have quickly upgraded the room. In fact, coloring out distracting elements in a room also makes it feel bigger. The greater the unbroken expanse of the same color, the more disparate elements connect to provide a sense of space.

Use monochromatic color schemes in light and bright tones. Avoid breaks in color that visually fragment sight lines. When the same color flows from room to room, the sense of space is visually extended.

Tip 103: Increase space by accenting the third dimension.

Most new homes today capitalize on volume ceilings. If you open up the ceiling and creat volume, the space feels bigger, even though the square footage is the same. If you have a high ceiling, accentuate that fact to buyers.

To emphasize the vertical dimension, strategically place track spotlighting and focus it up high. This draws the eye up to the ceiling and gives the room a much more open feeling even if it is a standard-height room. Tall bookcases are a good target for these spots.

To dramatize a cathedral ceiling, break the usual rules and hang an art arrangement high on the wall. Draw the eye up. Perhaps you have a towering palm or other indoor tree that emphasizes the drama of the room.

Tip 104: Use scale to create spatial illusions.

People don't perceive size in absolute terms. Items are seen in relation to one another. You probably remember optical illusions in children's books in which two objects in different environments seemed to be of different sizes, but were actually the same size. These principals hold in the house, too. The visual sizes of your rooms are more important than the actual dimensions. The more closely your upholstered fabrics and window treatments blend with their background, the more spacious the room feels visually. Your furnishings should be in proportion both to the size of the room and to one another, with a good balance of size and form, color, pattern, and texture.

Model homes are noted for using undersized furniture in order to make rooms appear larger. While you can't exactly go out and buy a whole new decorating set, you can scale your furniture appropriately for the room. Oversized furniture in a small room will make it appear even smaller.

Remove excess furniture in order to make the room feel more spacious. You don't want your prospects squeezing sideways past the sofa as they experience your house for the first time. How's that going to make your home feel grand? Now is the time to banish some furniture to other rooms, put it in storage, or become popular with your friends by giving it away. There is power in simplicity. Too often our rooms look as if pack rats lived in them.

Tip 105: Stop being square: use the room's diagonals.

Diagonal views offer more perceived space, thus greater perceived value. They make a room appear bigger, because the focal point is further away. You can also place furniture such as a bed on the diagonal, to give the room a larger feel. This forced perspective makes the room appear longer and wider.

Tip 106: Create a focal point.

To make a room work, establish a center of interest and work around it. This could be an architectural element such as a fireplace or a furnished element such as a large painting or piece of furniture. Try to locate the focal point at the farthest point in the room from the entry. Drawing the eyes to a distant point helps to increase the visual impact and stretch the surrounding areas.

> **Tip 107: Use furniture to open up a room.**

Rearrange your furniture. Furniture that sits against all the walls, dancing-school style, can make a room feel static. Placing furniture in a different arrangement can help add dynamics and excitement to a room and make it function better, too. The layout of your furniture can also make a room feel much larger. Experiment with moving the large pieces around. Remember, you are marketing your home, so do it all the way, and enjoy the process.

Make sure that the furniture enhances views and doesn't block them. Always be leading the eye. Don't "float" your furniture out from the walls, as this uses up valuable space.

There's no rule that says a dining table has to go in the center of a room. By shifting it over to one side, a small dining area can be made to appear larger as the buyer walks through a roomy isle, not dodging the backs of chairs.

> **Tip 108: Treat a room as more than one room.**

To expand the livability of small spaces, treat them as more than one room. When you subdivide a space to serve multiple functions, it psychologically becomes bigger.

One way to divide a room without shrinking it is by furniture arrangements. Grouping furniture in several clusters, especially if the areas are broken up by separate throw rugs, creates several "rooms" without creating the visual barriers that chop up rooms and shrink them. Another way to break up rooms is with a low wall of plants or books. A third way is to change the color or pattern on the wall covering or the material used for the flooring.

Try to make rooms multipurpose. For example, put a desk area in the kitchen. This helps make the house have more uses. Don't think about the main house only. Create additional uses in the backyard or patio.

> **Tip 109: Create rooms out of nonrooms.**

Create spaces out of corners and odd nooks. When leftover space is utilized, it becomes another room and mentally makes the house appear larger. You may only have seven rooms in the house, but if you have nine distinct "spaces," to the buyer you have eight or nine rooms.

By utilizing wasted space, you can pack more into a small home and still let it appear spacious. Squeezing bookcases into tight spaces, using the space under the stairway, creating window seats or utilizing corners and nooks are all ways to enlarge the space.

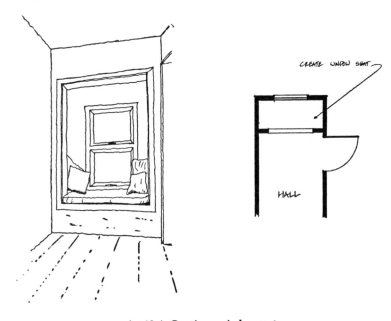

Art 10-A: Creating a window seat.
By taking the last 3 feet of this hallway and creating a window
seat, a special place is created from a useless hallway.

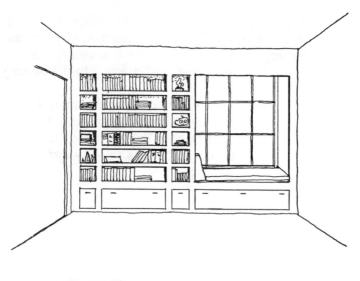

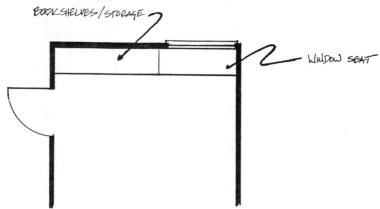

Art 10-B Creating storade and a window seat.
Removing 2 feet from this large bedroom hardly affects the room
size but creates both needed storage and a reading area/window
seat for the occupant.

In the early part of this century, the open plan came into favor in
this country. Without the visual barrier of walls, the house became more spacious in feeling, given the same square footage.
Although you don't usually want to eliminate rooms (more
rooms equals more perceived value), by using architectural elements such as half walls, level changes, or ceiling changes, you
can create "rooms" without needing full walls. Without the

visual separation of a solid wall, each "room" gets to steal a little space from the others, making the house feel larger.

Columns act as excellent dividers of spaces. They are elegant, define a room, and allow space to flow around them.

Tip 110: Bring the indoors out and the outdoors in.

You can go a step further in visually eliminating walls by opening up an exterior wall and placing a sliding glass door or French doors in the opening. By connecting the indoors to the outdoors you visually expand the space. Potted plants near a sliding patio door can connect an interior room to a deck or patio. By pulling the eye to the exterior, you make the interior appear larger.

Stress the indoor-outdoor orientation. People like to be outside. It reminds them of leisure and friends and the lifestyle they would like to lead. Since the outdoors is usually associated with the idea of "big," bringing the outdoors in makes the house seem as if it had much more space (and leisure space at that) than it really does.

Tip 111: Don't forget the floor.

The floor is one of the largest elements in a room. When decorating, use light or neutral floor coverings. Light colors enlarge a room; dark colors shrink it.

To visually enlarge a floor area even more, paint the baseboards as the floor is painted. Without a distinct color change between the horizontal floor and the vertical walls, the eye will bleed one into the other, making both appear larger.

Tip 112: Increased storage makes a home feel bigger.

Increase your storage capacity. Storage sells. One of the first things people look at when evaluating a house is the amount of closet and storage space it contains.

There are a few standard tricks to gain extra storage space:

- Use vertical space, and don't overlook height.

- Use organizers to increase the functionality of existing storage space.

- Create built-ins so that excess furniture is not necessary.

Built-in cabinets such as media centers can make a room more spacious and at the same time more livable and desirable. Wall treatments around fireplaces provide usable space that lessen the need for additional furniture.

Tip 113: Make small rooms appear larger with mirrors.

Mirrors can be one of the most useful elements you have in increasing the apparent size of your home. Artfully placed, a mirror can double the size of a room, make it lighter, and add a little element of play. Here are some possible uses of mirror in the home.

- A mirror strategically placed to reflect the outdoors will appear at first glance to be another window.

- Mirroring an awkwardly placed column can make it disappear.

- A mirror on the back wall of a display case doubles the size of the collection.

- Floor-to-ceiling mirroring on an accent wall can dramatically increase the apparent size of a small room.

- Mirroring the vertical wall space between kitchen counter and wall cabinets opens up closed space in a small kitchen.

- Mirroring bedroom closet doors enlarges the space and provides practicality for vain buyers.

Mirrors are a wonderful architectural device. But be careful not to overdo mirroring or the room may appear garish.

Tip 114: Create outdoor "rooms."

Making outdoor areas into usable living spaces increases the perceived size of the home.

A covered porch is an excellent way to create more experienced square footage in the home. Porches around the house can make 3,000 square feet feel like 4,000.

A trellis can add character to a deck and ease the transition between indoors and outdoors. Level changes can make a deck seem larger or gently glide the user down from the house level to ground level.

Tip 115: It is not how large the yard is, but how it is perceived.

With land prices higher than ever today, many builders are having to come up with creative solutions to make small lots sexy and appealing to the prospects that walk through their doors. Many builders today are making their backyards fantasy worlds, whether they be tropical paradises or ultramodern landscapes. Just as within the house, you must appeal to the senses and to the buyers' dreams and values.

Design the yard for active living. It's not necessarily the size of the yard, but how useful it is that makes it feel larger. Combine a gracious patio or deck with quality plantings and the size of the yard won't be such an issue to buyers. Many will appreciate the lower maintenance a small yard entails.

Use level changes. Steps up accentuate the spaciousness of a small lot. Just as many older public buildings used grand oversized steps up to them as a way to emphasize their grandeur, stepping up a yard will make it feel larger.

Strong horizontal or vertical lines can visually extend a yard. Optical illusions are useful in the exterior as well as the interior. Play with the eye's ability to perceive to make your yard appear larger than the square footage might suggest.

CHAPTER TWELVE

Make It Light

People like sunny, warm homes. They love homes bathed in natural light. All things being equal, people will pay more for a home that is light and airy over one with a cavernous feeling. Unfortunately, you're not designing a new home, but rather, you're working with what you have. Let's explore some ideas about how to make the home brighter and more appealing through lighting.

Tip 116: Add a window or a skylight to dark rooms.

Add a window or a skylight to dark rooms. The extra light will create lively spaces where before a cave existed. Skylights and windows, in addition to providing more natural light, can add to ventilation, giving the home a fresher feeling.

Windows that don't open, also known as "fixed windows," add a lot of light but cost significantly less than operable windows. The positioning of windows can also greatly affect the feel and layout of a room. An ill-placed window can interfere with the feeling a room conveys, conveying a subtle disharmony to the buyer.

You can balance the light in a room by placing a windows on two walls. Light from only one source tends to be less balanced and contain more glare.

Tip 117: Use mirrors to double your light.

Mirrors greatly increase the amount of light in a room in addition to increasing the space. They reflect light and bounce it around to previously dark corners. Mirrors can also balance the light better. When Hollywood cameramen film movies, they use reflectors to even out the light and enhance the starlet's features. Enhance the features of your rooms with mirrors.

Tip 118: Make a window into a door.

You can increase the light by increasing the opening from the house to the exterior. Many times, rather than adding another window, you can replace a window with a doorway to an exclusive private deck.

Imagine the difference in value of a master bedroom with one small window and another with two elegant French doors opening onto a private patio for morning champagne or coffee. Connecting to the outdoors also makes a room appear bigger.

Tip 119: If appropriate, add a greenhouse window or solarium.

Kitchens and bathrooms especially can benefit from the added light, space, and value that a greenhouse window provides. Not only do you get additional light during the day, plants thrive in greenhouse windows and give the house a more "living" feeling.

If you have a dark dining area, consider opening it up into a solarium. You not only get enhanced lighting; you create a wonderful dining space that rates high on buyer preference lists.

Tip 120: If you can't use natural light, use artificial light.

You can't always be cutting holes in the house, but you can increase the light by adding new fixtures. Lighting design can make a dull room elegant or a small room appear larger. Accent lighting can provide a mood that sells your home quickly and easily.

You can create rooms with light. For example, you can arrange a series of photographs along a wall and light them with halogen spots, creating the effect of a photo gallery from what might have otherwise been a useless corridor or an average wall.

Too many homes require a coal miner's hat to get around. Use hundred-watt bulbs and boost your lighting. You might also want to substitute full-spectrum bulbs for your regular incandescent bulbs in some of your lamps. Full-spectrum bulbs give off a light that is closer to sunlight and helps give the home more of a daylight effect.

Stage and restaurant designers are masters at lighting. They can create moods, focus attention, and create illusion by their use of lights. In addition, lighting is easy to control compared to more solid structures, such as walls. Good lighting supports favorable emotional reactions. Lighting has actually been used as a therapy to cure depression.

Dim light can create an intimate or cozy area. Observe restaurants to get some ideas about how lighting can create desired moods.

Tip 121: Use color to affect moods.

Color has a profound effect on the body. Studies have shown that colors such as pink or green have a calming effect while red agitates. This happens at a subconscious level and most people are not aware of the effects of color. For best results, keep colors monochromatic and neutral in the home. Select a muted tone for the background and then do as much as you can with that color. Use its various values, tones, and textures. This will help create a harmonious environment.

Bright colors can be thrown in, but as accessories. Never paint your walls in bright, bold colors. Bright accessories have an effect similar to bright flowers in a garden.

When planning your color schemes, remember some basic color principals. In general, rooms with north and east window light need warm colors rather than white. Yellows, apricots, peaches, and pinks warm up the soft bluish tones of northern light.

Paint the ceiling a light color. This not only lightens the room but also helps to enlarge it. White or light ceilings reflect light.

Some other color tips:

- The colors of the trim should be the same, or at least similar throughout the house. This helps unify the house.

- Strong, dramatic colors are best used in transient spaces such as foyers, halls, and bathrooms.

- When picking colors in the paint store, put at least four paint chips together, so that you are looking at a larger mass of color. And remember to look at the color chips in both natural and artificial light to get a true sense of the color.

- Dark or warm colors enclose a room. Light or cool colors open it up. If you want to make a small room appear bigger, paint it a light, cool color.

- Open up a cramped space by lightening the color on the wall you want to expand. You can help widen a narrow room to give it better proportions with color. Paint the short walls a lighter color than the longer walls, which can have slightly deeper tones.

Interior designers often say that color is perhaps the most important design element. A badly chosen color will poorly effect the best-planned room. Although rooms should have neutral backgrounds, it is color that helps give life to a room, like flowers in a field. As animals, people have a natural attraction to color.

CHAPTER THIRTEEN

Give Your House a Theme

Giving your house a theme will help you in decorating it for sale. It will help you get a handle on what improvements will add to the total image of the house and what ones will take away from it. Organizing around a theme can help give you a strong look, style, or image for your home. In a down market, you need all the help you can get making your house stand out from the myriad of other houses in your neighborhood.

If your house belongs to a noteworthy architectural period, you can accentuate it. This doesn't mean you need to put Victorian furnishings in a Victorian house (on the contrary, this usually makes your home look like Disneyland or a museum) but rather that improvements should have Victorian trim and details and that certain colors may work better than others.

If your house lacks an architectural style, there are other ways to come up with a theme for it. Most decorators of new housing developments make up an imaginary family (such as the targeted future buyers) and then decorate to fit that image. This helps attract people that either live in that way or that want to. When developing your plan, work from a strong sense of the house's functionality.

If you are having trouble conceptualizing, try imagining the ad you will place in the paper to sell the property. You might imagine something like:

> Beautiful 4-bedroom home in wooded setting. Relax on the deck and get away from the noise of the city.

With relaxation, entertaining, and leisure as your theme, you can decorate your home appropriately.

Tip 122: Keep the theme simple.

You might go into a new subdivision and find custom homes done up in ultratropical decor or Olde English style, but this will not work for the average homeowner. You have only one home to show, not a variety and so your one image has to work with the buyer. Developers have the luxury of being able to try out several themes. Some will work, some won't, but usually one will catch a buyer's attention. The others just help make the place memorable (a key goal).

Look for simple lines and try to pare down to basics. Then you can add features to enhance the home.

Pick a color scheme for the house and carry it through to provide continuity between disparate rooms and elements. Color helps tie together all the individual rooms and builds on the theme of the home.

Tip 123: Make the theme memorable.

In merchandising your home, you not only want to make it attractive to buyers and to appeal to their emotions, you want them to remember it when they go home. Do something unusual. Whether it is an outdoor deck with a wet bar or having a Jacuzzi with a view of the bay, it is these items that get people to fall in love with a house.

Of course, you want the theme to match the desires of the people who might buy your home. For instance, if you have a stately manor, you would tend more toward themes like Victorian and hardwood rather than bright and sassy. Likewise, if your buyers are likely to be parents of school-age children, themes might be climbable furniture or fun spaces for the family.

Tip 124: For maximum value, work in harmony with the house.

If your home has a particular style, working within that style will give you maximum value. Add-ons, tack-ons, and partial renovations don't add nearly as much value to the home as an appropriate change and tend to look like cheap parts rather than to create a harmonious whole.

CHAPTER FOURTEEN

Creating a Saleable Home

Other chapters of this book have focused on how to make buyers desire your home. Those ideas carry over to renovations since there are probably deficiencies in your house that can be remedied by adding or changing. This chapter describes items that can be improved by minor or major renovations.

> **Tip 125: Compare your house to others in your neighborhood to look at price breaks.**

One of the best ways to add value in your renovations is to fill a need that your home lacks but that is common or desired in your neighborhood. To illustrate, suppose you have a two-bedroom, one-bath house. There is a price ceiling for two-bedroom, one-bath houses in any given neighborhood. There is also a price ceiling for two-bedroom, two-bath houses (that is, your house with an additional bath), and a different one for three-bedroom, one-bath houses (your house with an additional bedroom). Find out the difference in the price ceilings. It may be extremely profitable to add a third bedroom—or it might not. The same is true of the second bath. See what is desired by looking at prices of comparable houses and fill it.

The mistake many people make is to add things like a family room without checking to see if that will add any value. You may find that a two-bedroom, one-bath house is worth perhaps $5000 less than a two-bedroom, one-bath house with a family room. Even though a family room may add $5,000 in value, may cost $15,000 to build. This is a prime example of an unprofitable renovation.

Tip 126: The things you must do to bring your house up to neighborhood standards may be small.

Sometimes, your house may only be lacking paint or a front porch that could significantly add to the value of your property. Sometimes a fence or gate can add to the feel of your home and make it fit in more with the character of the neighborhood.

Tip 127: Make the home say "quality."

People want to feel that the home they live in is well built. There should be no indications of potential problems when a prospect walks through your home. Doors should close properly, window should operate smoothly, and quality finishes should be placed in the most noticed areas. Unless your neighborhood is full of fixer-uppers (and this is especially unlikely in a down market), your house has to feel like a quality, finished home.

If the buyer develops the basic mindset that this is a quality home, he or she will start selling himself. If, on the other hand, doors stick as he tries to open them, or the knobs feel like plastic, the mental connection is made that the whole home is probably shoddily built and should be avoided.

Tip 128: Use moldings, trim, and woodwork to enhance the quality of the home.

You've probably noticed that moldings add definition and character to a room. What you may not have known is that the use of moldings is one of the least expensive ways to help give a home a feeling of quality. A room with no character takes on a new personality with the use of appropriate moldings. Moldings are a great way to join different materials, but their decorative function is the key to adding value.

Moldings include the look of your window and door casings and your baseboard. It is often the trim that defines a room's feel. The difference between a home with a Victorian feel and a modern one is often in the detailing, not in the room's size, shape, or construction.

When you look at other houses in your neighborhood, look at the details like the moldings and trim. Go to the most popular lumber store and ask what styles people have been using lately. Don't think that ornate finishings are always the best: fit in with the upper end of the neighborhood.

Tip 129: Use tile and other quality finishes to increase perceived value.

You can add value to the home by making good use of materials and finishes. Tile can be trite or it can be exciting for exactly the same cost. How you use materials will greatly affect the perceived elegance and value of your home. For example, you can tile a shower-surround all one color or you can throw in an accent stripe of a contrasting color. The first looks bland, the second adds some pizazz to your bathroom, yet both use exactly the same amount of material and take the same amount of labor. The choice is yours. Use quality finishes with a little imagination, or waste their potential value.

Local tile layers are a good source of information. Most tile layers can put down cheap or expensive tile just as easily and usually make much more money on labor, not materials. Ask a tile contractor what types of tile seem to be selling best in your area. Like other people who deal with homes, these people are often short of work in a down real estate market and would appreciate even an hour of consultation work that might later turn into a real job.

Tip 130: Accentuate the positive and neutralize the negative.

Every home has positive and negative aspects. No home is perfect. The key to your renovation is to look at the home with the renovator's eye. See the features that may be special about your home and then accentuate them. Also be critical, see the problems, and do your best to either correct them or draw attention away from them. Just as some women can transform themselves from ordinary looking people to great beauties with the proper use of clothing and makeup, you can make your home more appealing with the right use of illusion and skillful attention-shifting.

For example, most home builders in California put their focus on exterior detail on the front of the house and ignore the sides and back. They know that buyers will spend a long time looking at the house from the street and as they walk up toward it. But few will go around to the side and stare at the house for any length of time. So the energy is placed where the attention will be focused.

An example of neutralizing "problems" might be the case of foundation plantings. Most new homes look out of place rising straight out of the flat ground like a monolith. Foundation plantings not only hide the bare concrete, they act as a visual transition, softening the impact of the house on the landscape. Or perhaps you have an obvious burn in your formica countertop. Cut out the burned area and insert a wooden cutting board. Thus a liability becomes an attractive asset after you neutralize its problems.

Chapter Fifteen

Closets and Storage

Much of this book has emphasized home attributes that appeal to the senses of prospective buyers. However, there is another attribute of your home that will affect many buying decisions: the amount of storage space available. Closets and attics don't fall into the same categories as many other parts of the house, but they are sometimes even more important. Fortunately, they are easy to add or enlarge.

Insufficient storage can lose many potential buyers. If someone already has two or three closets full of "things," they will require at least that much in the next house they buy. Even if they don't, closets and attics can make a big difference. Many people have fond childhood memories of looking through their parents belongings, hidden away in their secret world of a closet.

Tip 131: Closet space is a universal need.

Few things help sell a house like adequate closet space and few things hurt as much as not having enough. Every room in the house needs a place for storage, and it is your job to provide it. A 6 x 8 bathroom with adequate storage is worth more than a 6 x 8 bathroom without enough storage. Good looking, efficient storage more than pays for itself in the marketing of your home.

There are many ways to create storage out of existing space. Some general ideas are listed below, although there are a wealth of how-to books that give you step-by-step instructions on creating space. If your house can hold more possessions than the buyer can acquire, you've gone a step closer to the sale.

- Use the space under the stairs as a closet.

- Install a new fireplace, recessed. A partition brings the side walls level with the fireplace and spaces created at the sides can be used as bookcases, cabinets, or storage. This gets you both a dramatic fireplace and the necessary storage.

- In the bedroom, build drawers and storage areas under a platform bed. You can also create a storage system in a headboard.

- Build a shelving-entertainment system along a wall of the living or family room. For added value, build accent lighting into the unit.

- In the bathroom, you can build storage in wall-storage units or the vanity and by using large medicine chests.

- If you have some attic bedrooms with sloped ceilings, you can create more storage going further into the eaves. Built-in shelving to house a stereo system or books adds character and quality to the room.

- Create a storage wall as a screen to divide areas of a room. Half walls can contain bookshelves, or an island of drawers and shelves can be used to separate two rooms instead of a solid wall.

- You can increase the usable storage space within your existing closets using closet organizers (see Tip 133).

Remember, people are concerned with where they will put all their possessions. The whole miniwarehouse–self-storage industry is based on the concept that people have too much stuff lying around. If you can meet buyers' needs for storage, you will have scored a point in your favor.

Tip 132: Steal two feet of space from a bedroom to create a wall of closets

---

If you have a large bedroom, one way to gain an impressive amount of storage is to frame a wall full of closet doors two feet in. Two feet is the recommended depth for closets. You now have an impressive wall of storage, even enough for a teenage girl, and you will barely notice the missing two feet of space from a large room.

You can use mirror doors on the new closet to help make the smaller room feel a little more spacious again.

Tip 133: Use closet organizers.

A whole industry has now sprung up to deal with our penchant for collecting things. There are closet consultants, closet companies, and closet systems sold in stores. The goal of all these is to (1) gain extra usable space in your closet and (2) eliminate clutter. You can do the same. Shirts don't need to hang 80 inches off the floor. Double hang them. Build some shelves for sweaters and shoes. *Voila*, a closet that is now twice the size as before.

Tip 134: Clean up your attic or basement before showing the house, so the space looks much larger.

If you have a large attic or basement, you have probably filled it with all sorts of stuff that you will throw away when you move. Consider doing that now, not later, so that the space looks larger. Even if you don't throw things away, move them around to maximize the open space so a prospective buyer will be more impressed with the added space.

Tip 135: Storage need not look like a closet.

Storage does not need to be in the form of a closet. Be creative. There are many good books on ways to steal space from a room for storage. For example, if you have a level change between two rooms, the space under the platform area can be used as storage. If you need to create a wall between two rooms, make it wide enough to contain storage.

CHAPTER SIXTEEN

Reducing Noise

Noise can be a significant nuisance in an otherwise attractive home. Many homes have sold for far less than what they otherwise would have been worth had the owner taken care of some noise issues or had the house been located in a quieter setting.

Why is noise such a problem? It is something that is very easy for buyers to detect, even people who don't know much about shopping for a house. To many people, it is a sign of what they can't control in a home. As you can see in this chapter, reducing noise is not very difficult or expensive, but you should be sure to do it yourself instead of assuming that the buyer would want to.

Sound control is cumulative. Each step you take will add a little to solving the problem. Several steps together can provide significant reductions in noise. Note that in successful soundproofing, workmanship is key. Also remember that the denser the material, the more it can absorb sound.

Tip 136: To hear your home as others do, close your eyes and listen.

You may get so used to where you live that you don't even notice distractions and conditions that might be bothersome to others. People living on busy streets can sleep through the noisiest of traffic within a few weeks of moving there. Somehow the brain determines certain sounds are not worth noticing, and you start tuning them out.

Be quiet for a moment and really listen to the sounds your house makes. You may find that there is a much higher noise level than you thought. You may have adapted over the years and are now blocking out many sounds (sounds which are turning off your potential buyers). There may be intermittent sounds such as the boiler going on and off or a car driving by. If you live in a condominium, you might hear conversations or sounds from next door. The key is to identify the problem sounds, the noise, and to focus on eliminating it.

Tip 137: Insulate exterior walls or build a second layer.

By insulating exterior walls, you are creating mass which absorbs sound. Increased mass is one of the best sound absorbers. After the insulation is in place, check for air leaks. Air leaks mean sound leaks. If there are any, fill them with an acoustical sealant.

If you can't find any air leaks but the noise is still a problem, the best solution is to increase the mass of the walls. This can be done by putting up another row of studs on the interior and then using drywall or plaster over them. A simpler solution is to line the interior with bookcases. Both these solutions eat up usable square footage but only the first takes away from marketable square footage.

Tip 138: Increase window glazing for both noise protection and better insulation.

In an otherwise solid house, windows and doors are often the weak links in sound transmission. With modern technology this no longer needs to be the case.

For windows, add a pane of glass, such as a storm window, to each window on the noisy side of the house. This can reduce noise as much as 50% while keeping your cost low. You can also replace single-glazed windows with double- or triple-glazed ones and make a tight seal with weatherstripping or acoustical sealant.

For doors, replace all hollow-core or lightweight exterior doors with heavy, solid-core doors. This one improvement can dramatically lesson noise penetration.

Tip 139: Landscape for sound resistance.

Noise control requires dense plantings of considerable depth and height to achieve a reasonable amount of sound insulation. To block unwanted traffic sounds from your home, plant thick hedges, bushes, and trees on the side toward the noise source.

If your house is downwind from a school playground or a factory, the best solution is to plant a windbreak to reduce the sound being carried. A tight evergreen or deciduous hedge will provide protection as far downwind as twenty times its height. So an eight foot-tall hedge can be planted as far away as 160 feet from your house and still provide some protection from wind-borne noise.

You can also build a fence and cover it with dense vines and plantings to help block sound. This has the added benefit of blocking a bad view and gaining privacy should those be needed also.

Tip 140: Interior noise is not as noticeable as exterior noise but can still bother many buyers.

In some houses, the greatest turnoff to buyers is noise not from outside but from the interior. Echoes, walls and floors that sound as if they are paper thin, and clanging pipes or heating ducts all serve to make your house appear cheaply built, less desirable, and worth much less money. When looking for ways to reduce noise within the house, first determine where the noise is coming from; within the room, outside of the room, or within the structure of the house itself. Once you've determined the source of the noise, you can do several things to reduce it.

A good way to prevent sound from spreading to other parts of the house is to absorb it at the source, within the room where the sound originates. Heavy draperies, wall-to-wall carpeting, and upholstered furnishings go a long way toward absorbing sound. Hard materials such as plaster walls, hardwood floors, and glass windows reflect and bounce sound around a room, making it appear noisier.

Wall coverings such as fabric can absorb much noise. Armstrong Soundsoak is a fabric over acoustical fiberboard that will absorb up to 60% of noise.

Tip 141: Increase the mass of your walls to reduce noise between major rooms.

To contain sound within a room, add mass to the structure. Replacing hollow doors with solid-core doors and adding another layer of sheetrock on resilient channels are two ways to add mass. Resilient channels are metal tracks that hold a wall surface in position away from the surface it is attached to. They are designed to isolate the two layers of sheetrock so that the outer wall will not transmit vibration to the inner wall, or the reverse. Putting better doors on the playroom or the room to the furnace can significantly reduce noise. Weatherstripping under doors will also help keep sound from traveling.

Double-stud construction can create the most soundproof wall possible with wallboard. It is the standard construction used between separate condominiums to restrict sound transmission between party walls. The drawback is that you will lose about four inches from the room. To create this wall, strip the surface facing into the room from the wall that requires additional soundproofing and erect the second wall in front of the first as described. Stuff it with insulation and cover the new wall with wallboard.

Electrical outlets placed back to back on walls are another source of interior sound transmission. If your outlets are not tightly installed, apply insulation around them. This may be in the form or a caulk, a putty, or a gasket. These items absorb sound as it works its way through cracks and openings from room to room.

↗ | **Tip 142: Fix squeaky floors or stairs.**

Squeaky floors and noisy stairs detract from the perceived quality of a home. They are so common that it is rare not to find them in older homes. Although they can be aggravating, they seldom indicate anything structurally wrong with the floor.

The squeak problem could be caused by loose or warped floorboards rubbing against each other. Depending on your floor, there are several ways to solve this. If you have access to the floor from below, you can pull the loose floorboards tight with screws inserted from below. If there is no access, you can drive in ring-shanked nails from above.

If it is a finished hardwood floor, first drill some small pilot holes to prevent the hardwood from splitting, and then drive in some finish nails at a 45° angle to grab the subfloor and penetrate a joist if possible. Alternate the directions the nails are aimed for the best grip. You can also try squirting some mineral oil between the joints or inserting some glazier's points.

Another common cause of a squeak may be warped or bowed floor joists. If the area under the floor or stairs is accessible, locate the squeak by having someone walk over the noisy area of the floor while you watch and listen below. Look for movement between joists and bridging that moves when weight is brought upon it. You can fill the spaces with wood shims to solve the problem.

If the squeaking area lasts for several floor boards, you can nail a cleat, consisting of a 1 x 4 or 1 x 6, up against both the warped floor joist and the subfloor. This will create the equivalent of a new, straight floor joist and should stop the squeak.

Squeaky stairs are treated similarly to floors. You can glue a squeaky tread to silence it, put in wedges from below, install wood cleats from behind, or try screwing the tread down.

Tip 143: Check sound transmission between ceilings and floors.

It's not only walls that transmit sounds. The way a house's ceiling and floor connections are constructed can have a great impact on the amount of sound heard in the room below. Fortunately, it does not have to be an expensive problem to fix.

You can hang a new ceiling on resilient channels below the old one. You can also place carpet or padding in the room above the ceiling. This is a solution which can both beautify the room above and prevent you from worrying whether potential buyers will think the house cheaply built as they hear footsteps from above.

Tip 144: If you can't get rid of it, cover it.

Sometimes the problems aren't great enough to warrant the cost of major improvements. All houses transmit some noise, but you don't even notice it. However, many prospects are looking at your house with a microscope, looking for every flaw. Like an older woman using makeup, sometimes it is best to apply a little sound cosmetics to help keep the home attractive. Some ways to mask sound include the following:

- Play soft music in the background during showings. Not only does it mask unpleasant sounds, it relaxes the body and puts prospects in a good mood.

- You can also mask noise with a gurgling fish tank with a filter and air pump.

- Water sculptures are excellent ways to mask noise, and the splashing water helps freshen the air, too.

CHAPTER SEVENTEEN

Health Hazards

Radon and asbestos are two potentially serious health hazards affecting most homes today. But these substances can have emotional impact all out of proportion to their actual health danger. You don't want to kill a deal because several weeks into the contract, the buyer's inspector discovers asbestos or radon in the home.

Tip 145: Decreasing levels of radon can be simple and inexpensive.

Radon is an element occurring naturally in the earth. As the earth shifts, small amounts diffuse up into the atmosphere. Because radon is over seven times heavier than air, it seeks the lowest level in the home (usually the basement) and lies there until stirred up by movement. It can then be breathed, in which case it is harmful. However, you won't notice it. It doesn't cause the eyes to water or the skin to itch, but over time problems develop.

Fortunately, special vapor barriers and proper venting can keep your home relatively free of radon. It is worth cleaning this mess up before a buyer sees your house. Depending on the scope of the problem, correcting a radon problem can cost as little as a few hundred dollars.

There are two basic techniques to controlling radon: seal the places where it enters the house and give more ventilation so that it moves out of the house more quickly. Sealing involves patching cracks, caulking around drain exits, and so on. Adding ventilation helps remove the gas more quickly since it is mixed with the air that naturally enters and leaves through windows and doors.

If your home has radon, don't assume it will cost you a huge amount to fix or that you have an unsellable house. Get some quotes from many professionals and have the radon problem remedied. It is worthwhile to talk to many contractors, since radon is a new scare topic and there may be unscrupulous people who will fix it for you, but at highly inflated prices.

Tip 146: Asbestos is a serious hazard and must be handled carefully.

Asbestos is a mineral that has been used in a wide variety of products because of its durability and heat-resistant qualities. In many of the uses of asbestos, it is unlikely it will ever cause health problems. The way asbestos harms you is when it separates into thin microscopic fibers that get into the air. When you breath air contaminated with asbestos, the fibers attach themselves to the lungs and can result in asbestosis or various forms of cancer.

Most homebuyers' inspections will discover whether you have asbestos in your home. Sometimes removal is the best way to get rid of it, buy many times sealing or encapsulating the asbestos is the best way to prevent it from getting into the air. Asbestos has a high scare value to it that exceeds that actual danger in most houses. Many buyers refuse to buy a home containing asbestos even though it may be perfectly safe. If you discover you have asbestos, getting a clearance or a certificate stating that no foreseeable problems will occur from the now-encapsulated asbestos will go a long way to quell exaggerated buyer fear of this element.

CHAPTER EIGHTEEN

Doing Major Renovations

There are many times when you want to spend thousands of dollars renovating your house before a sale. The best reason to do this, of course, is if you can profit from the renovation. The next best reason is to make your house more attractive, but this is not usually much of an issue if you intend to sell in the next few months.

The renovations in other chapters are usually of low cost. Of course, you can spend thousands (and even tens of thousands) of dollars renovating every part of the house. This chapter focuses on the higher-cost renovations. Most of them sound great, but you shouldn't even consider them unless you are reasonably sure that you will get a return on them higher than what you put in.

Tip 147: Get help from the professionals.

You will find that doing renovations takes much more time than you anticipate. Why else do you think construction jobs done by professionals are constantly going over time and over budget. You are probably already working at a job you enjoy and have better uses for your time than hanging sheetrock.

Quality is an important buyer concern. It takes many years to develop the expertise and skill to do smooth, complex construction details. Do-it-yourself jobs are usually a false economy because a home that looks amateurish in its construction brings up buyer concerns about the whole house. Buyers will notice the details, especially in a down market where they have the choice of many properties.

When starting any project that will cost over a few thousand dollars, getting professional help is necessary. Architects play a key role here in giving design advice that will increase the appeal of your home and its value. Your real estate agent can also be helpful in recommending what areas of the home should be remodeled to increase its value.

You don't always need to pay a premium for professionals. Many times quality workmen moonlight (especially in tough times when the extra money helps the most). These people, who might bill you at $15 per hour, are the same guys you'd get when you pay their company $40 per hour. Same quality, same people, different cost.

Remember, hiring need not be confined to large jobs either. Hire a professional cleaning crew to give your house a full once-over before putting it up for sale. Then you and your family can maintain it. But at least someone else did the grunt work. And wouldn't you rather be doing something else for eight hours than scrubbing out your oven and floors?

Tip 148: Let neighborhood standards dictate your remodeling.

Don't start creating a seven-bedroom, four-bath mansion with billiard room and private study in a neighborhood of two-bedroom, one-bath bungalows. Where you are located will have a significant effect on the upper limit of your remodeling jobs. If your home is located on a block of rundown, tired-looking Victorians, restoring yours to its original luster will increase its value, but by not nearly as much as it will cost you to do the work. The only time this is not the case is when the neighborhood is appreciating rapidly for other reasons, but from a cost-value standpoint, going too high above neighborhood standards is a loser.

When determining what would be an appropriate remodel for your home, look at other homes within your targeted price range for sale in the area. What can you do to improve on them without spending a fortune? If they all have family rooms and your house doesn't, than adding a family room might make sense. If none of them has a family room, running out and creating one in your home is usually a waste of money.

When looking at how to make your existing rooms better, such as remodeling the kitchen, take the time to plan. You may be able to increase the square footage in one direction for a much lower price than in another. How you tie into the existing roof and foundation will have a large impact on cost.

Tip 149: Analyze the floor plan without room labels on it.

Many times out of habit or because a builder labeled them a certain way, you have assigned rooms particular functions. But sometimes, either because of poor design in the first place, or because the home has gone through several remodelings, some rooms are not appropriate for their original functions.

There was a time, not too long ago, when the kitchen was a small room hidden in the back of the house. Today, kitchens are central to our modern lifestyle. Remodeling your kitchen, even with all the best techniques, still will not undo the design flaw if it is located in the far back corner of the house. Perhaps another nearby room would make a better kitchen and the kitchen could be converted to something else. Many of the best remodeling jobs require a reassigning of room functions. Don't be limited to your current scheme.

Tip 150: Use natural traffic patterns to dig for ideas and increase functionality.

Analyze the traffic effectiveness of your home by looking at how traffic moves through the house. If the kitchen is the focal point of the house, what rooms do people have to walk through to get there? Does someone have to walk through a public area after taking a shower before getting to his or her bedroom? Is the room you designated as the study in a quiet corner, or in the middle of the most traffic.

You will find that some rooms are overworked and some underworked. The underworked ones may be ripe for reorganizing. Draw a floor plan of your house on a piece of paper and then with colored pens, trace your family's traffic patterns through the house on a typical day during the week and on the weekend. What you will find is that some areas are almost black from color and others hardly have a colored line in them. This is your first clue. Areas that are hardly touched can be reclaimed for other uses.

Tip 151: Reclaim unused rooms for today's uses.

Many homes have a number of boxy small rooms that are rarely if ever used. Combining these rooms visually can add to the feeling of spaciousness in the home. The formal living room is often a rarely used room. Usually it seems that the room's only purpose is to get cleaned every so often. Many new homes don't even have formal living rooms. The trend is to combine the den and the living room to create a "great room" that better suits today's casual lifestyle. By combining these rooms, you can turn two nonfunctional rooms into a wonderful space, add some needed storage along a wall, and still keep the illusion of two rooms by the way you place the furniture.

In addition to attics there are carports, garages, basements, and even closets from which you can steal space. Such an area usually has a foundation, roof, and walls already. Thus you've cut your costs by at least a third in choosing these areas to remodel versus adding on with new construction.

Tip 152: Don't fix something that is functionally obsolescent.

Many homes have items that are uneconomical to repair. It might make sense to have a three-bedroom, two-bath house in your neighborhood. Those are the hot properties, and people pay a disproportionate premium for them. You have a two-bedroom, one-bath house, and you want to convert. Before you decide to go ahead, take a second look. How small is the living room? Will it support a larger household or look out of place? Will you have to repour the foundation to support the extra weight that your attic expansion will provide?

Many functionally obsolescent houses and items should be cosmetically dolled up and sold. Don't put too much money into these items

---

Tip 153: Add romance and character to homes that lack them.

Renovating old homes is no longer the frontier of renovation. Most older homes now will sell at a premium even without renovation because of the charm factor. Where value can truly be added is in renovating a bland, post-World War II tract home. Whatever they might be, Cape Cods, ranch homes, or Dutch Colonials, most lack the added spark that makes people want to buy new homes today.

Most cold war-era homes contain cramped dark kitchens, standard eight-foot-high ceilings throughout, outdated bathrooms, and rigidly defined rooms. Opening up the floor plan, reaching up into the rafters, and expanding the kitchen out into the back yard become major value points. Drama is the key to altering these plans. If you own a ranch house, you may have a gold mine with significant hidden potential.

Tip 154: Use those "return on major repairs" articles only as a guide.

Averages mean very little when they apply to the sale of your home. Just because the market is down 10% doesn't mean a house of your size in your price bracket is down 10%. And just because one article in some home magazine says that you can get only a 40% return on building a deck, that doesn't mean it is true.

The return you get depends on how the improvement impacts the overall perceived value of the house. In San Francisco, I've seen new siding add $30,000 in value to a house that was covered with ugly asbestos shingles before. But the magazines won't say that.

The basic principle is that improvements that buyers can see, feel, and experience add value. Improvements that enhance a buyers comfort or convenience add value—such as adding a fireplace or remodeling the kitchen. Putting in new plumbing rarely covers its cost.

Tip 155: Use the third dimension.

Adding drama to the home by creating volumes helps to make your home more memorable and seem larger to the buyer. People want high ceilings and lots of light. Vaulted ceilings give the perception of more space and make a room feel grand. Even the great cathedral at Chartres would lose its impressiveness if it had only an eight-foot-high sheetrock ceiling.

When creating your vaulted space, know that there are economical ways to work with vaulted ceilings. Analyze how new homes are being constructed. For example, stopping partitions at 8'0" to create plant shelves will add value while saving on drywall labor costs.

Start with what you have. Go up into the attic or crawl space above your ceiling and see what is there. Most homes are framed with traditional framing, consisting of rafters, a ridge beam, and joists. If your house was built within the last thirty years, it may have been built with trusses.

In creating a cathedral ceiling, what you have depends on what you find. If you have rafters, you can usually reach up all the way to them. You will need something to replace the collar ties. If you have trusses, you can also exploit them, rather than hide them. They can create bold, geometric shapes that frame the room.

If you are having trouble visualizing, work in three dimensions in planning. Building quick models will give you a better feel for the space and do much more than many sets of complex drawings.

Tip 156: Add a loft.

After you've created a vaulted space for drama and impact, you can gain some usable square footage by building a loft into the room. The loft can have a ladder or steps down to the room or it can be accessed from the second story. People like to use lofts as offices, libraries, or entertainment centers. Creating a vaulted ceiling in a family room could mean that an adult could supervise his or her children from the loft or attic office space while still having a separate work area.

Lofts are also a way to get around small bedrooms. By constructing a sleeping loft, you free up floor space otherwise taken up by the bed. A large bedroom subdivided into two smaller bedrooms may be too small for the usual amount of furniture. A sleeping loft might be the solution here.

Tip 157: Add a sunroom or solar greenhouse.

An inexpensive way to add some square footage and make an awkward or small space work better is to bump out a few feet of space and create a solarium or sun room. This can be done using one of those premanufactured kits, or you can actually frame it with lots of windows and skylights. By creating a true sunroom rather than just adding some square footage to the house, you are creating another "room" that adds value.

People love sun. When adding an addition, such as a family room where none currently exists, create a sunroom, with windows on two or more walls. A high ceiling and lots of glass can give a small room a sense of volume far in excess of its square footage.

Tip 158: Enclose a porch.

Obviously, one way to gain extra living space is to expand the exterior boundaries of your home. Of course, you could do a major addition, but at today's prices, after you build a foundation, roof, and other components, you could find yourself renovating your home for a loss. A less expensive alternative is to enclose an existing porch.

Many porches actually are located in prime sections of the home. A porch may overlook the back yard, or perhaps it can become a prime solarium at the front entrance. Porches have been successfully transformed into breakfast rooms, libraries, and even master bedrooms. Closing in a porch doesn't require building from scratch. But you may need to strengthen the foundation.

Tip 159: Reach up and create an attic room.

As potential new living space, attics contain two very desirable, easy-to-get qualities, light and ventilation. Many attics have the potential to be easily converted into quality living space. By adding a few skylights, finishing the walls, and carpeting the floor once-wasted space becomes usable square footage.

Not every attic is a good candidate for conversion to living space. You have a good start if your attic contains the following features that help keep the cost of a conversion down:

- A stairway over two feet wide.

- At least half the space you wish to convert can accommodate a finished ceiling with a minimum height of seven feet.

- The floor joists are strong enough to support a floor and people walking on them.

Put down a thick plywood floor and cover it with a carpet for good sound insulation.

Attics are perfect for creating a variety of built-in storage spaces. The low walls provide excellent storage for clothing and books, as well as using otherwise wasted space.

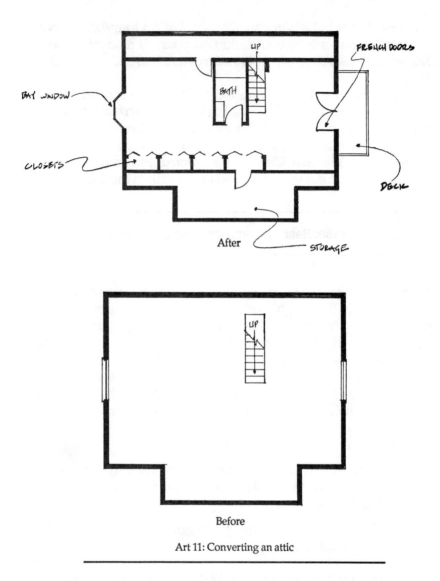

Art 11: Converting an attic

If you find that your attic is just short of becoming a wonderful living space, think about popping a dormer into the roof to create added living space and an interesting roof line. A dormer creates more than a treetop view; it adds extra headroom and helps diminish the cramped feeling that steeply sloped ceilings create.

Dormers can be framed in a variety of ways to suit many architectural styles. Gable dormers and shed dormers are the two most common styles. Gable dormers have two sloping roofs that meet at a ridge running perpendicular to the main roof ridge. A shed dormers has a single sloping roof which follows the direction of the main roof ridge. Shed dormers are simpler and less expensive to construct but in many cases don't harmonize with the home's architectural style as well as gable dormers do. Choose the one that is appropriate for your home.

Tip 160: Convert the garage into a room and add another garage.

Sometimes the garage is located more appropriately for people than for cars. An attached garage can easily become more living space such as a family room or extra bedroom. Building a new detached garage is relatively inexpensive and in many cases, not even necessary.

When planning a garage renovation, look at the home's entire floor plan and see if some room uses should be rearranged. Garages are usually not in the main flow of traffic and without a shift of use, the renovation can appear as a cheap add-on. Garage conversions make excellent family rooms. In many cases, the old garage door can be replaced with a row of windows and a french door.

A garage can also work well as a new bedroom. The garage can become a wonderful master suite in an otherwise small home. With its large size and usual proximity to the kitchen, the garage can easily be turned into a master bedroom with an elegant bath. Shift the focus from the front of the house (where the old garage door used to be) to the rear by cutting large openings in the wall.

You might also want to turn the garage into a home office. Garages make ideal home offices with their separate entrance and separation from other family activities. Also, the large size creates enough office space to actually house employees, too. Check with your local planning department to see if an office is allowed, especially if you have a business that generates a lot of traffic in a quiet residential neighborhood.

One possibility if you don't wish to convert the whole garage is to subdivide it. A home today often comes with a two- or three-car garage. In many cases these end up being used more for storage than for cars. If you convert the equivalent of one parking space into useful living area, you can gain some valuable living space at a low cost. Make sure you meet fire codes with your wall, as the partition between the garage and the home is usually of extra-heavy construction.

Tip 161: The number of bathrooms can significantly affect value.

The number of bathrooms is one of the few items that appear in real estate listings. Usually you see a home advertised as a four-bedroom, two-bath house. The lot size isn't advertised, the formal dining room isn't advertised, but the number of bathrooms is. Therefore it stands to reason that adding a bath can add value.

First see how many bathrooms are the norm for your area. You don't want to create a three-bedroom, seven-bath home in a neighborhood of three-bedroom, two-bath homes. The next step is to compare the sale price differences (*not* the asking price differences) between, let's say, homes with three-bedrooms, two-baths and three-bedrooms, three-baths. Notice if there is a significant difference. If so, the added bath will more than pay for itself.

Because of the high cost of running pipes, in many cases the best place to locate an additional bathroom is next to an existing one or near the kitchen. Sometimes this means relocating a bedroom, but that is usually a less expensive option than creating the bath far away from existing plumbing. Whenever you add a bathroom, be sure to use as many of the appeal elements described in this book as possible.

An extra bath will add value if you are curing a deficiency in your home relative to the neighborhood. One time an extra bath is always a good idea is when there's only one in the house. An extra half or full bath will go a long way to adding value.

Tip 162: Avoid overimprovements.

You know this one already, but it is important to emphasize it again and again. With few exceptions, values in an area tend to cluster around a certain value for a certain size and type of home.

It's like those bell curves we used to see in school when professors graded us on a curve. Housing values often don't go more than 20% above or below the area's median.

Overimprovements are in the eye of the beholder. Use market savvy when planning your renovation and you will avoid 90% of overimprovements just by being in this frame of mind.

CHAPTER NINETEEN

Renovating with the Trends

Every few years, a new trend in home design becomes popular. If you happen to have a house that can fit the current trends, you are in luck since you can offer something that the average home buyer associates with "what everyone wants." If not, you are not at a significant disadvantage since these trends are usually for wants, not needs.

This chapter covers the main trends that have popped up in the last few years. Do not feel that your house needs to conform to all (or even any) of the trends. You should first analyze whether your prospective buyers desire these trendy items and only implement those that they might.

Home Offices

Tip 163: A home office appeals to young couples, independent types, and those who want to get out of the corporate world.

There are two types of people who want home offices: those who want to work full-time from home and those who want to spend part of their work week out of the regular office. These people have different needs in a home office, but they both have something in common: they don't want to have to put an addition on the house themselves.

If your house has a small garage that isn't really functional for cars (because it was built for Model Ts) or a large family room that can be divided, you should consider creating a home office. In these cases, a home office adds a great deal of value to the house for people who are too busy to put one together themselves.

Even if a home office is desired in your market, don't simply change a bedroom into a home office. Since house prices are heavily dependent on the number of bedrooms, removing a bedroom can drive the price down. However, if you have more bedrooms than your target buyer will probably want, do consider turning one of them into a home office.

Tip 164: Decide on the most appropriate look for the home office.

Whom are you appealing to? How does the office tie in with the look of your home? Do you want the overall tone to be classic, elegant, or casual?

You need to coordinate the office. Look at professional offices: see how each creates an image. You want to have one here, too. The furniture, wall coverings, window coverings, lamps, and equipment must work together to send a coherent message.

Decide what has to go and what can stay. You don't need to buy a whole new set of furniture. Just decide what is consistent with the image you want to convey. Remember that a few inexpensive accessories such as photos and books can go a long way in conveying a certain image.

Tip 165: If you can't afford to give the office a whole room, steal a niche out of another and make a pocket office.

Home offices have become so popular today that homes with them have a decided advantage over homes without. Even if the buyers work at conventional jobs, most appreciate a place to do the paperwork or put the computer at home. You can create an office space out of all the little nooks and crannies that abound in most homes. Staircase landings, parts of the kitchen or living room, and even closets have been transformed into excellent working spaces.

When you create an office out of a landing or other formerly wasted space, you are creating another "room" in the mind of the buyer and gaining usable square footage.

Tip 166: Not every room is suitable for a home office.

Before you start tearing up a part of your home, work out on paper the kind of office space that your buyer would be looking for. Obviously, you won't know the kind of work prospects do, but you should consider some of the following points:

- Is there adequate electrical power for all the office equipment likely to be used?

- Is there adequate heating, cooling, and ventilation? Beware of locating a home office in a poorly venti-lated or uninsulated attic. At extreme temperatures, these spaces are unusable. Basements are often damp and poorly heated and make poor offices, too.

- Is there a separate entrance to the exterior of the home? That way a person can entertain clients without interfering with domestic life.

- Is the space pleasing to be in?

In-Law Apartments

Tip 167: If your target market has older parents or want to make extra rental income, an in-law apartment will look very cost-effective for them.

There are two main reasons for installing an in-law, or accessory, apartment in your home. One is to allow extended families to live under the same roof economically while at the same time maintaining privacy. The other is to provide the prospective buyer with extra income and a way to keep his out-of-pocket mortgage expenses lower.

The first place to look when contemplating the design of the second unit is to look at underutilized areas such as the attic, basement, or garage. Check for adequate ceiling heights and access to plumbing to determine whether or not the project is feasible at a reasonable cost.

Many in-law apartments are small, dark, and poorly built. They have a cramped feel. If space allows, construct at least one bedroom in the apartment. People prefer separating their public spaces from their private ones and are willing to pay higher rents for the privilege. Constructing more than two bedrooms is not recommended in an accessory apartment.

Tip 168: When planning the in-law apartment, determine the market value of the house with and without the apartment.

You want to make sure that you are adding value and not just keeping yourself busy by adding the second unit to your house. The simplest way to determine the value of the apartment is to look at comparable houses. See what houses have sold for that contained a second unit versus those that didn't. Compare square footages to make sure they are similar in size.

Another way to determine the value of an apartment is with the capitalization approach. This is how most commercial real estate is valued. Take the income stream produced by the apartment, and then, by determining what a return on the investment should produce, apply a value to the unit. For example, assume you want a 7% return on your money, similar to the rate available on CDs. If the apartment brings you $400/month (that is, $4,800/year), its value is $68,571 since $4,800 is 7% of $68,571. If you need a 10% return, the value of the apartment is only $48,000.

Even exclusive neighborhoods can use in-law units, only there they are referred to as *au pair* units. Second apartments need not be just for income. They can house servants or relatives or allow two friends to move in together. The key is how they are marketed.

Tip 169: Use your design skills to make the apartment appear larger and lighter.

The accessory apartment should also be appealing to the senses. Although the finishes need not be at the level of the main home, the apartment must appeal to both your prospective buyer and, of course, the prospective renter. This is particularly true if the buyer is going to put his or her parents in the unit. Use mirrors, lots of natural light, and optical illusions to make the apartment feel homey and spacious.

If you are turning a bedroom or a storage room into an apartment, you have lots of opportunity to use the tips in other parts of this book as you create it. Keep the apartment design similar to that of the house so that the potential buyer thinks of it as an extension, not an addition. The nicer the apartment, the more the buyer will be able to rent it for, thus making your house more attractive.

Tip 170: Preserve the appearance of a single family home.

Many people are still against putting in accessory apartments, even when the zoning laws allow it. They have a feeling that it lowers their property values, even though they have no data to confirm this. In order not to offend the neighbors, and to make it easier to get your permit approved, it is best not to let it appear from the street that you have an accessory apartment, aside from perhaps two addresses or mailboxes.

Barrier-free Living

Tip 171: Remodel all parts of the home to be wheelchair-accessible.

As our population continues to age, the importance of barrier-free environments is becoming greater and greater, as are the demand for them and their marketability. Because so few homes are accessible to those with physical disabilities or impediments, a home that is accessible can be sold in a market where others sit stagnant—if the demographics are right.

The modifications needed to make a home accessible are often not that great. Each doorway needs one foot of space next to it to allow a space for a wheelchair to back up while the door is being opened, doorways need to be at least 32 inches wide, and a ramp should replace the front step. Standard faucets should be replaced with ones that have wrist blade handles instead of knobs.

Many people feel that an accessible home has to look antiseptic and be full of ugly gadgets. This is not true. Just paying attention to details such as counter height, knobs on cabinets, and lowering thresholds may be all that is necessary to make the home accessible. Even grab bars are now being manufactured in decorator colors.

Tip 172: Even if your home is not wheelchair-accessible, make it appealing to the elderly.

Even people who are not yet old are planning on getting old and want a home they can still live in if they become less mobile. Vision that is not as good as in youth, fragile bones, and sometimes painful joints are some of the common effects of aging that many buyers have seen in their parents and grandparents. Plan your accessory apartment to be able to accommodate these needs by using contrasting color on a wall, non-skid surfaces in the bathroom, and knobs and pulls that are easier to work. These are some ways to make the apartment more desirable to a large and financially stable part of the population.

The "Healthy Home"

> **Tip 173: If you have an older home, play up its health advantages.**

The history of housing has been a progression of more and more innovations and conveniences. One hundred years ago, indoor plumbing was still a rarity and household electricity did not exist. Since the late 1940s, many new products have been introduced to homes such as plywood, synthetic carpets, particle board, and foam insulation. Many of these newer materials have had a detrimental effect on our health.

One in three people in the United States now has an allergy severe enough to require him or her to go to a doctor. One out of every five people now living will get cancer. Birth defects are on the rise. Although still not a large proportion of the population, the people who have awakened to this realization are strongly affected by how "healthy" your house is in making their next purchase. You can improve the healthiness of your home for not much money, often significantly. Telling prospects about the healthy quality of your home will help make it distinct from many others on the market.

Some items are easy to change, some items you can do nothing about. If your home is located under high-voltage electrical lines, it will take a lot of convincing to sell your home as healthy. Be realistic. But if your home seems to appeal to that type of buyer and is a likely candidate, it is time to get to work.

Many people are now becoming aware of the problems of "sick buildings," homes that actually cause headaches, nausea, or illness because of outgassing of the materials that it is made of. Most of the products causing these illnesses are in post–World War II homes. That is when plywood glues, synthetic materials, formaldehyde, and other substances became common in building materials. Older homes, if not renovated, do not have any of these products or problems. If a buyer has an allergy or sensitivity, this is a good selling point.

Many older homes contain plaster walls. Newer ones contain walls of sheetrock and joint compound. The joint compound causes a lot of problems for allergic or sensitive people. It contains mica, talc, polyvinyl alcohol, and perlite; these newer compounds can cause health problems.

Tip 174: Use filters to purify the indoor air.

Few buyers would ask you, "Have you done anything to make the air here healthier?" Air purification is a feature you find in very few homes. However, it is very inexpensive to add and, if your buyers have allergies or are worried about the air, telling them that you added air purification will certainly make your house stand out. This could be a make-or-break item for people moving from cleaner climates or people who have severe allergies.

Placing particle filters into your ventilation system can help remove spores, pollen, and other pollutants from the air. Activated carbon filters remove toxic gases and impurities; gasses adhere to the activated carbon instead of to your lungs. You can buy a combination filter kit with motor and blower that attaches to your mechanical ventilation system. The air will be healthier, you'll feel better, and you can market the health benefits to others.

Negative ion generators, although they do not purify the air, contribute to cleaner indoor air. They send out electrons which bond with particles in the air and make them adhere to various surfaces. Negative ions have been shown in a number of studies to have beneficial effects on health including increased energy, friendliness, and alertness. The air in your home can actually enhance people's moods.

Tip 175: Filters can improve the water quality.

The water you drink these days has been routinely chlorinated to disinfect it, whether it needs it or not. Our water is commonly treated with other chemicals as well. Several studies have shown a link between chlorinated water and increased cancer risk. Several types of filters are available: carbon, reverse osmosis, distillation. All have one thing in common, though: the goal of removing toxic substances from the water. If your city's water supply has a bad reputation, a water filter that costs a few hundred dollars is an inexpensive way of showing the buyer that you care about quality.

Water quality has become an item of concern to developers and homeowners alike. Recent surveys show that water quality has become a hot topic. In questioning buyers about what they wanted in a home, 45% chose a water filtration system. When asked specifically about water quality, over 90% said they want more control over the quality of their water. Water-filtration systems will be one of the hot kitchen appliances of the 1990s.

Tip 176: Make your house safe.

Making a home healthy also means making it safe. This is especially important to families with small children. Making your home more childproof can be a tactic for marketing to families with young children or for older couples. Marketing safety works well with many buyers who want to know that the seller cares about how they live.

Falls

Falls are the number one type of accidents in the home. As you show your home, many people will be coming through. You are liable if they hurt themselves. Before you can get rid of the hazards, you must know where to find them.

You would be surprised how likely it is that you have unsafe floors. Beware of waxing floors to a slippery shine. Never use a throw rug at the top or bottom of the stairs. If carpets or rugs don't lie flat, be sure to restretch them.

Exterior hazards are also significant and easy to take care of. Patch all holes in sidewalks and driveways. Clear wet leaves and ice off of all walkways and driveways as often as possible (certainly every day when you are showing the house). Provide plenty of lighting, especially near the ground on walkways.

Fire

More people are killed in residential fires than in fires anywhere else. Fire prevention is welcomed by all buyers, although few would be willing to pay much for it. Pointing out the fire-safety features of your home reinforces the sense of quality buyers feel for your home and for you. The following are some of the items you should take care of in your home are:

- Install smoke detectors. Because smoke rises, the best location for smoke detectors is on the ceiling or high on a wall near the ceiling. Install at least one on each level of the home, usually two or three a floor.

- Place a fire extinguisher in the kitchen, and probably have one in the garage. This shows attention to safety and is a good practice for all homeowners.

- Use a wire screen in front of the fireplace to keep sparks from flying into the room and remember to clean the chimney and fireplace when carbon build-up becomes too great.

Other hazards

There are many other hazards to be aware of, such as:

- Electrical shock. Install GFCI electrical outlets, especially in bathrooms, kitchens, and workshop areas. These contain their own circuit breakers and can prevent death by electric shock. They help show your concern for safety.

- Physical dangers. Have a minimum of sharp corners. If you are getting a new countertop, it should have rounded edges. Make sure bathroom floors and tub have nonslip surfaces.

- Earthquake. If your home is in earthquake country, bolting and bracing it properly can be a strong marketing tool and insure your investment in your home. After the 1989 earthquake in the San Francisco area, homes that were properly earthquake-protected sold much better than unsupported ones.

CHAPTER TWENTY

Making the Exterior Special

Most houses in need of help suffer one of three problems:

- Not enough detail. A home without interesting architectural details is rarely memorable. Details can be added with shutters, window boxes, trim, moldings, or other features. Paint can be used to accent present details or to create new ones.

- Too much detail. Some houses contain too many materials and styles. Bringing this type of house back to basics will increase its appeal. Strip away oddball elements. Paint mismatched materials the same color to help hide the detail.

- Poor proportions. Use landscaping tricks or a new color scheme to help shape up a house with awkward lines. Adding an entry porch, dormers, or shutters can help balance a house.

To help visualize changes, enlarge a photo of the home's exterior. Then put tracing paper over the photo. Trace the house, then sketch in features or colors that are being considered. When considering color, keep the roof color in mind in the plan.

Tip 177: Nothing is more important than curb appeal.

The look of your home starts with the neighborhood but then works its way to your yard and eventually to the front of your house. Earlier, you read how to plan the tour of the house in order to guide buyer expectations. Now we need to talk about the next step: the yard. The key to planning the yard is to get the buyer excited and create a good first impression for the whole house.

Someone visiting your house sees the view from the curb at a time when you are not around to point out a nice highlight. Thus, your house must present itself well from the curb or you may not even get the person through the door.

Tip 178: Use gates and fences to give your home the look and feel you desire.

Fences can be inviting or stately, warm or cold. Many wealthier areas have fences around the homes. Studies have shown that a barrier in front of the house makes it appear more valuable to buyers.

When planning your fence, look at what the homes in the better parts of town do. Contrast that with the gates in the poorer sections and you'll have a good idea of what to do and of what not to do.

If your house seems bland and unattractive from the street, a nice fence with a welcoming gate can draw buyers in who might otherwise have driven by. People are curious to see what is behind a fence and will get out of their cars to look. Once out of their cars, they will tend to come into the house since they "are already there."

Fences can also be used to screen unsightly views or to create outdoor rooms. Most importantly, they make the house appear bigger by extending the facade to the lot line.

A lattice can be used to help partially screen a view. This is especially important on small lots where an imposing fence might seem overwhelming and actually shrink the apparent size of the lot. By growing a flowering vine or ivy on the lattice, you can brighten and enhance the appearance of your home, adding value, and screening out unsightly views.

How can the prospect buy your house if he or she can't find it? Make sure numbers are clear and look classy. Polished brass numbers are a favorite. Look at your house as an overall picture. In fact, cut out a cardboard frame and look at your home in just this way. Notice what seems out of place or what is lacking.

Look at the overall concept. How do the plantings relate to the house? Are the colors of the flowers working with the house color? Connect all the elements as in a masterpiece painting and soon the whole will be much greater than the sum of the parts.

Tip 179: Landscaping usually adds more value than it costs.

Twenty years ago builders would bulldoze their housing developments to expedite the work. They soon learned that buyers place a huge value on mature landscaping. Now they pay landscape architects thousands to carefully plot out which trees should be saved and how to enhance the curb appeal of the home.

Mature trees can add a lot of value. It has been estimated that homes with well-kept, mature trees can add 10% to 15% to the value of a home. If you have large trees, consult a tree trimmer to see if you can enhance their appeal and the value of your home.

Tip 180: Use landscaping to guide the eye.

Landscaping can be used to steer the eye from the unattractive areas of your home to the attractive ones. Color tends to draw the eye more than plain backgrounds and an asymmetrical item in the midst of symmetry sticks out.

You can also use landscaping to hide ugly foundations and to soften the effect of the house against the ground. If your home sits fine on the lot without foundation plantings than don't waste your money. Trees and shrubs help anchor the home to its site.

The entry should be focused with the help of landscaping, but you don't need to put on a plant show either. Using flowers and a variety of plants makes the walk to the home friendly and interesting. Don't let the plants encroach on the walkway or entry itself, though. The psychological effect you want is one of welcoming, not fighting off insects and briars.

Tip 181: Plants are living things, so timing is important.

In a down market, homes do not sell as quickly as you would like. Also, buyers are becoming more concerned about the maintenance required to keep up landscaping. Each plant has its season. If you plant items which flower only briefly, than the time when most buyers are seeing your house might be the time when the plant that looked so beautiful at the nursery looks like a giant weed in front of your house.

Tip 182: Use plantings to screen out eyesores or unsightly views.

If the house next to yours looks bad, you may need to build a fence and then soften it with ivy or flowering vines. If you are having trouble finding plants that grow fast, look good, and are hardy, look along the freeways and contact the transportation department to find out what they use.

Chapter Twenty-One

Renovating Room by Room

Renovation can add significant value to the house over and above the money you put into the renovation. When preparing to sell your house in a down market, your primary motivation for renovating is to make your house memorable and attractive to buyers at a reasonable price.

However, you may have decided by now that you are not ready to sell just yet. If you are reading this book in preparation for selling in six months or a year, you have plenty of time to renovate for the second-best reason: to make money. Even in a down market, you can more than double your investment dollar by renovating intelligently.

This chapter describes smart ways to renovate the most important parts of your house. Following these suggestions, you can increase the value of your house by at least the amount of money you put in. This is even true in a down market, since many carpenters, tile layers, and so on are short of work and will often work for less than they normally would. Note, however, that there is a potential down side to renovating now. If you decide you want to sell quickly, you can't start showing your house while it is being renovated. Think carefully about timing before you start renovating a room in your house.

Entranceway

> **Tip 183: The first impression of the inside of your house is your entrance or foyer.**

The entrance can set the tone for a home. Adding a front porch where their currently is none or opening up the entry vertically to create a soaring effect can often add value significantly above what the nominal gain in square footage would imply. Working on the entrance can also help cure design flaws common in many homes. Many houses lack transition areas from the outside to the inside. You are thrust directly from the walkway into the living room. Creating an elegant transition area allows for a place to linger, to hang coats, and to give the home an enlarged feeling.

If you have a consistent interior design in most parts of your house, be absolutely sure that the design is reflected in the entrance or foyer. It is common for designers to forget the entrance since there is usually no furniture there and it is not a congregating area. Home buyers, however, will receive many first impressions the moment they walk in the door.

If you have spent time and money on a theme for the house, be sure to take that theme into the entrance. Let the buyers see what they will see throughout the rest of the house as soon as they come in.

> **Tip 184: Make buyers feel welcome with hallway amenities.**

How many times have you walked into a warm house wearing a heavy coat and had to carry the coat halfway across the house before you got to the "guest" closet? When you are showing a house, you will have many strangers coming and going. Cater to their comfort even more than you might already be catering to that of your usual house guests. An inexpensive but tasteful coat rack makes everyone feel at ease, especially during seasons when coats are worn but not always needed. If there is any chance of rain, also have an umbrella holder, not just a corner where people can stick them. Of course, if you have a furniture style in your house, be sure the coat rack and umbrella stand match that style.

Entrance amenities don't have to be useful. If you have decorated your house with houseplants, be sure to have one in the entrance. Be careful here, though: make sure the plant in the entrance does not stand out from the ones around the house or the buyer will notice it. Also, if your entrance is small, don't put a big plant there that will make the entrance look smaller.

Remember, most people want their homes to impress house guests. They dream of dinner parties for friends and business associates at which everyone admires their house. If they don't feel comfortable just as they walk in, they won't feel that other people will either.

Start your home's presentation with items that call attention to a buyer's values. These might be a rocking chair on the porch, a welcome mat, some plants and other items which call attention to home and family and allow the buyer to make good associations from the moment he or she walks in the door.

Tip 185: Light in the entrance makes buyers think there is light throughout the house.

As is noted in other parts of the book, most buyers want houses with lots of light. Even in places where too many windows may indicate energy inefficiency, almost everyone wants to see a cheery entranceway. Due to the way most houses are constructed, this is often easy and inexpensive.

If you already have a small window, consider enlarging it. Making a small window larger is much less expensive than putting a window in where there was previously just a wall. Many home developers used to put small windows in big spaces to save on costs; take advantage of that by knocking the walls around the window out to the nearest joists and putting in the largest window possible. For example, if you have a window that is 24" high and 18" wide, replacing it with one that is 24" x 24" lets a third more light into the hallway.

Do not overlook tall windows. Since many hallway windows do not open anyway, consider replacing a small window with a floor-to-ceiling window. For instance, replacing the same 24" x

18" window with one that is 96" x 24" increases the light by more than four times!

If you have any natural light in the entranceway, you can usually double it for under $100 simply by adding a decorative mirror. This mirror not only brightens the entrance, it lets strangers entering your home adjust themselves a bit before meeting you. This in turn makes them feel better about how your house will feel after they buy it and guests come to visit them.

Tip 186: Adding a window to a door adds light from another direction.

The front door is one of the most familiar objects in your house for a very good reason: it is one of the most used. As such, it may be one of the most worn. If you are going to replace the front door due to normal wear and tear, strongly consider one with a window, especially if there are no other windows in the entrance hall. The way most houses are designed, the front door has no windows near it, so a window in the door adds light were there was none before.

If you are concerned about security, think about a door with a window at the top. Many door manufacturers now make doors with windows high enough that a burglar could not break the glass and reach the deadbolt, yet these windows still let in lots of light. Remember, the purpose of the glass in this case is to lighten the foyer, not necessarily to let people see in and out.

Tip 187: At the very least, use artificial light.

If you have been following the tips in other parts of this book, you know how important artificial light is when natural light is not available. Most entries have a ceiling light: keep it turned on, even during the day. This is especially valuable for buyers coming at dusk or on a rainy day, since it creates a feeling of warmth inside your house. If you have no ceiling light, consider adding one. At the very minimum, you should have a floor lamp, preferably one that matches the style of the other lighting fixtures in your house.

Tip 188: Buyers always look at the floor in the foyer, so make it especially bright.

Most people entering a stranger's house wipe their feet on the doormat, so their eyes are already on the floors. This is unfortunate since the floors and carpets in an entrance are more prone to scuffing and excessive wear. The most important part of the floor in the entire house is in the entranceway: be sure that the floors or floor coverings look their best.

With wall-to-wall carpeting, it is difficult to replace one piece that is worn more than others. Consider using a different material such as wood or marble for accent. If you do not want to replace worn carpeting in the entrance, consider a tasteful throw rug to cover the spot. Even though you have shampooed the carpets throughout the house before you start selling, you should vacuum and possibly clean the carpet and rugs in the entrance every week.

Tip 189: Consider what the potential buyer sees after he or she has been impressed with the entranceway.

Every room in your house is connected, and a buyer will notice the connections as he or she walks through the house. You have a buyer in the entrance and you have made an impression: what next?

Think about how strangers entering your house feel as they leave the entrance way. Are they drawn in a particular direction? Is that the direction you want them to be drawn? If not, consider placing some bright or interesting object in the direction you want them to look in. If they are drawn directly into the living room, is the living room arranged in a way that invites them in? A common mistake that is simple to fix is arranging the first room after the entrance in such a way that someone has to walk around furniture, usually the back of a sofa, to enter. Make the transition from the entrance to the first room natural and in a straight line. If there are many choices, make them all inviting. Lead the eye of the buyer with color and furnishings.

Tip 190: Remember the entranceway when you renovate adjacent rooms.

Since every room is connected to others, it is important to think of the connections as you renovate a room. Since the entranceway is the most important room for first impressions, keep it in mind when you renovate adjacent rooms. For example, if your entranceway leads to a living room, be sure you look carefully at the intersection if you decide to renovate the living room. Could you add light to the entranceway by knocking out a living-room wall?

If your entrance leads to a long hall that connects many rooms, think about the hall when you renovate any rooms. Is the hall really necessary? With a major renovation, could you eliminate the hall completely, making the entrance a way to get to many rooms at once? If someone walking into your house has many views at once, your whole house will seem that much bigger.

Living Room

Tip 191: Almost everyone expects the living room to be the most formal room in the house.

Of the many fantasies that buyers have of the houses they look at, one of the most pervasive is that of the formal living room. In this country, the living room carries more emotional luggage than other rooms because it is often the one associated with old-style families. It can invoke the image of a hearth, family togetherness, and so on. Families with limited money for furniture often spend the most on the living room, purchasing nice sofas, stuffed chairs, and fancy stereo systems.

You may not subscribe to these lofty images, but there is a good chance that your buyers do. Thus, you may have to make some concessions to their fantasies in the way that you present the living room. If you must, rearrange the furniture in the living room to reflect the formal feeling that buyers want.

Tip 192: $1000 spent in the living room can easily turn to $2000 in the buyer's eyes.

A formal feeling is very easy to attain, although it often costs more than you might want to spend. Try to think in terms not of costs alone, but of benefits minus costs. $1,000 might seem like a lot of money to put into a house that you are about to sell, but you should think of how much more it will make your house worth.

What can you do for $1000 that will make a big difference?

- Molding. Even if your house already looks nice throughout, it is still important to make the living room look better. Adding molding to the living room does not detract from the pattern of the whole house but adds a sense of formality to this one room.

- New paint. This is very important if your old paint has yellowed or discolored unevenly around bookcases and pictures. It is also important if the walls have lots of holes from picture hangers.

- Accent lighting. Your living room may already have special features that make it seem formal, such as a mahogany chest or family pictures on the mantle. Emphasize them with spot or localized lighting. Show buyers that you share their values and want to emphasize them yourself.

- Formal doors and windows. Again, keep them in tune with the rest of the house, but adding doors or tall windows to the living room makes it seem like a special place.

Tip 192: Nothing says "living room" like a fireplace.

Like everyone, home buyers look for traditional icons when they walk through a house. A fireplace is about as traditional as you can get for something that says "living room," so it is very important that the fireplace state the theme of the whole living-room space.

If you have a fireplace, be sure that it is appears clean. If your fireplace tools are old or battered, consider buying a new set for around $100. If you have firewood in the living room, be sure that it is stacked neatly and in abundance so that the area has a feeling that you really appreciate your fireplace.

You may even want to have the chimney professionally cleaned and inspected. Any smart buyer will ask if the chimney is in good condition, since a leaky chimney is a fire hazard. "Yes, we just had it checked" sounds much better than "Well, it seems to be." Being prepared with an answer to such a basic question shows that you use your fireplace and that you care about it. Having it cleaned also shows that you are anticipating the needs of the buyer, something that few other sellers do.

Dining Room

Tip 193: If your dining room is small, tear down the walls.

Because a dining room is required to hold a large table, often one that expands with leaves, a hutch, and side tables, a small dining room can easily become more of an inconvenience than an asset. Many homes today don't even have separate formal dining rooms, but rather combine the dining area with other living areas to create a large room. The dining area then becomes defined more by materials and flooring. This allows you to borrow space from the living area if necessary, making the dining room roomier and more functional.

If your dining area has a nice view or is conveniently located near the yard, think about opening up the wall to a deck or patio.

You can use French doors to create an elegant transition from the inside to the outside.

Tip 194: If you have no separate dining room, create a dining area.

Although formal dining rooms are not required, especially in smaller homes, a separate eating area is a must. This area must feel like a separate dining room to achieve the desired added value. This can be accomplished through a change of materials in that area (such as switching from linoleum to a wood floor), a change of level (such as an elevated platform), or a change of lighting (through a skylight, enlarged windows, or special artificial light). It is important for people that there be somewhere other than a kitchen table or snack bar to entertain guests.

A quick trick: if you're afraid that buyers won't recognize the area you have set up as a separate dining area, set the table as if guests were coming. To heighten the effect, put some fruit and maybe a bottle of wine in the middle of the table. Since you are relying on visual cues to make this a dining area, use all the help you can get.

Kitchen

Tip 195: The kitchen is the center of the house.

Kitchens are a big part of what sells a home today. They are the heart of the home, the most-used room, and the eventual gathering place for every party on the planet.

Kitchens must have an impact. They must wow the buyer and make your home memorable. Much of what homeowners want today in a kitchen is to convey their upscale taste and lifestyle.

Kitchens are not only becoming more luxurious, they are also opening up to the spaces around them. One reason for this is the lifestyle changes many American households have undergone, particularly the rise in the number of two-income families.

Today, spouses are sharing more of the cooking duties, replacing the traditional separation. When they come home from work, parents are more likely to combine their time preparing food with spending time with the children.

The paradox is that even though the kitchen is being used less for cooking, it is still an exciting area for buyers. Perception is the key. Whether or not buyers actually use the kitchen, they think they will

---

Tip 196: Everyone wants a big kitchen, so make your kitchen appear larger than it really is.

There are many ways to make a small kitchen appear larger with minor renovations:

- See-through cabinets between the kitchen and dining nook allow for storage while also allowing for views and light to continue on and connect the two rooms. This creates a separate identity.

- Glass between the countertop and the wall cabinets connect you to the outside and open up a small kitchen.

- If your home is located right next to another house, a glass block wall or backsplash can add pizazz while still maintaining privacy and separation from other homes.

- Turn a window seat into a breakfast nook. This adds a custom feel to the home and takes up less space than chairs.

- Add a bump-out window (greenhouse window) in front of the sink. This situation creates a counter 30" or more wide while creating views to the outside. This adds disproportionately to the feeling of space generated and gives you something nice to look at when you're doing the dishes.

> **Tip 197: You can define spaces without closing them in, creating a larger feel to the kitchen.**

You can divide spaces with walls, but in a kitchen the fewer walls the better. Use low walls or even just different lighting to separate the kitchen from other parts of the house while still giving the illusion of large spaces.

For example, you can use peninsulas and overhead cabinets to divide the area physically. Use pocket doors, partial walls, or columns to suggest separate areas while retaining lines of sight. You can even repeat design elements to unify a space or several spaces.

If you are doing a major renovation on an adjacent area, use changed ceiling heights and floor levels within the space. You'd be surprized how well a simple one-foot step-down in the ceiling gives the impression of a different room while leaving the rest of the space open and giving both rooms a much larger feel.

> **Tip 198: Keep the major elements simple.**

The kitchen is the most complex room in the house. Aside from having the most electrical, plumbing, and ventilation concerns, in terms of surfaces, there are more disparate elements here than any other room. You have appliances; countertops; cabinets; flooring; task, general, and accent lighting; and small appliances and specialty items. In order to keep things from getting out of hand, keep these elements unified by theme.

> **Tip 199: Increase the usable storage space.**

Like closets, you can never have too much storage in a kitchen. Make sure you have adequate cabinet space. Less than adequate space will turn buyers off quickly. Pantries and broom closets also provide good places for storage and for hiding items. You can carve out a small walk-in pantry from most kitchens without sacrificing space, creating a hot button for buyers.

You can also purchase premanufactured pantries from cabinet companies. These cabinets, which have become more popular in recent years, can hold a large number of items, far greater than one would suspect from their size.

If your cupboard seem too crowded, first empty all excess items. You don't want buyers to think you have inadequate storage. Than look at other options. Perhaps a hanging pot rack will add to the look of the kitchen while freeing up a whole cabinet for other items. Restaurant shelving has a slick look and can make a blank wall into a great kitchen display instantly.

Tip 200: Accent your eat-in area or create one.

At the top of buyer preference lists is the ability to eat in the kitchen. A larger kitchen has plenty of space for a breakfast table, but smaller ones have to get creative sometimes. The island can do double duty as an eating bar. All that is required is a 12" overhang at one end so stools may be placed alongside it. You can emphasize this area even more by dropping the counter height to table height and create an actual table with chairs.

If you are planning a large remodeling job, you can create a sun space which can become your breakfast nook. Buyers love breakfast areas awash with sun. Make sure it is insulated, so you can eat comfortably at night too.

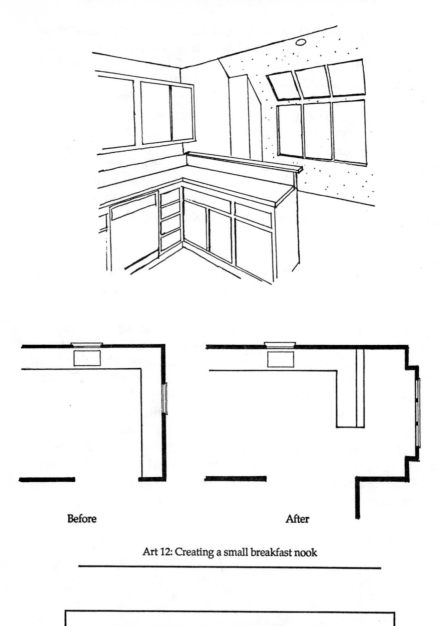

Before   After

Art 12: Creating a small breakfast nook

Tip 201: Differentiate your kitchen from the competition.

Making your kitchen memorable is also a key home merchandising concept. This is particularly important in neighborhoods where there are only three or four basic interior layouts. If you think that your kitchen looks too much like those of your competition, you can add touches like these:

- Put in a fireplace or wood stove to make a warm "hearth" in the home. Of course, this works only in a large kitchen, but it is sure to be remembered by everyone who sees it.

- Create a "recycling center." This appeals to the environmentally conscious. A small compost container in the kitchen can lead directly to a discussion of your garden. Linking the kitchen to the garden in this way will certainly attract people who are moving from more agricultural areas.

- Create an office nook that can be converted to an eating area. This is very useful, especially if your target audience would like a home office but you couldn't put one in your house. The space could hold a personal computer and books, but be easily rearranged for parties.

Tip 202: Make sure you incorporate the items buyers want most.

Every year surveys are done by builders and remodelers to keep up with what today's buyers want in a kitchen. Some of the most requested amenities in recent years have been these:

- Lazy Susans in the cabinets
- Microwave oven, preferably built in
- Pull-out shelves
- Garbage disposal
- Appliance garages
- Walk-in pantry
- Breakfast nook or eating area directly adjacent to kitchen

- Island cabinets
- Sink placed for panoramic view of outdoors
- Pass-through counters

Of course, it is better to stay ahead of the trends than to follow. Some of the hottest trends for kitchens in the 1990s will include these:

- A preference for gas cooktops with five or more burners
- Multifunctional cooking units that offer gas and electric cooking, indoor barbecue, and deep frying all in one
- Double-wall ovens and built-in refrigerators
- Corner sinks and cabinet organizers to maximize space
- Roof windows and skylights
- Environmental appliances such as electronic air cleaners
- Small media centers for VCRs, TVs, and music.

Bathrooms

> **Tip 203: The design of the bathrooms is probably the key difference between a new home and a "used" home today.**

No room in the house has been so transformed in the last four or five years as the bathroom. The bathroom has become a place to satisfy our fantasies and our needs.

Bathrooms with soaking tubs, fireplaces, spas, and top-of-the-line fixtures have become the norm in new homes. The design of the bathrooms is probably the key difference between a new home and a "used" home these days. By appointing your bathroom luxuriously, you can capture a share of the market that might be looking somewhere else.

Make the bath special by focusing on the details. An oversized medicine chest, a glass shower enclosure, and lots of natural light are just some of the elements that will excite buyers. Look at what builders are offering in new homes in your area and determine what elements you can easily incorporate into your own bathroom.

Remember, if you are planning a full renovation, don't skimp on the bathroom.

Tip 204: Buyers know the hassle of renovating a bath.

Buyers are usually aware of the costs and hassles involved in renovating a bathroom, so the value a good one will add, a poor one could take away. Dark and dingy bathrooms turn off many buyers more than one rationally would think they could. Having an attractive bathroom is a must in a down market to move the house quickly.

The flip side of this argument will help you: if you renovate a bathroom, the buyer will know that you put in a lot of work that they don't have to. Be sure to mention any plumbing that you did so that the buyer recognizes that the plumbing won't fail any time soon.

Tip 205: The bathroom must feel light, airy, and clean.

Nothing turns buyers off as much as a dark and moldy bathroom. It is crucial to your success that you focus on increasing light and spaciousness in the bath, no matter how small it is. Do everything you can to increase the light, from knocking out a hole in the wall to create a window to adding a skylight. If you are concerned about a lack of privacy there are many creative solutions. You can use glass block, translucent glass, or stained glass to allow light in but block the view in. Some other solutions include these:

- Placing a clerestory window above head height is another solution that retains privacy.

- Use a greenhouse window at the edge where the wall meets the rafters. This makes all vertical glass above viewing height, and the part along the ceiling acts as a skylight.

- Creating a porthole window allows for privacy. Set it at a height that allows for viewing out while showering but does not allow for views in.

Artificial light is also a must. A good set of recessed cans in the ceiling or a central fixture are excellent for increased general lighting. However, the real selling point comes with accent lighting. Linear tubes, Hollywood lights, and sconces all add to the sex appeal of the bathroom.

Tip 206: Use architectural features to create drama and impact.

The trend in the 1990s is to create as much of an architectural impact in the bathroom as in the more public rooms. Bathrooms with level changes, lots of space, and vaulted ceilings are exciting buyers all over the country. Use building elements such as columns, arches, and glass blocks to update and add drama to your bathroom. Window treatments also add style from oriental shoji screens and stained glass to shades and shutters.

Create a focal point. It could be a fireplace near a tub or a dramatic view. Ceiling height changes in the bathroom, skylights, dramatic steps up to the Jacuzzi, or a window overlooking the yard are all ways to add excitement to a large but blase bath. Set a theme for the bathroom to keep it consistent.

Tip 207: Go with buyer's hot buttons.

Every year builder's and remodeler's magazines conduct surveys about what home buyers are looking for. Some of the items that top the lists are these:

- Two sinks
- A makeup area, or a knee space in the vanity for a chair
- Linen closet
- Mirrors
- Lots of natural light
- Dressing areas
- Vanity storage
- Ceramic tile
- Shower adjacent to tub with a glass enclosure

Incorporate these elements into your design to achieve maximum impact and desirability.

Tip 208: Create a look for your bathroom.

Luxury and fantasy have crept into the bathrooms of America. Romance now plays a key role in bath design. The key to creating an exciting bath is the use of exquisite materials, artfully placed. Fancy "European" faucets and hardware will dominate the bath of the 1990s as will other custom appointments such as brass towel bars and decorative ceramic tile.

The bathroom is now the ultimate stage set in the house. Create a theme whether it be soft and homey or high tech and slick. A bathroom that is dramatic makes the home memorable.

Tip 209: Focus on the dressing areas since these say "luxury".

Focus on the separation of his and her spaces and the transition areas. Pay some attention to powder rooms as buyers like to lavish a lot of attention on themselves in this space.

The bathroom is becoming the stress-reduction and health center of the house. Exercise rooms should be located just off the bath area.

Tip 210: Make up in detailing what you lack in size.

Detailing is becoming increasingly important to new-home builders as construction and land costs force bathroom sizes to shrink. If you have a small bathroom, you can use expensive, quality materials, since the amount of them will be quite small. Small elements like brass towel bars or a three-sided mirror don't require too much money or work, but they make your bathroom special. Some inexpensive items that create a luxury feel include large medicine chests, built-in dressing tables with drawers for make-up and other paraphernalia, and book or magazine racks near the toilet.

Bedrooms

Tip 211: Focus on the master bedroom.

The person spending the money cares about one person most of all, and that's him- or herself. Since your renovation budget is limited, focus the money on the master bedroom rather than the smaller secondary bedrooms. Spend as much as you need to to make the master bedroom seem large and comfortable and have lots of closet space.

A fireplace, a separate study area, and lots of storage are all desired elements in a master suite. Adding a skylight or replacing the existing window with a bay window or seating area will enhance and brighten the space.

Try to create the feeling of a private living room in the master suite. This is usually done with furnishings, but you can add renovation touches such as high-class moldings, expensive windows, and built-in cabinets.

Tip 212: Create private outdoor living areas.

Private outdoor decks or patios off the master bedroom create excitement for most buyers. Who wouldn't like to be sipping orange juice in the morning sun on his or her private deck, away from all the cares of the world? Not only is this a convenience, it makes the bedroom look much larger than it really is.

You might be surprised how inexpensive it is to add a small deck that will hold a few chairs, especially if the bedroom is at ground level. It certainly costs less to add a deck than to actually expand the room. If you are adding a deck, make sure to get doors or windows to the deck which complement the deck's luxury.

Tip 213: Focus on the closet space.

In the master bedroom, closet space is even more important than in the other rooms. Deluxe closet space with all the amenities helps add sales value to the room. Ideally, you should have a walk-in closet and a dressing area. Use closet organizers to further increase the usable space of the room. Some builders even go so far as to use motorized carousels of the type dry cleaners have in order to add pizazz.

Other Rooms

Be sure to think about the small areas, too. The little extras can add up to create the impact you want your home to have with a buyer.

Tip 214: Make the laundry room as inviting as possible.

What? The laundry room? Does that really rate up there with kitchens and entrance ways? You bet it does. Remember, you are not trying to spend the most money, you are trying to spend a little money and have it turn into the biggest profit or, at least, the most positive memory. Putting $100 into the laundry room can do just that.

Face it: everyone dislikes laundry. There is a very good chance that your prospective buyers do their laundry in their basement, their garage, or a tiny closet. If you have a real laundry room, make sure they know it. Even if you have only a laundry closet, make it as useful and inviting as possible. It will cost you only a few dollars.

Provide space for folding, sorting, and hanging. Add a fold-down ironing board to a door to show efficient use of the space. If you are leaving the washer and dryer behind as part of the house deal, be sure they look nice and are not dusty.

Structural Issues

> **Tip 215: If there are water stains, find the source of the problem and fix it.**

Water stains are another problem which can make people panic. Water damage can be very expensive, although the cause may be something as simple as a five-cent washer. In order to protect yourself from liability, repair all sources of water stains before covering them up. But then, do cover them up. If a buyer senses damage in one area, he imputes it to the rest of the house.

> **Tip 216: Repairing all termite and wood rot will save you money.**

After you have your full inspection, repair any termite or wood rot problems. Structural pest-control inspection companies charge a very high markup to fix work like this. In most cases you can shave 30% to 50% off the cost just by hiring a contractor who is not a licensed termite-repair contractor and get just as good or better work. This can translate into thousands of dollars on a large repair.

PART III

The Sale Itself

CHAPTER TWENTY-TWO

Strategies of Successful Selling

Most people believe that selling a home is a matter of getting the right person to walk through the door and then "closing" them: convincing them this is the right house. It is analogous to how one would expect a used car dealer to sell cars. A couple walks in and then is persuaded to buy.

The difference between the average real estate agent or home seller and the most successful professionals is that the successful sellers know this is not the way it really works. Just as with the accomplished athlete or actor who makes the performance look easy, a lot of preparation goes into the act behind the scenes.

Tip 217: Follow the sales strategies of successful salespeople.

Some of the strategies of successful sales people are these:

- Managing your mental and emotional state
- Understanding the market through preparation
- Managing the prospect's state of mind

- Developing strategies for effective prospecting
- Creating interest and drawing attention to the home
- Building trust
- Qualifying the prospect

These must all occur before the "close." Relying solely on the fact that you listed your home with a broker to guarantee a sale is foolish in a competitive down market.

Most people skip the first three strategies right off the bat. Many skip all seven. Aside from a quick appraisal of the property by the listing agent, little more thought goes into who is buying the property. A housing developer would never risk this, or he would go bankrupt. Successful ones know every nuance of the market they are in and who their buyers are. Treat your real estate for what it is: your biggest asset. Don't shortchange yourself by skimping on your preparation.

Tip 218: Manage your mental and emotional state and stay positive.

This is probably the most important precept of all in a down market. These are trying times for most sellers. It can be frustrating waiting for a buyer and watching the days go by. You must do whatever you can to keep yourself in a positive frame of mind and avoid anything that will cause you to become a "don't wanter" or "motivated seller" willing to slash his price 20%, 30%, or 40% just to get rid of it.

A negative or passive frame of mind will not help sell your house more quickly. Keeping alert, positive, and creative will allow new ideas to flow which will help sell your home quicker.

As stated in earlier chapters, you must put yourself in the shoes of the potential buyer. If you were out looking for a house, how would you feel if you came across someone who was depressed or resigned to the idea that you weren't going to buy his or her house? How would that make you feel about that home? On a more positive note, think of the buyer who has encountered a negative seller just before coming to your house. If you are cheery, the prospect will certainly be more interested and a bit relieved at not having to deal with your problems.

One way to put yourself in a negative frame of mind is to buy a new home before you sell the old one. There is a strong temptation to buy a home in a bad market when you see all the "bargains" out there. Your house will become a bargain, too, if you suddenly find yourself with two mortgages and a debt burden ready to swallow you. This will make you an emotional and financial wreck.

Don't believe everything you read in the newspapers. The business of a newspaper is to sell more newspapers, not necessarily to give an accurate portrayal of the news. When real estate is hot, the papers make it really hot by writing articles about multiple offers on houses and other homes getting $30,000 above asking price. Articles about crowds lining up outside housing developments appear in a good market. This only fuels the fire as people jump in before "prices rise more and it is too late." It works the same way in reverse. Articles begin to appear about how bad the market is, people read them, and then those that panic begin slashing their prices.

In 1990, Northern California was inundated with articles about how bad the market was—stories of sellers stuck with two mortgages, others letting their homes be foreclosed on because they couldn't sell, and still others about homes sitting on the market for six months. You'd think the area was in the middle of a depression with stories like that. Yet housing prices had actually fallen only less than 2% in the year preceding the articles. Some crashing market! Always analyze the facts before panicking. The papers may be reporting isolated cases in order to make the articles sound more interesting or vital. Remember, these are anomalies; that's why they are news.

Tip 219: Be better prepared than the other people in the market.

This is exactly why you are reading this book. Most sellers haven't done their homework. This puts you at a distinct advantage. Preparation means knowing what the competition has to offer, being able to show the benefits and future potential of your home to buyers. Preparation means merchandising the home effectively, looking at it from the eyes of the buyers rather than your own viewpoint.

Preparation means knowing enough about the various items which interest different buyers. For example, if you have a golf course nearby, even if you don't play golf, inquire about the fees, the hours, whether it is public or private, and so on. You might just find a buyer who loves golf, and you can inform him intelligently about the nearby course. In the same way, you should find out about the local schools, even if you don't have children, or the nearby cultural and entertainment facilities.

Preparation means understanding the role of emotions in home buying and how to trigger them in buyers. It means practicing what you will say on the phone, taking the time to learn about the competition, and general sales skills.

Understanding financing options, what is happening in your community, and how people buy are all part of the preparation necessary to have a sale at a price you want in a down market.

Tip 220: Manage the prospect's state of mind.

You need to focus on managing the prospect's state at both the conscious and the unconscious level. How you prepare the home for a showing will have a great impact on directing unconscious motivations.

You need to overcome the buyer's fear of commitment. In a down market, one of the greatest problems is convincing buyers that it won't get worse. They read the newspapers and see the scare headlines, and they feel that if they wait a little longer, an even better buy will come along. If you make your house unique and special, buyers start to realize that they can't afford to wait because they may not find a house quite like this again. If you've targeted your buyers, then when the right one comes along, you will stand out from the competition.

Emotions drive sales, but logic is necessary as a backup. You need just enough logic to justify the emotions. Have some facts and statistics available that are believable to the buyer. You can show them how your neighborhood has held its value, or how the SAT scores are the highest in the community. By giving logical reasons after appealing to the emotional ones, you can cement the commitment by the buyer.

Tip 221: Form strategies for effective prospecting.

Once you know who your buyers are, the questions become, "How can I locate them?" "How can I gain their interest?" and "What can I do to induce them to buy my home?" Effective prospecting is going fishing where the fish are, not where you want them to be.

Even untrained home sellers will look in the standard places by placing newspaper ads. Be more creative than they are. Is there a bulletin board in a high-class supermarket that you can post an ad on? How about the local coffee house? Is there a fair taking place near your house? Keep thinking of ways that others wouldn't so that your advertising will be the only one some prospects see.

Tip 222: You have to create interest.

To people who havn't seen your house in person, your house is a nonimage. If they've already looked at other houses in your neighborhood and been unimpressed, they assume that they won't be impressed by yours, either. It is your job to have them look at your advertising or marketing and think, "Hey, this one seems different. I'll check it out."

In a down market, there are many more homes for sale. Homes very much like yours may already have been for sale for months. You must take the initiative to make your house more interesting than the others.

How can your advertising draw people in? What can you do to your home to make it more appealing, more desirable to buyers? There are many ways to make a home interesting and to get people to look at it. Effective marketing will draw them to the address, and good curb appeal will get them to want to look inside. There is a great deal of focus on this step, but remember, it is only one of seven which you must follow.

Tip 223: Build the potential buyer's trust.

In order for a prospect to become a buyer, a bond must be formed. People don't buy from people they can't trust. This is why the buyer's real estate agent becomes handy in many sales situations. Since the agent becomes a trusted advisor to the buyers, if the agent recommends your house, he or she is acting as a neutral third party in their minds (despite the fact that she technically works for the seller and is working on commission). For the agent to say that the house is a great buy, and to show what comparable houses cost, goes a lot farther than the seller saying it.

Building trust is an essential element in selling. It is the difference between having a forced closing where the buyer feels hammered into a deal and one where the buyers feel they truly decided on what they want. Getting their interest gets them in the door. Bonding with them makes you their friend. People buy from a friend, even if the friend is a lousy salesperson, much quicker than they'll buy from a slick wheeler-dealer.

It is not impossible to build trust in direct buyer/seller situations, but it does require a bit more work. Opening up a friendly dialog, getting to know the person and giving sincere compliments before getting into the sales situation go a long way.

Tip 224: Qualify the prospect.

This is an essential step. You might get a couple to fall in love with your house, like your price and terms, and be ready to talk about how great you are all over town, but if they can't afford the house, you've wasted your time. Many agents know that qualifying is a key step. You don't want to get into a contract only to have the bank turn down your prospective purchaser. After you've gotten them to want to buy, make sure they *can* buy.

Unqualified buyers not only waste your time, they waste their own. In this case, however, yours is more important, because you are trying to sell your house quickly, while they can afford to take their time buying.

Some people say that disqualifying people and therefore not spending time with them is mercenary and cruel. However, if you are wasting time with a buyer who can't really buy your house, you are spending less time with people who can. You "owe" your time to the people whom you can make happy by selling them your home, not to the dreamers who really wish they could afford it, but can't.

When you are qualifying potential buyers, be very sure not to let any prejudices you may have get in the way. Disqualifying people because of race is not only illegal, it is also stupid. In a down market, you find savvy buyers in all shapes, sizes, and colors, and turning any of them down for nonfinancial reasons simply means that your house will be on the market longer.

CHAPTER TWENTY-THREE

Finding Buyers

In a normal real estate market, buyers often come to you. They look in the classified ads or call a few brokers in the area and see what feels right. If you bought your house in the last ten years, this is probably how you did it.

This isn't a normal real estate market, it's a down market. The rules change, and the buyers change with it. There are fewer buyers, since many people can't afford to sell the homes they are in now or can't afford the increased monthly payments needed to get out of their rental. Also, there are many more homes per buyer.

Buyers won't be throwing themselves at you as they might have a few years ago: you have to go out and find them. They are out there, of course. A quick look at the local sales charts tell you that *someone* is still out there buying. To sell your house, you must go out and find those people.

Tip 225: If you want to catch fish, you go where the fish are.

Once you've chosen your target market, target it. Suppose your house is aimed at first-time buyers. Where do you find them? Go to apartments, or perhaps even condominiums where owners want to move into single family houses. Be creative. Do you have an executive home? Find actual executives, or even better, those aspiring ones that would like to feel like they've arrived. Target the clubs they belong to or the gyms they work out at.

Many real estate companies targets apartment dwellers. One recently sent out mailers that tease the reader ("Five Reasons Not to Pay Your Rent Next Month") and then launch into the benefits of home ownership, of course emphasizing their homes.

Tip 226: Sometimes you need to bring the fish to you.

There are times when, despite creative advertising and good targeting, you still need to induce likely prospects to your home. You might work with your real estate agent and other home sellers to run bus tours for groups of home shoppers. You can get together with several other sellers, provide cocktails and hors d'oeuvres, or successive courses of a meal (a progressive dinner). This may sound way out, but it may also get your house sold. The key is to be creative. Nothing is off limits. Those that use conventional methods will get conventional results; in a down market, that means no sale.

If your home is located near a church, the church membership can be an excellent source of prospects or referrals. Perhaps you could have a special open house after services, with refreshments. Having a hundred pairs of eyes on the lookout to sell your home will go a long way.

Another novel method is to advertise at local garage sales. If a neighbor is having a garage sale, be sure to give him of her a stack of flyers for your house.

Tip 227: Start with your neighbors.

You could go around spending thousands of dollars on advertising and overlook what might be the best source of sales around, and it is free! It's your neighbors and friends. Let the neighbors know the house is going up for sale soon. Often, they have friends who want to move into the neighborhood. You can help them by preparing the fact sheet in advance and handing it to them.

While you're talking to them, ask them if they know of any places that you should advertise. For instance, someone's company may have a good bulletin board, or someone's social club may have an upcoming event.

Give them the feeling that they'll be doing themselves a favor by finding a person to buy your home. Use phrases like "It would be great if you could have your friends move close by" and "I'm sure you know people who would love to live near you." Make them think that they can improve their neighborhood by bringing in their friends.

Think about who else might want to live in your home. Target neighborhood businesses. People like to walk to work and avoid the daily traffic nightmare. What better way to find prospective purchasers than to target the businesses near your home?

Find the center of activity in the area. These are places where people congregate. Perhaps there are several. Look into bulletin boards at the local ice cream parlor or coffeehouse.

Tip 228: Word of mouth can be the best advertising.

Many more homes get sold by simple word-of-mouth advertising than you might at first think. People trust a recommendation from someone they know much more than one from an advertising or a real estate agent.

Community involvement can accomplish more than just good deeds. The people with whom you volunteer, attend PTA meetings, work on fundraisers, or play in little leagues are an excellent referral source of potential buyers. Even if they don't know you well, there is a positive bond between you that will reflect well when they tell a friend about your house for sale.

Talk to your doctor, banker, CPA, and lawyer and everyone else you know. Tell them you are selling you house and mention your next open house event. If you get the word to enough people, eventually someone will know someone looking for your type of home.

Have a party. Inviting people over to have a good time and letting the word out that the home is for sale will get them thinking of who they know that might be interested in a house like yours. Be sure to pass around a suggestion book for both ideas for the house and names of prospective buyers.

Tip 229: Relocated executives and employees are motivated to buy.

According to the Internal Revenue Service, 1.5 million people make a job-related move each year. Wouldn't it be great to tap into that stream of potential buyers who can't spend a whole lot of time looking for a new home? These people don't just want to buy, they have to buy.

There are many firms and brokerages that specialize in relocations. Get hooked up with one of these firms. Let them know what you have available. Also be sure to tell them who you think your target market is (executives, first-timers, large families, and so on).

Contact companies in your area that regularly transfer employees in and out. The business section of the local paper often covers major hiring and firings. Some companies even buy homes outright to place their executives in. Let the personnel department know that you have a house for sale; they'll use that information to try to lure people to make the move instead of leaving the company.

Tip 230: See if your employer can help sell your house.

If you work for a large company, it may be planning on transferring people into the area. See if the company will buy your home for an incoming employee or executive. You may have to search around for the right person who would know what the company offers people as they arrive.

If you have been transferred to another city by your employer, ask for assistance in selling your house. Most big companies have relocation assistance programs that include help with both selling your current house and buying a new one. If both people in a couple work, both should approach their employers.

Tip 231: Finding buyers through advertising is great but not sufficient.

You should never overlook effective advertising as one important tool in marketing your home. Writing good ads, putting up signs, and getting flyers out are all necessary to let the world know what you have to offer. In a down market, though, your advertising is diluted by all the other ads that people are placing. An ad that brought in twenty prospective buyers three years ago might bring in only five or ten now. You can no longer rely on ads, even great ones.

Remember, though, that advertising is just one tool in your box. You wouldn't build a house with only a hammer, even a good hammer. You'd need a saw, some nails, and other key tools. Advertising when done correctly is a powerful too, but relying solely on it will diminish your results greatly.

Tip 232: Add high tech to your marketing.

The U.S. now has a whole generation of video-literate people: the high-tech, high-touch baby boomers. So how can you tie video into your sales? Real estate agents have started selling high-end homes on TV with videos!

Other home sellers are turning to cable TV. There are shows which display homes on video, allowing a buyer to "walk through" the house on TV. This opens you to a large market that because of time constraints might not make it to your open house. If your home shows well, this can be an effective tool, although you should carefully consider the value, since the videos often cost $500–$1000 each to produce and broadcast.

Portable radio transmitters on which buyers can tune into a sales presentation as they drive by your house are another way to sell homes. Costing from under $200 to $800 new, such a transmitter emits a weak signal that can be heard for about 1200 feet. You place the information on your "for sale" sign and let potential prospects tune in 24 hours a day. Even at open houses, some prospects are hesitant to enter a home and this helps get them excited enough to enter. And this can build excitement at odd hours.

Transmitters are also good for homes that have special features people can't see from the street. Buyers can tune in to find out about the Jacuzzi in the master suite or the two level living area. Since they feel comfortable in their cars, you should be sure to use phrases that make them want to come into the house, not simply judge it from the outside.

Tip 233: Use the tight market to your advantage.

With housing prices through the roof, and times getting tougher, economic pressures are forcing young people to stay at home. As we noted in discussing the granny flat, multigenerational living arrangements will become more common. You can use this to your advantage, if you have a large house or one that's adaptable to a large multigenerational family, by properly targeting these groups.

In this case, be sure to emphasize the family values of your home even if you aren't using the house that way yourself. For instance, you can say, "We were going to have my father move in to this room but he found another place, which is why it is an office now." Tell them about how you think the room can be used in your own family. "Well, the kids are gone and my parents haven't moved in yet, but we kept the room open for them in case they changed their minds."

Tip 234: Focus on special issues or concerns.

Focus on special issues in a timely manner and you may attract concerned people and get their sale. After a disaster, sales tend to drop. You can counter that effect by emphasizing how well your house did during the disaster.

After the earthquake that hit the San Francisco bay area in October, 1989, homes which were bolted to their foundations and properly braced to resist earthquakes became much more valuable, while homes that weren't became less desirable. Sales were lost because people didn't want to be in a home that had not been earthquake retrofitted. Savvy real estate agents and sellers quickly had the earthquake work done to their homes and then marketed it.

The same is often true after devastating hurricanes. If the hurricane is still on everyone's mind, use positive words to tell the buyer why your house is still attractive. "We sure are glad that we had these new style storm windows added a few years ago: look how well they did in the storm." Show that you are also concerned about damage. "After it blew over and we helped out our friends, we went all over the attic and found only one leak, which we fixed ourselves."

CHAPTER TWENTY-FOUR

Reducing the Buyer's Maintenance Costs

Keeping maintenance costs down is always a favorable selling point. A house, if marketed properly, can fetch a higher initial price if it can be shown that in the long run it is less expensive than a similar house with higher maintenance costs. Energy efficiency is probably the most common area to focus on in this regard, but there are several other key maintenance-cost areas which should not be overlooked.

Making your house energy efficient need not cost a lot, and the savings, especially during the winter, could be capitalized in talks to prospects about the home. Remember, you need to make your home stick out from the crowd.

Energy

As energy prices have gone up again, there is a renewed interest in energy-efficient homes. These are not the superinsulated homes of the 1970s which don't allow for fresh air to flow in and out, but rather homes that stay warm in the winter without draining your bank account. If your home is leaky, not insulated, and currently an energy black hole, running out now and trying to make it energy efficient will not be a profitable investment. You will not get all your money back in resale value. If, however, you are performing some renovations around the house, than it is highly recommended that you use energy-saving technologies. These usually cost only a few dollars extra, and their payback is immediate both in energy savings and in resale value.

If a homeowner can save $500 per year on his or her energy bill, what is that worth to the value of the house? If that $500 represented a return on investment, it could easily add several thousand dollars to the value of the house and the homeowner would be getting an excellent return.

Tip 235: Emphasizing low operating costs can be a big plus in times of high utility prices.

No one likes to pay the monthly utility bills, especially during the hot summer or cold winter months when the bills can exceed several hundred dollars each month. You can make your home more energy efficient and use this as a marketing tool to distinguish your home from the crowd. An energy-efficient home that costs a few thousand dollars more will quickly pay for itself in cost savings each month.

Most people like to feel intelligent and to believe they are doing something good for the environment. If you can link the energy-saving features of your home to these beliefs, the extra emotional pull will help connect you to the buyers and produce a sale.

If you spend money to make your house more energy-efficient, be sure to tell the buyers about it. For instance, if you added insulation a year ago, make a chart of your heating costs for the last few years and show how far the bills dropped. Calculate how much the new owners will save over the next few years due to your expense.

Tip 236: You can have lower bills and enhanced appearance with new appliances.

One way to produce lower utility bills is with new, energy-saving appliances. Most older appliances were energy dinosaurs. They assumed gas and electricity prices would always be incredibly low. By purchasing new appliances, you will bring your home up to date, have a true marketing feature to show buyers, and be producing lower utility bills which you can show as a low-operating-cost item.

Your local large-appliance store will usually have brochures that tell which appliances are energy-efficient. The two major appliances people think of as potential energy eaters are refrigerators and water heaters. In a colder climate, a new furnace might be much more efficient than the one you have now.

Tip 237: Gas is usually cheaper than electricity.

If you have a gas line in your house already and you are planning to update your cooktop or your dryer, think strongly about gas as an alternative. Electricity is a poor use for producing heat since so much is wasted. Gas appliances initially cost more, but produce a considerable savings during use.

Most people who cook prefer gas burners on their ranges anyway. If you have a gas range, be sure to talk about both energy and convenience advantages.

Tip 238: Get a home energy audit.

Many utility companies now do free energy audits on homes. A utility representative comes to your home and shows you where your home is wasting the most energy. Use the results of the audit to pinpoint where you need to improve the house before putting it on the market.

If the energy audit shows that your house is already very good, be sure to leave copies of the audit with your fact sheet. This shows not only that you think you have an energy-efficient house, but that the local utility does also. This is also a good way to score points with buyers who are ecologically concerned.

> ### Tip 239: Look at window placement as a way to cut heating and cooling bills.

When you are adding or replacing windows, the location of the openings can affect the eventual heating and cooling bills significantly. For example, if you are adding a window on the north side of the house, chances are you will have a net energy loss. However, if you are adding it on the south side, you will most likely increase your energy gain. If you are in a cool climate, the location of the window will affect you in real dollars every month. It could be a very expensive choice.

Plan the locations of your openings to provide for good cross-ventilation in the summer months or year-round in warm climates. A larger area of "outlet" window versus "inlet" window will increase the air flow and allow for greater circulation. A combination of openings can direct air flow as desired.

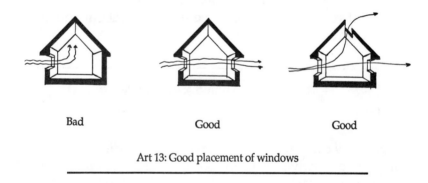

| Bad | Good | Good |

Art 13: Good placement of windows

> ### Tip 240: Cut energy costs with electronic innovations.

Electronic thermostats now allow you to program times when heat should be high and other times when it should be low in order to suit your lifestyle. This can save you money throughout the year without sacrificing an comfort at all. All the thermostat does is lower the temperature while you're gone and then gets the heat back up just before you arrive home. With the cost being only about $150, it is an investment with a very quick payback.

Tip 241: Start with proper insulation and watch the bills drop.

Insulation value is measured by a rating called *R* value. The *R* number refers to the resistance a surface has to winter heat loss or summer heat gain. The higher the *R* value, the higher the resistance and the better the insulating value. The recommended *R* value is different for the ceiling than it is for the walls, and it differs in different parts of the country. This is because most heat is usually lost through the ceiling, so a higher *R* value is recommended. In coastal California, *R*-19 is a typical ceiling insulation number, while in New York, *R*-30 or 33 is the recommended insulation.

Insulation costs very little but, if it can decrease your energy bill significantly, you can use that in your marketing. The first area of defense is to caulk and weatherstrip around windows and doors. Caulking and weatherstripping costs only about $50 for you to perform and might save you that much your first winter. There have been many technological advances in these products in recent years. Check out the selection at your local hardware store.

The next line of defense in the energy battle would be proper insulation in the roof. Most heat is lost through the roof. A good *R*-30 insulation should do the trick. Insulation has one of the best payback rates. You can probably save $100 a year on heating and cooling costs with $300 of ceiling insulation.

Tip 242: Insulating properly can solve other problems, too.

Replacing old single-paned windows with new thermal double-paned windows not only dramatically increases the insulating power of the house but also serves as a sound insulator. If you face a noisy street, replacing the street windows with double-paned windows can make the interior of your home almost silent. When you tell prospective buyers about the windows, be sure to mention both effects.

You can also enhance the look of your home while making it more energy-efficient. If you need to replace the drafty old windows, think about whether there are things you can do to enhance the value of the room. Perhaps this is a good time to convert those windows into French doors. Or perhaps you need more light and you can enlarge the windows or put in a bay window.

Tip 243: Look at high-tech energy-saving ideas.

Technology has jumped by leaps and bounds in recent years. Personal computers are now common in the home, and solid-state technology seems to run the cars too these days. High tech is finally making its way into the home, too. Old, manually adjusted thermostats are being replaced with ones with special features. Zone heating systems have separate thermostats in each zone or room in your house. A tiny computer in the furnace channels heat to each room only as needed so that bedrooms stay warmer than an unused dining room, for example.

Tip 244: If you are replacing a fireplace, think about energy efficiency.

Fireplaces are hot items these days (no pun intended), and one that's combined with energy efficiency will be a double sell. Energy-efficient fireplaces send more heat into the house and less up the chimney. They are also usually safer. Talk to a local fireplace specialist or chimney sweep about costs.

Tip 245: Energy savings are not confined to the building alone.

How your home sits on its site affects its ability to retain heat. Homes exposed to strong sun or wind will be less energy-efficient than those that have the elements tempered for them. You can improve the energy efficiency of your home by doing some basic site work.

Trees can provide excellent protection from sun and wind. One common use of plants is to place deciduous trees between the path of the sun and the house. In the summer, when the leaves are their largest, the trees shade the house from the hot sun, reducing cooling costs. In the winter, the trees lose their leaves, allowing the badly needed sun to help warm the house on cold days. Note that the sun travels along different paths during the year so that trees may provide house shade only during some seasons.

Fences and low walls can break or divert wind away from the house. They can also be used to divert breezes to the house on hot days or in warm climates.

Plantings can also provide tempering of the environment. Not all heat is direct heat. Much is reflected from white sidewalks or street asphalt. Plants can help provide a surface which does not reflect all this summer heat toward the house.

Tip 246: Don't forget the basics.

Insulation, caulking, and weatherstripping are all low-tech ways to save money and energy in your home. Many good books are out showing you how to do it yourself in order to keep your costs down to a few dollars. Most utility companies around the country perform energy audits free of charge or for a nominal fee. These will show you where you are losing energy the most and what you can do to stop it.

Typical energy conservation measures include these:

- Attic insulation
- Exterior wall insulation
- Floor insulation beneath crawl spaces
- Insulation of heating and cooling ducts
- Insulation of water heater and hot-water pipes

- Caulking around windows and doors, and at points where electrical or plumbing fixtures break wall surfaces

- Window and door weatherstripping

- Shower-head flow restrictors

- Storm windows and doors

Time, Gas, and the Long Commute

> **Tip 247: If you are located near public transit or shopping, sell that fact**

With traffic jams appearing daily, locations near transportation hubs and public transportation are becoming more valuable and will continue to appreciate. Sell the extra benefits of no more hassles in traffic, being able to read on the way to and from work, less wear and tear on the car, and so forth.

Few people stop to think about all the money they spend on gas, car repairs, insurance, and plain old depreciation on the vehicle. But this can add up to literally thousands per vehicle per year. Demonstrating to your prospect how much more it will cost him to live in that "less expensive" suburb may garner you a sold home.

Buyers prefer to hear real stories instead of scenarios. If you used to commute but now use public transportation, calculate your savings in hours and dollars and list them on your home fact sheet.

> **Tip 248: Sell location near work.**

In these increasingly busy times, the time lost on the road away from the family can be incredibly painful. Many people commute one to two hours each way. For an eight-hour workday, they are really gone closer to 12 hours from their family. Point out the added benefits of living close to work. Get them to think how much more they could earn if they worked instead of commuted all those extra hours or just how much more time they would have to relax and enjoy their families.

Water

Tip 249: In the arid West, water savings will enhance value.

After several years of droughts, builders in California have started using native plants, drip irrigation systems, and other ways of cutting down on water use. These measures have been strongly marketed with excellent results. With water prices increasing and the threat of water restrictions hanging over people's heads, not having to use much in the garden is a real sales plus.

If your area has had water shortages in previous summers (as have areas in the South and West), be sure to point out why your house is better than the typical house in your neighborhood with respect to water. Don't be shy about comparing your house to others, since a buyer will be glad if you are the first to mention water shortages.

The reality is that water doesn't cost that much. Even in drought areas, water bills might vary only by $10 or $12 for a heavy user versus a light user. Installing low flow showerheads and toilets that don't use as much water won't save you that much in terms of dollars, but can go a long way in connecting your home to the larger picture of conservation of the environment.

Other Low Maintenance Features

This is a busy society. With long workdays and two-income households, leisure time has become a very valuable commodity. Few working people relish the idea of spending their weekends working in the yard or cleaning the house. These items are usually downplayed when a real estate agent shows a home to a buyer. If your home is truly low maintenance, you need to point it out and contrast it with the other homes the buyer has seen.

Tip 250: Make the yard low maintenance.

There are many ways to make your yard into a low-maintenance yard, depending on your circumstances. If you have a smaller lot than other comparable homes, that would normally be a detriment. However, by making part of the yard a usable outdoor room and carefully landscaping the rest with plants that don't require constant attention, you can make the small yard more desirable than a larger one.

The types of plants you choose is crucial. There are many beautiful flowering plants that don't require the care and attention of beautiful orchids or even the weekly maintenance of a lawn. Talk to the people at your local nursery for some suggestions. You can often even hire one of the people who work there to come out on their off hours and consult for a very low fee.

Tip 251: Use easy-to-clean surfaces in the home.

Tile looks beautiful, but cleaning out the grout lines takes time. Use surfaces such as Corian that are easy to clean, and then sell that fact to the prospect. Images of working all day just to keep the house up will affect them emotionally and get them to reevaluate other homes they have liked.

Tip 252: Keep the house in good condition even if it is a high-maintenance house.

This one goes without saying. But a house that looks well kept is assumed to be easier to maintain than one that's not. Perhaps buyers feel that if you were able to keep it up, they will be, too. If the house and yard look very good, the issue of maintenance seldom comes up.

Tip 253: Use long-life materials.

Which costs less, over the long haul, an asphalt shingle roof with a life of 15 years or a fiberglass roof with a life of 25? If your home is built of quality, long-life materials or designed to reduce wear and tear, this is a marketing point and should be pushed.

Tip 254: Lower maintenance costs with financing.

This is a key "cost to buy versus cost to run" item. Improper financing can add thousands if not tens of thousands to the cost of operating a home. When money is scarce and the market is against you, financing is one of the strongest weapons you have to sell your home. Sell at affordable terms and you can even raise your total price.

Insurance, special assessments, and property taxes vary from home to home and neighborhood to neighborhood. If your home rates favorably in these categories, it may be worth noting. Remember, savings of $500 dollars a year on lower taxes and insurance adds up to many thousands over the length of a typical home ownership. Although the buyer doesn't get the whole savings in one lump sum, he should be willing to pay something for an extra $500 per year.

CHAPTER TWENTY-FIVE

Appraisals, Inspections, and Warranties

Whether you like it or not, appraisers and lending institutions play a key role in determining your pricing. You need to take appraisers into your confidence. Appraisers are human, and are probably not as familiar with the area as you are. Do your homework, get the sales information on other homes—their square footage, lot size, terms of sale, and so on. Armed with this information, you can usually positively influence the appraiser.

Appraisal is about value. The first measure of value is one side of the old supply and demand equation: demand. Value is highly dependant on demand. If you have the only Tudor castle and people want that, it is worth more. If you live next to Three Mile Island, there is less demand for your home, and value plummets.

You can usually find a reliable appraiser by asking around. Certified appraisers are designated either MAI (Member of Appraisal Institute) or ASA (American Society of real estate Appraisers). An appraiser can help you set a value that carries a lot of weight at a cost only about $300.

Tip 255: Before doing any work on your house, think like an appraiser.

Thinking like an appraiser means looking at the market before you begin any improvement work. You need to know the neighborhood values before you can calculate your own in relation to it. Sometimes neighborhood values are obvious. If you have a mansion in the South Bronx, you won't be able to increase its value much, since you are probably already above the neighborhood median. In most neighborhoods, however, doing an appraisal is often difficult, since appraisal is an inexact practice. Your real estate agent may have good information about recent appraisals or may have access to written material that appraisers use.

By appraising your home's value compared to other properties in the area, you can get a sense of where you can add value.

Tip 256: The biggest mistake many sellers make in a down market is overpricing.

Appraisal is the skill of determining market value. Few sellers act as objectively as appraisers in setting their asking price. There are certain basic rules you must follow in pricing your home. The first is to forget about what you paid for the home. Whether you got a good deal or a bad deal it's irrelevant. The buyer doesn't really care; he or she is interested only in what type of deal he or she will get.

The second is to forget about what it was worth last year. Just because the house was "worth $300,000" a year ago and market value is $275,000, don't think you've lost $25,000. Bear in mind that if you sold last year and then bought another house, it probably would have cost an additional $25,000, too. Stop carrying that emotional baggage around and face reality.

Third, remember that most buyers are looking for a good deal, so try to pass on a little something in the way of compromise so he feels he's doing well. Holding out for the last nickel and being petty will turn off a buyer and cost you time, energy, and money in the long run.

In the end, the market value of a home is the price that a willing buyer will pay for it. The more it fits the buyer's needs and the more the buyer wants it, the higher the price the buyer is willing to pay. In your tours, in the physical makeup of the home, and in every encounter you have with a prospect, you must make him or her really want the home. Then you will be able to set your price in a down market.

Tip 257: Price it right the first time.

Whatever you do, don't try listing your house too high and then chopping the price little by little. It will only annoy buyer's agents who will tell their clients that you are not a serious seller. By the time you get to the "right" price, they will all be ignoring you.

Sellers don't seem to consider carrying costs when setting prices. If you have to carry the house for an extra six months and that costs you $20,000, you would have been better off lowering the price initially, generating buyer excitement, and moving it.

Tip 258: Use appraisals as sales aids.

Americans often believe what they see in writing far more than what they are told. A written appraisal for your home, showing its value as higher than your asking price, sitting on the dining table alongside the pest-control and other reports gives you an edge in the logical part of convincing a buyer of the value of your home.

Most sellers are pushing their price to the appraisal limits, far from selling it "under value." If you sell below appraisal, are you really leaving money on the table? Appraisal is an art, not a science. It is a best guess by an individual. This is an imperfect market in an imperfect world. Market value may actually be below appraised value. Look at the problems that the federal government is having trying to sell properties at appraised value: no one wants to buy.

Work the appraisal to your advantage, then sell the house "below appraised value." Buyers will feel they're getting a bargain.

Tip 259: Market your house to the appraiser.

Since appraisers are human, they have the same desires and work the same way as the people you will be marketing your home to. In other words, there's no law against trying to give the appraiser a positive experience and view of your home.

Show him the list of attributes your home has. Tell them what you think it is worth and why, and have data to support that viewpoint. Give him a list of comparable sales in the area, especially high ones. Most appraisers don't know of every sale and might miss some that are very important in determining your home's value. Show a list of comparable houses (you can usually get this from your real estate agent).

Tip 260: Don't forget, appraisals are opinions.

Buyers of homes are not rational. Appraisers try to be. Just because an appraiser thinks your home is not worth much, don't just assume he or she is right. You should carefully evaluate your home against the marketplace and possibly get a second appraisal. Also, appraisers have not seen the insides of comparable houses which have been sold.

Tip 261: Use inspections to help sales.

If you get an inspection before you ever think about putting your house up for sale, you've made significant strides ahead of other sellers. Instead of getting lots of questions about what condition your house is in, you can hand over an inspection report (preferably, a second, clean one) and a warranty on the home. You've just knocked out that concern of the buyer.

Spending $200 for a home inspection before you put the house up for sale is an excellent investment. First, you catch the inevitable unexpected problems that the buyer's inspector will find. You are not a building contractor: you probably don't know everything to look for. Second, if you do get a clean bill of health it can be a strong selling point. The buyer now knows everything in the house is up to snuff.

Even if you do find problems in the first inspection, after they are repaired the inspector will usually come back and give you a signed inspection form showing the house is OK. If the buyer finds termites, it could kill the deal. If you find them, have the home treated, and then get a five-year warranty, you have turned a potentially devastating negative into a positive sales aid.

By doing a home pre-inspection, you will save money. Buyers seem to want more in credit than a repair will actually cost. Many pest-control problems can be repaired for half the quoted value. And even general contractor reports estimate repairs at full general contractor prices, not the handyman price you are likely to get. If you have any repairs to do, you will save much more than the cost of the $200 inspection.

Tip 262: Warranties sell, too.

Homeowners' warranty programs can also be a good marketing tool. These programs guarantee repairs should any major part of the home break down. It's like getting an extended service contract on a car. By showing buyers that your home is sound enough that you will put a guarantee on it and that they won't have to lift a finger for the next year, you have made your home significantly more appealing to many buyers who don't want to fuss with fixing the heater on their Saturday off.

CHAPTER TWENTY-SIX

Selling It Yourself

Selling a house yourself in a down market is harder than it looks. Except in hot markets, even the professionals spend many hours marketing and showing a home. That probably explains why over 90% of homes are sold through real estate agents. However, whether or not you do sell it yourself, you should know all the necessary skills both to help your real estate agent and to help yourself.

The tips in this chapter are old hat to most real estate agents. They do this sort of thing every day. If you are selling your home by yourself, you are competing with dozens of real estate agents in your area who are selling other homes, probably much more professionally than you can.

Tip 263: Selling your house by yourself often changes the type of buyer you attract.

Many buyers for For Sale By Owner (FSBO, or "fizzbo") properties are vultures and bargain hunters. They expect the commission discount to go into their pocket, not yours. It's hard to market your home for top dollar when the people you are attracting are all bargain hunters.

Think carefully about whether you want your potential market to change. Even if there are many "regular" buyers who still come to look at the house, you have to deal with this new type of buyer at the same time. Your sales energy will be split between bargain hunters and "regular" buyers, and you may find yourself adopting multiple personalities depending on who is in the house. Of course, it is often difficult to pick out who is looking only for a bargain and who isn't, especially in a down market.

Tip 264: Evaluate carefully before deciding to sell it yourself.

There is one good reason why you should sell the home yourself:

- You save a lot of money, as much as 7% of the selling price.

There are also several reasons why you should *not* sell the home yourself:

- You may not have a sales personality.

- You may not be able to build motivation in people as well as a professional.

- Most buyers are more comfortable working with professional real estate brokers.

- Buyers' agents especially don't like dealing with amateurs.

- You probably won't have access to the MLS (multiple listing service).

- Your lack of knowledge of real estate will hurt you.

- Agents provide some legal protection for errors and omissions.

- Crooks and sharks target people selling their own homes.

Imagine you are the marketing director for the your home sales company. When times are bad you have two choices: lay off your salespeople and do the sales yourself, or hire the best salespeople you can possibly find, pay them well, and let them use their skills and talents to help sell the home for top dollar while you run the marketing side. The latter is usually the best strategy.

If you still want to go it alone, you need to figure out how you want to market your new-found financial cushion. You can use that commission as your negotiating room, thus allowing your house to be priced below market, gaining the attention of some buyers, or you can keep the price where you would have had it and spend a little extra on marketing to attract buyers.

Tip 265: Commit yourself to being a professional.

You must have confidence in yourself and be persistent when you take on the obligation of selling your home yourself. Most agents ask for a minimum of a 90-day listing. Yet most homeowners try for a few weeks and then give up and list the property. If a professional doesn't think he can sell it in a few weeks, why do you think you should be able to?

You can't treat this as a game. You must do your homework and be properly prepared on pricing, how to show your home, how to handle buyer objections, and how to close the transaction. Remember, thousands of dollars are on the line. Decide whether you really want to sell it yourself or whether it should be listed with a broker.

Tip 266: Access to the local multiple listing service is critical in a down market.

Potential buyers go to their real estate agents to get the largest list of available houses. In a down market, there are plenty of them. If you aren't on the MLS list, they'll never notice your absence.

Many cities have agents or services that get people listed in the MLS and provide general assistance in selling their own homes. It is imperative that you at least get listed.

Tip 267: When selling your own house, it is more important to put yourself in the buyer's shoes every day.

When you have an agent selling your house, it is easy to let the agent take the steps necessary to be objective. When you are selling it yourself, it is much more difficult. But the best way to reach buyers is to pretend to be one. Spend at least an hour a day, before people come by, thinking like a buyer. Drop your sales pretensions so that you can see how they want to buy.

Stop talking and start listening. Your goal is to get your prospects to imagine how wonderful your home will be for them, not to tell them how great it has been for you. Ask them questions such as, "What would you use this room for?" which help them imagine themselves in the home. If they have problems or special needs, see how you can solve them. Is it a cash problem? Work out some financing. By asking questions and learning the buyer's needs, you can help the buyer to solve their problem of which house to buy.

Focus your questions on the prospect. Ask if the quality of the schools is important. Or perhaps all they care about is whether the dining room is large enough for entertaining. The more you know, the more you can see if you can make your house work for them.

Tip 268: Ask qualifying questions on your tour.

Unlike the situation in which you hire a real estate agent, you can't just hide in the corner somewhere. You've got to make things happen. The first step occurs in the way you show the home. Remember, the decision to buy occurs in the buyer's mind, and your job is to help the buyer associate positive feelings to your home.

Walk a prospect through a few rooms, let him or her touch the appliances, try the cabinets, and peek into the closet. Let each prospect also have some time by him- or herself. You don't want anyone to feel pressured. Listen to what people say, but don't necessarily have a quick rebuttal.

While showing each prospect around, you can qualify him or her. The problem with many FSBOs is that you have not had the advantage of prequalifying the buyers thoroughly before they got to your door. All they've read is an ad. You don't know their tastes, or what turns them on. So, as you walk with them, ask some questions to see how much this prospect is worth pursuing. Questions like, "Have you seen other houses you liked?" "What did you like about them?" "How much money would you have for a down payment?"

Buyers are often reluctant to discuss their personal financial information and may intentionally give you wrong information. Be wary of anything you hear, but be open to their circumstances.

Find the motivation in your prospect. The best way to find this out is to ask directly, "Why are you in the market for a home?" The answer will give you a valuable clue as to what to emphasize as you show your home.

Tip 269: Qualify the buyer financially.

In addition to determining what the buyer wants, you need to know if he or she can afford your home. Many times buyers will spend hours with sellers looking at houses they just cannot afford. If you permit this to happen, you will have wasted a good deal of your valuable time.

If the buyer seems serious, you can start talking finances. Find out how much he or she can put down and if he or she has enough to cover standard closing costs. If not, you can decide if you want to try a nonconventional financing method.

Tip 270: Ask questions that put them in positive states.

Because buying a home is such an emotional issue, you want to get the positive emotions associated with your home. Remember, logic is the smaller part of the buying equation. Let the prospect talk about his or her wants and needs and connect your home to fulfilling those desires.

As a seller, you are at a disadvantage showing the home compared to a real estate agent. You have one and only one function in the buyer's mind: to sell that home. The real estate agent, on the other hand, is a friend who is helping the buyer make a decision. He or she might be taking them through this house just to show them how much better some other house is for their needs, or may be qualifying them. You are trying to sell, and they know it.

Don't sell a house, sell solutions. Sell solutions, and you will have buyers.

Tip 271: Orchestrate the tour.

As you walk a prospect through the home, have the layout planned. You want to show the best parts first to keep up the excitement you've generated with all your planning and directing them to your home. Each room should build on the others, enhancing the prospect's image of your home. You need to orchestrate this dance ahead of time. Try to imagine which rooms would make the most powerful positive impressions.

Bring an associate or friend through if you can't imagine it on your own. Decide ahead of time which room would be the best to linger in to answer questions. Make sure it is a wonderful space, either a room with a great view or one with the best features. You want buyers to linger in the good sections and go quickly through the less desirable parts of the home.

Tip 272: Make the buyers mentally see themselves in the home.

Remember, people don't buy real estate, they buy the benefits that owning real estate will give them. Sell the benefits, not the house.

When walking through the house with prospects, don't say, "This is the living room" They *know* it's the living room! Don't be a second-rate tour guide. Sell the benefits. You might say "Isn't it great how this living room opens onto the patio? It would be great for parties." Don't say, "This is the master bathroom," rather say, "It feels great to relax in that Jacuzzi tub after work."

Put the prospect mentally into the home. Instead of saying, "The schools are nearby," say, "Your son's new school is only three blocks from here."

You can even reframe a negative by focusing on the positive side, for example, as, "I thought you would appreciate how easy it would be to take care of this (small) yard."

Don't oversell. Owners have a tendency to talk about how wonderful the house is, how great the location is, and how much they've enjoyed living there. Remember, focus on the prospect's needs, not yours. Get him or her imagining how much he or she will enjoy the home. Don't talk about how much you enjoyed it. Don't oversell. Many of the outstanding features of the home will speak for themselves.

Tip 273: Avoid selling an empty house.

Buyers have a difficult time imagining furnishings in an empty home. They also have trouble really picturing accurately the sizes of the rooms they are in. Model units sell quicker than empty units in new housing developments.

If you are moving, try to leave most of your furnishings behind for now. It will help sell your home more quickly. If you must move it, use some rental furniture to help sell the home. Furnish one or two key rooms and the entry to give buyers' imaginations some fuel as they walk through the rest of the house. The furnishings will only cost a few hundred dollars per month to rent but may save you thousands in mortgage costs and a higher sales prices.

Tip 274: Accentuate the positive and neutralize the negative.

Every home has positive and negative aspects. However, what makes them positive is your point of view, or the way you frame the situation. If your home has some characteristics which might seem less than desirable to you, try to think of some positive aspects about it. Because buyers are certain to ask you questions about it and if you sound hesitant in your answer you will invoke fear in them rather than reassurance. Here are some examples of positive speaking:

If your house is located near the freeway, say, "It's great being near the freeway, since you avoid the long commute." If your house is located far from the freeway, say, "Isn't it wonderful being so far away from the noise and dirt of the freeway."

Sometimes it is necessary to change the buyer's perception of a problem. If the buyer says, "This house is only one block from the freeway; it must get awfully noisy," then you wouldn't say, "It's great being near the freeway since you avoid the long commute." You need to address his concern and soften it. Don't debate or argue with him. Agree: "You know, we felt the same way when we first bought the house, but after a few days we no longer noticed any noise." You've acknowledged his concern, but you've also reduced its magnitude.

> **Tip 275: Prepare your presentation, but don't make it obvious.**

For some reason, most people feel they are being false if they've prepared their "pitch" in advance. Yet studies show that that is what many of the best salespeople do. Knowing what you want to say in advance and crafting an appropriate way of saying it leaves your mind open to really observe and listen to what the buyer has to offer. Your text does not need to be memorized word for word, but how much better to be able to have an intelligent, persuasive answer than to be sitting dumbfounded at some buyer's question.

It may sound silly, but people want to help friends. A person would rather buy a product from a poor salesperson he or she likes than from an ultraslick salesperson. Be likable and you're a step closer to the sale.

**Tip 276: Handling buyers' objections is as
important as showing the positive side of the
house.**

Almost every prospective buyer will have objections. You need to ignore minor objections. Many times people express objections out of habit. Ignore one and it usually goes away. Sometimes all you need to do is hear out the objections and the prospect will run out of steam.

If the objection seems more serious, question it. This is how you get information. ("I know you must have a good reason for saying that. Do you mind if I ask you what it is?")

Make it a final objection ("If we could meet x, y, and z, would you want to buy this house?") If someone complains about the master bedroom, ask, "If it weren't for this master bedroom would you buy the house?" You'll find out the real reasons this way.

Have you ever seen a home without any weak points? Every home has them. Buyers make objections. Study the weak points of your offering in advance and learn how to handle the situation.

Finally, after handling the objection, confirm it and shift gears to something else. You don't want to linger on the objection too long.

**Tip 277: Get the buyer to know the property and the
neighborhood.**

You must be able to answer the following commonly asked questions. In fact, you should think of creative ways of getting the buyer to want to know the answers.

- What are the local school facilities?

- What is the reputation of the local schools?

- What is the driving time to the nearest shopping?

- What are the local cultural facilities?

- Who originally built the house. When was the house built?

- What local recreational facilities are nearby and what is the driving time to each (pools, golf course, tennis, and so on)?

Tip 278: Use the buyer's senses.

As you lead buyers through the home, stimulate them to use all of their senses. Experiential reactions are stronger than intellectual reasoning. Get their whole body into it.

Let the buyer touch things. You can lead them with your comments or actions. You might say, "Feel how easily this door glides" as you work the sliding glass patio door. Or you might say, "I really like that the doors are solid," as you knock on one, "not like those hollow-core doors builders use these days." Be careful how you do this. You don't want to be too blatant or insult the buyer's intelligence.

Behavioral scientists have shown that, unless blind, humans receive the major portion of their information visually. In other words, what you see is significantly more important than what you hear. As a seller, you have to work very hard to overcome visual negatives which have already found their way into the potential buyer's brain. The immediate reactions to a neighborhood, a street, or neighboring houses often determine whether or not the customer even gets out of the automobile to inspect your house.

It is not always possible to mask unfavorable neighborhood influences, but it is necessary to do so whenever possible. If you are near some real estate in poor condition, you need to attempt to isolate yourself from that environment. This can be done through several ways. When giving directions to your house, steer prospective purchasers away from blighted elements. Try to have them drive by parks on the way and to approach the house from its best side.

Tip 279: You must separate the buyers from the lookers.

It's fun to show a home, but it is a lot more fun to sell it. Before you spend too many hours on any one buyer, you want to make sure he or she is serious. You can do this by talking about money. If they are serious, they are usually willing to talk about finances, although many people have a hard time talking finances with a stranger, especially someone who is not a professional.

Not every prospect is a real one. Some are house addicts who look at houses for something to do and as a way to socialize, some are wishful thinkers who back out at the moment of truth, some think they are qualified but really are not. Others may be professional thieves looking at what you have where and checking out the exits.

Tip 280: Sell the neighbors.

People like to know who's in the neighborhood with them. Talk about the neighbors. If the buyers have children and your neighbors have children the same age, mention that they might be in school together. If the prospect works at a certain company, ask them if they know your neighbor, Mr. Jones, who also works at the same company.

Some buyers are impressed if prominent people or celebrities live in the area. If this is the case, mention it.

Tip 281: Do effective follow-up work.

You need to be doing effective prospecting. In a down market, you have to chase after the buyers. Follow up on all the fact sheets you gave out and with the people who dropped in with a phone call within a week.

Tip 282: The little things help to make a showing work.

Here are a few little details that make a difference on buyer's reactions to your home and on your chance to follow up.

Have a pen and a visitor sign-in sheet. Be prepared to ask visitors to sign in, giving both name and phone number. This can be useful for many reasons, such as following up on prospects to see how they reacted to your home, for security, so you know who came through, and since most agents will give you their card instead of signing in, to get a good feel for the number of agents who have seen your home and can promote it.

Have a sheet available with complete information on the house. You want to give a potential buyer all the information he or she needs to make a decision to go ahead.

Have a sample offer worksheet out where a buyer can see it. This should show price, proposed financing, and other information to help the buyer visualize how to make an offer.

Some people like to be led, most prefer to be left alone. You need to arrange the house so that you don't have to comment on the features buyers might miss, such as cedar-lined closets, built-in shelves, the view from the bedroom, and so on. Draw the eye to these items, or it you must, point them out.

Encourage prospects to do things such as turn on appliances, try switches, use cabinet pulls, and open doors. A house that a buyer actually touches and reacts to is one he or she will remember more.

You could have copies made of a map of the area, featuring amenities and the location of your home in relation to them.

Tip 283: The buyer's trust must be gained, whether by you or through their agent.

You don't have the advantage the buyer's agent has of being able to take the buyer by the hand from house to house showing him or her why yours is better than the others and comparing one property to the other as the buyer discloses his or her reactions. So you need to build up rapport as the prospect enters and walk through your house. Talk with each. Go through some small talk not related to selling your home. Compliment each or comment on something he or she is wearing. The key is to get past being a "seller" and become a real person.

Note that selling the property yourself leads to dealing with many unqualified prospects. Sorting them out is what you pay an agent to do. You may find yourself warming up to many dead-end deals. Use this as practise in gaining the buyer's trust.

You need to overcome the unfamiliarity most buyers have of dealing with the seller directly on a home purchase. Most are used to dealing through agents.

If a prospect is using an agent, warm up to the agent. Then the agent will be more on your side. It's human nature. Getting trust is very important. Become a friend. Talk about things outside of selling the house. Connect on a personal level.

Tip 284: Handle inquiries with enthusiasm and in a helpful manner.

Whether the buyer first encounters you by phone or by dropping in, the manner in which you answer questions will determine greatly whether or not he or she continues to the next step. Many buyers are nervous about asking questions. They are relatively inexperienced at buying homes and don't know exactly what to ask. Even if they've owned previously, most likely it has only been one or two times before. Contrast two different ways in which a prospect is greeted and the different feelings that come out of the transaction:

Seller: Hello.

Buyer: Hello. I'm calling about the home you advertised in the paper.

Seller: Yes.

Buyer: It says it has four bedrooms. Um, are they good sized?

Seller: Yes.

Buyer: Oh. OK. Does it have a nice yard?

Seller: Very nice.

Buyer: Are the bathrooms in good shape?

Seller: Fine. We remodeled one two years ago.

The seller is forcing the buyer to pry for information and putting him in an uncomfortable spot. It is much better to calm the buyer's fears rather than reinforcing them by making him or her decide mentally your house isn't worth the struggle. Even if you are not naturally talkative, you must be talkative on the phone. Prepare a speech in advance, if you must, that describes the merits of the house. Consider how much more effective the responses below are:

Seller: Hello.

Buyer: Hello. I'm calling about the home you advertised in the paper.

Seller: Yes, I'm glad you called. It's a large, four-bedroom house with views of the bay and a two-car garage. The kitchen in wonderful. We remodeled it only last year and put in all new appliances. The bathrooms are nice, too, and one even has a Jacuzzi. Would you like to see it?

Buyer: Yes, it sounds nice.

Seller: We're at 32 Bayou Vista. My name is Dan Lieberman; what's yours?

Buyer: David Patterson.

Seller: Great, David, what time would you like to come by?

> **Tip 285: When handling objections, act like a real estate agent, not the home owner.**

Remember your goal, which is to sell your house. Most of the objections that people make may offend you since, after all, this is your house and your sales job. Don't take objections personally: turn them around and treat them as a professional salesperson would.

Answering price objections is usually easy. Always clarify the objection, attempting to reduce its importance. Remember, a buyer will overstate the importance of an objection in order to get you to come down in price or give up some of the commission you are saving by selling the house yourself.

The most common objection is "The price for your home is too high." The best clarifying response is, "When you say too high, could you be more specific?" or "Is there a reason why you feel we aren't justified in asking more than the competition?" You want to dig deeper. Price is only one of many variables. Your price might be too high for this buyer. But don't take a surface "no" as a final answer.

You should also try to create an agreement frame for an objection ("I can appreciate your feeling that way") before probing deeper ("Let me ask you a question, though; if you were selling this home, how would you go about determining its value?"). Another response to, "The price for your home is too high" is "We looked at the comparable houses in the neighborhood and we feel we priced it competitively: what do you think it is worth?" This gives the buyer a feeling that you want to come to a meeting of the minds. A typical response would be, "About $20,000 less." Don't start bargaining: let them know why you priced the house as you did.

Tip 286: Use proactive strategies to avoid price objections.

You can often head off price objections by being ready with responses that indicate that you didn't just pick the price out of thin air. If the buyer seems ready to object, start talking about how you determined the price and how fair it really is.

To prepare a proactive strategy, you must first do a market analysis. What are the current trends in your market? What are the demographics of buyers. Look into the projected growth for the town, industries, and so on. Also, if you are selling the house as prime for an addition, find out how much building permits cost.

Next, you need to do a competitive analysis. Which homes are selling well and why? Which neighborhoods are hot and why? What are your competitors doing? What do they have to offer? By making note of what is selling and what is not, you can give buyers good reasons why your home is worth the price you are asking.

After these objective analyses, you should do a careful self analysis. What do you offer that is unique? In what ways am I vulnerable and how can I avoid them? What objections do I normally hear from prospects? Why would someone not buy this house? Answers to questions like these will help you put a particular buyer's financial fears to rest.

Of course, it is good to know your prospects well, too. What conditions prevail in the prospect's mind? What has the media been telling him or her? What are buyers looking for? Who is the key decision maker?

Tip 287: You must get buyer's agents to show your home or you will be left with only a few walk-ins.

How does a buyer get to your home? Obviously, he must follow a path. This path will play a role in setting up buyer expectations. Some prospects arrive on their own. Many come with the aid of a real estate agent. But agents won't bring someone to your home unless there is something in it for them.

Instead of lowering the price, try raising the commission and adding it to the price to motivate agents. If agents are your main source of buyers, you need to appeal to both the agent and the buyer. Note that their two motives may be very different.

Tip 288: The buyer may expect help on financing, so you must be prepared with facts.

In order to facilitate the sale of your home, you need to make it easy for the buyer. This includes handling the elements of an escrow and finding financing for the buyer. There are many sources of information.

Most cities now have loan brokers who help a buyer find the best loan and often recommend an escrow company. Ask recent buyers in your neighborhood whether or not they recommend their loan broker. Banks, of course, can also be good sources of information on financing. Most escrow companies are similar, so any good recommendation should be sufficient.

Tip 289: Get a good lawyer.

If you go it alone, a good attorney is a must. It is the attorney who will guide the transaction and make sure that all legal requirements have been obeyed. Check around for an attorney and compare fees. You're not beating a murder rap; you're selling a home. So as long as the attorney is reasonably competent, you don't need to go with the most expensive in town.

Tip 290: Nothing lasts forever.

If you have tried to sell your home by yourself but failed, you should strongly consider listing with an agent. This could serve many advantages. You got a good feel for the market for your home. You may have found an excellent agent among the many that either came to see the home or hounded you for a listing.

If you feel that you've made some good contacts with prospects and that one of them might turn into a buyer, consider an exclusion in the listing agreement that lists these people. That way, if one comes through, you are not obligated to pay a commission on work you did before signing the agreement.

Tip 291: Expect a few shockingly low offers.

This is unfortunately common. Ignore them, and certainly don't let them deter you from your goal of selling at a fair price. People who offer these low figures are often trying to cheat you out of your house so that they can turn around and sell it for a quick profit. Some are just malicious and enjoy seeing people hurt. Either way, don't take them seriously. Thank the person for his or her consideration and quickly show him or her to the door.

CHAPTER TWENTY-SEVEN

Value-added Selling

No product is overpriced unless it is not desired. Therefore, if you get a price objection, it is generally because the real value of your home has not been communicated to the buyer. If most buyers balk at the price, either your selling is not good enough or you have overpriced the home for its value to them.

The stronger the relationship between buyer and seller, the less important price is. This is where the buyer's real estate agent can help you sell your home. Note that, even with high value, price is still very important.

Tip 292: Ask appropriate questions for information.

The key to selling is to gather information about the buyer's needs and then show how your product fills those needs. The best way to do this is through the tool of asking questions.

Probing for buyer needs helps bring to the forefront the buyer's nonprice variables. Letting the buyer talk at length about nonprice items makes price less of an issue and the value your home offers more of one. If you and the buyer talk about quality of life, the importance of good neighborhoods and schools for the kids, how much he likes the kitchen, and how the guest room would be perfect for Aunt Ida's stays, than the price lessens in importance and becomes only one issue of many.

Tip 293: It's your job to break the ice.

Few relationships are like love at first sight, especially in a down market when there are so many houses on the market. Most conversations, especially business transactions, need to be eased into. That's why phrases like "breaking the ice" and "warming them up" are so common. They reflect reality. By probing, you gain more information and the buyer appreciates that you care enough to listen.

When questioning, use open-ended questions. You want the buyer to elaborate or expound, not just answer yes or no. Here are some examples of open-ended questions:

- Why do you feel that way?
- Tell me about what you've been looking for?

Examples of closed-ended questions:

- How long have you been looking?
- How much money can you put down?

Tip 294: Good questions help the sale.

Most home owners are not practiced salespeople. If this is the case with you, good questions might be your salvation. Questions allow the prospect to feel important because of all the attention you're giving him while allowing you the information you need to help sell the home.

Questions also prevent you from talking too much and dominating the conversation. They also help the person who is naturally a little reticent, since you don't have to think of engaging conversation to fill the silence. All you need to do is let the prospect speak.

Questions can also be used to change the prospect's state of mind. Questions like, "Don't you love sitting by a warm fireplace at night?" or, "Isn't the view beautiful?" help alter what the buyer focuses on and put him or her in a more receptive state. Questions like, "How much money do you have?" can do the opposite.

```
Tip 295: Sell the value that is relevant.
```

You may never have even noticed the maple tree in your back yard, but if that tree is bringing back happy childhood memories to your buyer, you need to talk about how nice it is to sit in the backyard under the tree. Don't talk about your remodeled kitchen if all he or she ever does is bring in take-out food. You have to focus with the buyer and step out of what you think is valuable about your house.

Remember, value is in the eye of the beholder. What may be valuable to you may not be valuable to your customer and visa versa. If you want to charge more than the competition, you need to create a greater perceived value.

```
Tip 296: You don't need to own it to sell it.
```

You don't need to own amenities to market them. If you are marketing to couples with children, it would help to advertise that you are near the park or near good schools. Focus on their needs. Empty-nesters would be attracted to security, while first-time buyers might feel it is an unnecessary expense. Recreational amenities such as nearby tennis courts or a golf course are an added sell.

```
Tip 297: Sell the value that is unique.
```

Remember, you want to make your home memorable and to stick out from the crowd. The only way to do this is to sell the unique attributes of your home to the buyer. Sure, they all have formal dining rooms, but this house has a built-in hutch. Yes, their kitchens are larger, but when the sun shines through the windows in the breakfast nook, you're in heaven.

Real estate is unique. Every home and every location is a little different. That difference will make your home more valuable, because if buyers pass on it and it sells, they will never be able to get quite the same thing.

Tip 298: Create solutions.

Some people say that if the railroad companies had understood that they were in the transportation business and not the railroad business, they would still be in business today. Understanding what your role really is is the first step to understanding how to do value-added selling.

Understanding how to sell your home begins, paradoxically, with forgetting about the home, and focusing on how to solve the buyers' needs. Whether the problem is lack of cash or any number of other problems, understanding your role as a problem solver will get you past many "deal killer" issues.

CHAPTER TWENTY-EIGHT

Choosing a Real Estate Agent

A good agent should possess as many of the following characteristics as possible. (Note that these are also the qualities and standards you must have if you are selling your home yourself.) It is much easier to find an agent with all these qualities (or at least most of them) than to find them in yourself.

- Good understanding of the needs of buyers
- Lots of preparation, with deep knowledge of both product and market
- Ability to prospect for qualified buyers
- Ability to present your home in the best light
- Proven ability to close prospects effectively
- Good follow-up of unclosed prospects

Whomever you choose has the tremendous opportunity and responsibility for getting you the highest price in a down market. This is not an easy task. Be careful whom you choose.

**Tip 299: Spend some time to find the best agent
you can.**

The importance of finding the right agent to sell your home cannot be overemphasized. You must find the individual or firm that is the most creative and imaginative in its marketing and innovative in its solutions to financing problems with buyers. The better the salesperson, the less the burden on you will be to perform the functions of a seller. You can't afford to waste time with those who do not meet top standards.

One of the best ways to find a good agent is to ask your friends who have recently bought or sold. They'll usually tell you exactly what they think about their agent. Take advantage of that honesty and be sure to tell your friend if you go with the friend's agent.

Look through the paper and see which brokerage is advertising the most. Some firms don't advertise much, especially if they have had bad luck selling in the past few months. Successful ones market carefully.

Drive around the neighborhood. See whose name appears often on the listing signs. Real estate is a local business: see who knows your neighborhood. If you don't see one particular agent's name, call the firm that seems to specialize in your area (the one with the most signs) and ask the broker who their three most successful brokers are, such as the ones with the highest sales or the most awards. When you call these people, ask for proof: you don't want to have had the brokerage send you some average agent just because they felt sorry for him or her.

Look for a salesperson who hustles. You can usually find one by reading the agency advertisements and see who is most frequently named salesperson of the month. Make sure you're getting someone who is knowledgeable and who specializes in homes within the price range of your home and within your neighborhood. Call several title companies and ask the officers who are the best agents to work with. Title companies deal with the agents in the complex parts of the transaction.

You want to have an experienced agent, especially in a down market. No matter how good an agent is, an experienced one, especially one who has been through a down market before, will be able to protect you when buyers come up with creative financing or other unusual offers. You want someone who's been through this type of market before.

Real estate is a people business. Pay particular attention to how your prospective agent relates to you and others.

Ask the agents to make a formal proposal and presentation. See which one is most convincing to you; after all, this is the same one who will be convincing your potential buyer to buy. In a down market, it may be difficult to get many agents to make proposals since they already have so many homes they are trying to sell, but others will treat you the same whether the market is up or down.

When you ask for an estimate of your home's value, notice how detailed and thorough the questions are. Does the agent do a thorough inspection of the house, ask about any defects, and ask about other relevant details, or does he or she just pull a number out of thin air because he says he "knows the market"?

You can't choose a salesperson without considering the agency he works for. Different brokerages have different advertising budgets, and some will expose your property better than others. But, more importantly, individual brokerages have different reputations within the real estate community, and many agents have qualms about working with certain brokerages.

The largest brokerage may have the most sales, but how many sales per agent are they getting? This is a better gauge of how good the salespeople are.

Check out the brokerage office. Visit it. How does it make you feel? A realty office should be attractive, accessible, and open seven days a week for residential business. Does the office seem to attract buyers? Are there amenities you would expect as a buyer?

> **Tip 300: Make a bond with the agent so that he or she will sell your home harder than others.**

Get a personal commitment from the sales person to use all his or her ingenuity and drive to sell the property. It's amazing how personal commitment works. Let the agent know that you want someone with energy, even in a down market.

At the same time, be sure to tell the agent that you will be helping by doing independent marketing and beating the bushes for additional prospective buyers. By showing them this type of resolve on your part, you will make them more interested in your house than in the other houses they are selling.

Always ask how you can help. Your agent probably has lots of clients who don't lift a finger but always complain about how long it is taking. If you show you want to help, your house will be in the front of their minds every time a prospective buyer comes in the door.

Working on the sale of your home is a team effort and requires cooperation and trust. Even if you find a hot-shot real estate agent, if you don't like each other, you are not going to work well together, and you are not going to get top dollar for your home in a tough market. Make sure your personalities mesh.

Tip 301: Watch out for unscrupulous agents.

In a down market, there are agents who take advantage of panicking sellers, get listings below market, and pass them on to their friends before the properties ever hit the public viewing. The best way to avoid this happening to you is to do your homework. Get at least three agents to give you an estimate of market value, or have your appraisal done.

Be wary if your agent wants you to sell for significantly less that the value the house was appraised at. Ask to see other listings that were recently appraised by the same appraiser and see if they are selling at the same discount your agent is suggesting in your case. If not, consider getting a new agent quickly.

Tip 302: It's not just the agent, it's the brokerage.

In deciding which is more crucial to the sale, an excellent agent is more critical than the brokerage. But don't discount the importance of the company this agent works for. Does it have a good reputation in the real estate community? Will other agents work with it, or do they avoid it?

In many cases, the seller of a home is at an advantage going with one of the syndicated real estate firms. These franchises often deal with relocating executives and employees from other areas where the franchise operates. Also, many of the better franchise operations provide marketing training for their staff. But it is the coast-to-coast referral network that is the strongest plus.

Tip 303: Qualify your agent as you would qualify your buyer.

When choosing an agent, be sure that he or she is qualified to sell your house. A good agent for executive homes, for example, may be totally unqualified to sell a condominium.

In a down market, you can still pick and choose agents. If you follow the tips in this book, you will help sell your house much faster than the average, so agents will want you as a client. Feel free to ask questions like the following:

- Are you a full-time agent?

- How long have you been in the business? Have you been through a down market before?

- Do you have any professional designations?

- Do you have any homes listed in my neighborhood? What homes have you sold in this neighborhood? How recently?

- What percentage of the listing price have your homes been selling for?

- Will you give me the names and current addresses of recent selling clients as references?

- How much will you spend on advertising? Where will these ads appear?

- What other marketing techniques do you propose for a house like mine?

- What other homes do you currently have for sale outside my neighborhood? Are they similar to mine? Which ones have you recently sold?

- What solutions would you have if a buyer could not qualify for conventional financing?

- Which banks and lending institutions have you used? Has their experience been extensive?

- Would you take back part of your commission in the form of a short-term note if it was necessary to close the deal?

- What would you sell my home for? Why?

- Why do you think you can sell my home better than anyone else? What makes your firm special?

Tip 304: Always check an agent's references.

Remember, these are salespeople. If you ask for references, they know that there is a good chance you won't follow up and call the people listed. Don't end up with an unscrupulous agent by not doing your homework.

Questions to ask the prospective agent's references include these:

- How long did your house stay on the market? Why?

- How many people were shown the home?

- What was the original list price? What was the sale price?

- Were you satisfied with the transaction?

- Did the broker help you all the way through the transaction?

- Would you use this person again? Would you recommend him or her to a good friend?

Tip 305: You don't have to pay retail for your agent's services.

Most sellers never question the commission rate that real estate brokers charge. Although most brokerages do have standard fees, these are usually negotiable. In many states, the law insists that they be negotiable. In a down market, many brokerages are more flexible on commissions if they feel they have a house that will sell quickly and easily. Since you are going to help the agent much more than the average seller, use that fact to help get a lower fee.

When negotiating a lower commission, be especially sensitive to how much the buyer's agent makes. A lower commission might attract fewer buyer's agents. For example, if you sell your house for $100,000 with a 6% commission, the listing brokerage gets $3,000 and the sales brokerage also gets $3,000. You could reduce this commission to 5% but change the shares to $2,000 for the listing brokerage and $3,000 to the selling brokerage. That way other agents are still just as motivated to bring buyers.

Examine all the factors that you can use to lower your agent's commission before agreeing to a commission schedule. Many factors can work to your benefit in negotiating a lower commission. For instance, having a property in the hottest price range in your community makes a sale easier. Higher-priced property makes a small percentage still a large number. Having a desirable property (following the renovating rules in this book) means a quick and easy sale and may be used to negotiate a lower fee.

You should be careful that, if your agent agrees to reduce his commission, he's not silently agreeing to reduce his *service*.

Even after you agree on a commission schedule, it can be negotiated down in special circumstances. You might be able to make the broker give up part of the commission if he doesn't get you a price within a certain percentage of the listing. If your broker brings you an offer with a low price and pressures you to accept, you may be able to have him or her reduce the commission, too.

Try talking in terms of dollars, not percentages. A 6% commission doesn't sound like much, but on a $250,000 home, it is $15,000. See if the broker will drop it to $12,000 or $13,000. The numbers still seem large and the broker may be more amenable to discussing a discount.

Tip 306: Discount brokers can save you money, but be sure that you are getting enough services to sell your house.

Discount brokerages for stocks and bonds have become popular in the last ten years, and many have appeared in the real estate market as well. Choosing a discount broker can save you money, but all discount brokerages are not alike.

Some brokerages help with the paperwork, but the buyer deals directly with the seller. With some, the seller must pay for his own advertising.

When you consider a discount brokerage, be sure you're getting adequate advertising, showings, and help in negotiations with buyers. Also make sure you're working with a full-time salesperson, and make sure other brokers will work with your discounter. Get references. Ask previous sellers if they were satisfied.

Ask others in the full-service real estate community how they feel about this firm. They may have negative stories about working with the brokerage, such as botched sales due to bad paperwork.

Tip 307: Flat-rate agreements may work to your advantage if you are sure your house will sell quickly.

In a down market, it is usually best to use traditional real estate agents in traditional settings. However, it is possible to pay agents by the hour instead of by commission. Good uses of hourly pay include:

- Getting information on sales of comparable houses in the neighborhood

- Reviewing all paperwork to make sure it meets industry standards

- Going through the escrow process with a seller

Some real estate brokerages offer certain services for a set fee rather than a commission. For a flat fee, they will usually put you in the MLS book, give you a few signs, and leave you on your own. You can also unbundle the package of services a typical brokerage offers and pay for only the ones you want.

Tip 308: Put it in writing.

You'll soon know if your agent keeps all his promises, but until then, get him to put everything in writing. If he promises he'll do so much advertising, get him to write it down. If he offers to take care of and maintain your vacant house for sale, put it in writing, and detail exactly what that means.

In a down market, an agent may be carrying more properties than he or she normally would, since the properties are selling more slowly and there are fewer buyers. This causes some agents to get a bit sloppy or to overextend themselves. Having the agreement in writing prevents this problem from occurring.

Tip 309: Be considerate about your agent's time.

You should be talking regularly with your real estate agent, but you must keep in mind that a good agent will have several clients and several listings going on at any one time. The average agent may call you once or twice a week to give an update on what has happened.

Most agents take off only one day each week. Find out what day that is and then be considerate: leave him or her alone that day.

On the other hand, you want to keep in touch with your agent. You want to find out everything that happened during the week. How many people called, where from, how many came by. Two heads can brainstorm better than one, and you may see things that your real estate agent missed.

Tip 310: Make the house always available.

Many homes don't sell simply for lack of exposure. How are the Joneses going to be able to buy your house if they can't even see it? Too often sellers say "show my home only during business hours when we're not home. We don't want to be bothered with people walking through the house." Well, those people are your prospective buyers, and if you want to sell your house in a down market, you'll roll out the red carpet for them.

Agents make notes of how easy it is to call you on short notice and get someone in to see your house. And if you're not easy, they'll go somewhere else.

Keep the house in "open house" condition at all times. If this means hiring a housecleaner to keep the house looking nice, do it. What's an extra $100 per month compared to the thousands extra you will receive by being able to sell your home quickly at a premium price. This will prevent your agent from being embarrassed when he or she brings prospective buyers by only to find that the house is not showable.

Tip 311: Market your home to the agents.

Using the network of real estate agents in your community is like having a thousand employees working for you. You want to make it easy for them to see and show your home and you want to keep them motivated to remember your home over others when showing houses to clients. Make sure you are on all broker's tours and then do something special for the agents coming through. Have a food spread or some special treats. Make it interesting for them and make sure your house is fully set up when they come through. Real estate agents are people, too, and they have emotions you can appeal to.

And remember, market it right the first time. It's a lot harder to entice real estate agents back to your home for a second broker's tour. They assume they've seen it already and that nothing has changed. Make sure the home is in perfect shape first, and then watch the crowds of agents go to work for you.

Tip 312: Tell the agent everything.

You need to tell the agent all the negatives about your house in addition to the good points. Seller disclosure laws are becoming more stringent all the time. Getting a few extra dollars today is nothing compared to losing it all in a legal action.

Tip 313: Before you fire an agent, determine if he or she is not doing a good job.

In a down market, it can take a very long time to sell a house, or you may have to keep cutting the price. You may get itchy and decide that something is wrong. It's easy to blame your real estate agent (and it's easy for the agent to blame you). However, that's often not what you want to do.

If you have been working with an agent for a few months, don't drop the agent just because the house hasn't sold. If you get a new agent, you're starting new with someone who is unfamiliar with the house. Also, the new agent will know that you dropped the old one and may worry that you will drop him or her as well.

Before putting the onus totally on the agent, think about the following:

- Is my price too high for the market?
- What has been the quality of the prospects we have attracted?
- What is the condition of my home in relation to others?

When you observe the agent in action, ask yourself:

- How is his or her style?
- Do prospects get turned off?
- Is the broker cooperating? How easy has it been for other agents to get information on your home?
- How much follow up has been performed?
- How good is his or her record keeping?

When your broker calls for an appointment, do some qualifying on your own to see how much he did. Ask what he knows about the people. Are they likely to qualify for financing? What size houses have they been looking at? Have they been looking in the area?

If you don't work well together, don't worry: get a new agent. In a medium-sized or large firm, it should be fairly easy to find another agent within the firm so that you don't have to change brokerages. In a small firm, this may be more difficult, especially if there are only two people. You may have to move to a different brokerage. One caution: If you signed a long term listing agreement, you might be stuck with that bad agent for a long time. Be careful of how long your listing agreements are for.

CHAPTER TWENTY-NINE

Negotiating

Negotiating is a part of every real estate transaction, but it is a skill rarely taught to or experienced by most Americans. People are not used to haggling at stores, but pay what's on the price tag. In a down market, few buyers, if any, will pay the "price tag" on your home without some skillful selling and negotiating.

Tip 314: You are not doing a hard sell.

Negotiating is not a hard sell to close the buyer. In fact, good negotiating is very subtle. You want the buyers to sell themselves. You are there to show them why and to help them make a commitment.

For many reasons, buyers have a hard time making offers. Either they don't really know how, or they are scared, or they need some reassurance. Get the ball rolling by at least soliciting an offer.

Tip 315: Always encourage the other party to speak first.

Your price is on the fact sheet; it is now up to them to make you an offer. If they ask you, "What price will you take?" tell them that price is not the only issue and that they should make an offer.

Listen carefully to what the buyer is saying or objecting to. Keep the communication open. Hear what the buyer is really saying.

Tip 316: You are negotiating from the moment you meet the buyer.

In his book *You Can Get Anything You Want*, Roger Dawson states that there are three stages to any negotiation:

- Clarify the objectives. You need to find out what the other side wants. Why do they want to buy your home? Note that what they say they want and what they really want may be two different things. They might tell you that they are just looking, but they might have sold their home and need to be in another within the month.

- Gather the information. You should be doing this from the moment you first make contact with the buyers. Who are these people? What is important to them? Remember that countries spend millions to have spies gathering data. You need to invest a little of your own time to find out about your buyers. It could easily save you thousands during the negotiations.

- The agreement stage. This is what most people think of as the negotiation, but jumping into this without the two preceding stages can hamper your negotiations seriously.

By properly preparing for the negotiations before they start, you have a strong jump on the other side and put yourself in a stronger position.

Tip 317: Price is not the only item on the menu.

The main items that can be negotiated include price, financing terms, contingencies (such as recognizing that the buyers need to sell their house first), date of possession, and what personal property is included with the home. Use some of these other items to keep your price. Everything has value. Focus on what is valuable to the buyer but not to you.

Use trade-offs. Trade-offs are a series of concessions you make to be matched by similar concessions by the buyer. "If I let you have four extra weeks to close escrow, then I would like to get your father to co-sign the note."

Never label a position you take as definite or carved in stone. Don't say, "$175,000 is as low as I'll go," say, "I could take your offer of $169,000 if you'd pay 16% on the seller carryback note." Trade off terms and conditions.

Tip 318: Know what you want before entering the negotiation.

Prepare a list of "must haves" and "like to haves" in advance before ever entering into negotiations. This will prevent you from getting off track because of emotion.

Tip 319: Ask good questions and look for hidden assumptions.

According to Gerard Nierenberg's book *The Art of Negotiation*, there are three aspects to questioning:

- What question to ask

- How to phrase it

- When to ask it

He illustrates this by telling the story of a clergyman who asked his superior, "May I smoke while praying?" He was turned down. Another clergyman, approaching the same superior, asked, "May I pray while smoking?" and was given immediate permission.

There are many assumptions people make as they encounter each other and enter into business transactions. Check the way ideas are conveyed to you. Are the buyers assuming you're desperate because it is a down market and making appropriately low offers? Are they assuming you would never go for creative financing? Try to put yourself in their shoes to see how to make a deal work.

Tip 320: Use the power of legitimacy.

The written word provides legitimacy. Years ago, hotels were having trouble getting guests to check out on time. Then someone came up with the brilliant idea of placing that little sign on the back of the room door saying "checkout time 11a.m." Those signs have helped raise compliance levels to almost 100%.

You have seen how to use appraisals and inspection reports. Using documents to convince the buyer that your price is right is a very convincing tactic. Any statistics about sales prices in your area, if they come from someone perceived as a neutral third party, help bolster your case. Think about what documents, articles, or other written communications you have that can help sway a buyer's viewpoint. You should also question the power of anything the buyers present to you.

Tip 321: Use time to your advantage.

Time is one of the crucial elements in a negotiation. Selective foot-dragging can have a positive use in the negotiations. If the buyer feels that you are desperate and have a sense of urgency, he may conclude that you must sell now and try to ram down the price.

In a down market, the buyer has the advantage with time, usually. You want your house to sell quickly because there are so many other homes on the market. Try to turn this advantage around. If you can get a contract which becomes noncontingent in a short time, you can have a longer closing, because a buyer who backs out loses his or her deposit.

You can also put time to your advantage is if you know the buyer has a time limit. Perhaps the buyer is in a tax-deferred exchange and so must acquire your property by a certain date. Once that date is past, the buyer will be stuck, so you have much more negotiating room.

Listen. You might hear them talking about spending Thanksgiving in the new home with all their relatives. If this is an important point to them, you can promise a quick close if they are flexible on some other issue, such as price.

You are desperate to sell, you have made some concessions, and now it's over, right? Wrong. As long as the buyer has time on his side, you may find yourself giving in time and time again to little requests and concessions.

Tip 322: Use the prospective buyer's experts as a guide to negotiating.

It is unlikely that the prospect will walk into your house once and then make you a full-price offer in writing. More likely, a prospect will come back a second or third time, usually accompanied by relatives or "experts" they know. Use these visits as a chance to learn something about the buyer. Who are they? Where do they live now? What do they like about the house?

This information will be invaluable later when you are negotiating. Since the buyer trusts these people (probably more than you), you can target them the same way you target the buyer. If you can convince them about your house, they will help you convince the buyer.

Tip 323: Use the art of persuasion to help the buyer see what you want.

The simple key to persuasion is to not to sell but rather to induce the buyer to buy. Although the two sound similar, the difference in the syntax and the point of views they contain are worlds apart. Part of inducing the buyer is to set the proper stage. You have done that by making the home merchandisable and targeting the product and program. Now the key is to continue showing the buyer why this is the right home and to put him into a contract.

Tip 324: Listen more, talk less.

Stop talking and listen, really listen, to what the buyer is saying. You might find that items that are important to him or her mean little to you. Perhaps you could get the buyer to stop cutting your price if you throw in your old rusting Wedgewood stove. All some people want is for you to listen to their problems.

If you are to be a good negotiator, you must be a good listener. When you listen, you want to be objective so that you pick up accurate messages. Try to understand not only what a person says, but what that person really means.

Tip 325: In a down market, the first offer is often the best offer.

When your home first hits the market, all the buyers that have been looking for one, two, or three months will hear about it. Once it has been out a few weeks, only as new buyers come into the market will they learn of it. Thus, there is usually an initial stampede to a new listing relative to the amount of traffic it gets a few months later.

If you get a reasonable offer early in the listing period, give it some serious attention. It may save you a lot of headaches and hassles later.

However, don't jump at the first offer just because it is an offer. This may sound contradictory, but it's not. Even if the first offer is what you want or will accept, it is in your best interest to respond to it but to take your time, or else counteroffer with terms very close. It's just human nature. When people jump at the first offer, the other party assumes they could have gotten a better deal. You'll wind up being nickled and dimed for the rest of the sales process, through every inspection, and before removing any contingency.

Tip 326: Start the negotiations slow and build momentum.

You want to catch and keep the buyer. The best way to do this is not to press so hard you scare him away initially. Work with the buyer and get him to commit himself mentally to buying the home. As he spends more time doing inspections, telling his friends about the house, and generally buying it in his own mind, he is less likely to back out, even when you ask for some concessions later.

Tip 327: Be able to walk away.

If you are so set on this buyer and you must sell now, you have seriously weakened your position in the negotiation. Remember, you can always walk away from a negotiation and start over. Those that can't walk away are bound to give up much more than they have to.

Prevent yourself from telling all your friends and associates that you've sold your home before it actually closes. If everyone thinks you've sold it and your ego is riding on this sale, then when the buyer decides he wants you to cut your price by $5,000 at the last minute, it is going to be very hard emotionally to say no. You have too much invested in the sale. Being able to walk away is one of the strongest tools you have. Use it.

Tip 328: Don't win the battle to lose the war.

Don't get so caught up in the negotiations that you lose the big picture: to sell your home for a reasonable price. You don't want to send the buyer away in a down market where buyers are usually few and far between.

CHAPTER THIRTY

Going Beyond the Ordinary

Alternative Sales Techniques

In a down market, there are too many houses and too few buyers. In a stagnant market, you may need to resort to very different sales strategies in order to sell your house. Some of these are very risky, but many people feel that leaving a house on the market for too long is also risky.

Tip 329: Consider auctioning your house if you absolutely must sell.

Auctions were once used almost exclusively to unload foreclosed homes, but recently many sellers have taken to auctions to try to unload their stagnant homes. Roughly $26 billion in residential and commercial real estate was sold at auction in 1989, up from $10 billion in 1980.

Most people think of auctions as places where desperate sellers go when they can't sell their homes any other way. This is often the case. However, what professional auctioneers know that most buyers don't is how to build up a bidding frenzy where you can actually get more for your home in a short time than you could have by leaving it on the market. There have been many auctions where the initial bid for a property was a bargain price, but by the time the bidding was done, the unwary buyer had actually bid over market value because he'd gotten so caught up in the auction frenzy.

As with choosing any professional, you need to look around in order to choose the best auctioneer. Does he or she specialize in real estate? Does the auctioneer advertise extensively, and to whom? How successful has he or she been at getting good prices?

If you are putting your home up for auction, try to offer the house with a "reserve" option. A reserve option gives you the right to reject the winning bid, even if it exceeds the minimum price advertised before the auction. This way, if the auction is not going as well as expected, you are not forced to sell your home for a song.

Auctions are good at stirring up interest in depressed markets. Often, even if your home sells for less than market value, you are really saving thousands of dollars which would have been spent in carrying costs while the home languished on the market.

Most people still believe that auctions are a way to pick up real estate at fire-sale prices. Auctioneers play on this belief, knowing that they are really skilled sellers who are able to get people into "auction fever" bidding prices up higher than they should. Most homes sell at around market value at auctions.

Tip 330: Consider using incentives to help move the property.

Special offers, gimmicks, and that little extra push have helped sell homes in down markets. Although not usually a recommended part of the marketing strategy, they do serve the purpose of getting your home noticed, making it memorable, and tapping into many buyer's wants and psychological needs. Success with incentives amounts to being able to read the mind of the consumer and tap into what might excite him or her.

In a tough market, you need something to make your house stand out. Sometimes people suffer from "homebuyer's amnesia." They've seen so many homes, they can't even remember them all. They forget the ones they like. If you can't make your home memorable, you can't sell it.

By making it easier to own a home, you open your market to more people. You might want to improve the financing terms, using methods such as:

- Paying the buyer's closing costs or points

- Paying for appraisals, credit reports, deed recording

- Creative financing with balloon payments

You also might want to provide bonus incentives to salespeople. These are the people who will bring you most of your buyers. Make your home stand out from the crowd. And remember, money does motivate. You can offer incentive commissions to agents with a time limit. More traditionally, you can offer a free trip to agents who bring a full-price or near-full-price offer.

Give the buyer more for his or her money, *if they buy now.*

- Supply a free electronic security system

- Pay for automatic sprinkler systems

- Throw in free appliances, such as a new washer and dryer

- Pay for landscaping or provide free maintenance for a year

- Promise a cleaning service for a year

- Maybe offer a free trip, possibly in conjunction with a trip you offer to the agent

Other creative items include these:

- Prepayment of condo maintenance fees for a year.

- Promotional items: One company recently gave away suntan lotion with the message, "Don't get burned and buy at the wrong place."

- Throw in the cost of commuting from the new home to work for a year.

- A free car.

- Zero coupon bonds or T-bills. You get to buy them at a discount but they get marketed at face value.

Chances are a trip to the Caribbean isn't going to sell a home, but the incentives can attract attention. Conversely, they can signal that there is room left in the price for negotiating. However, aggressive marketing and creative incentives are not new to real estate. Incentives seem to appear in every downturn. And when something keeps reappearing, that usually means it works.

Unusual Situations

In general, most houses must be sold as houses, and frankly will fetch you the highest price as houses. Not always. Many homes that were once built in nice residential areas are now on the edge of commercial development. Rents and sales prices for commercial property are significantly higher than for residential property. If your home can be put to a higher and better use, its value may come from that.

Tip 331: Consider converting the home to other uses.

Many homes have been converted into doctor's or lawyer's offices. Often a professional doesn't want to be located in a steel and glass building but prefers the coziness of an older home. The amount a professional can pay for your home, although higher than another buyer might pay, may still leave the mortgage payment considerably lower than the rent for a fancy office space.

In many cities, homes abut commercial property. Usually, these homes can be rezoned to become retail establishments. In San Francisco, Union Street, one of the highest priced shopping areas, was mostly residential at one time. Most of the buildings are converted houses with storefronts. The retail area just crept down the street, building by building.

Homes have been turned into lovely restaurants, in which each room offers a different dining experience. Restaurants are not always big money-makers, so this plan is not as likely to draw top dollar.

Bed and breakfast inns are the travel rage of the 1990s. If you have a large, historic home near a popular area, converting it to a B&B can reap you a high return on sale. Be sure to do most of the legwork for the buyer, checking city and state codes and so on. There may be a B&B owner's association in your area that will give you additional information.

You may even be able to take a house with a large lot and turn it into a profitable urban farm, as has been done in some cities. The owners grow fresh gourmet vegetables for fancy restaurants and have created quite a profitable enterprise.

Tip 332: You might be able to subdivide the lot and get two sales.

Many people live on large parcels studded with several smaller buildings. Some just live on lots which are large for the area. In many cities, if you have a house on a 50-foot-wide lot, it's considered a double lot by most real estate agents. By splitting it into two 25-foot parcels, you can turn an extra 30% to 40% in profit. Sometimes you can sell the primary residence and hold onto the other lots for future sale when times are better and the prices higher.

Although bigger is usually better, it may not bring the best value for the land. Every area has an optimal lot size. It is the typical lot in the neighborhood. If you have a smaller lot, your home seems poorer or less desirable, if you have more, you have excess land. Look at how much similar homes sell for on different-size lots. Does the larger lot add a proportionately higher value, or is it just a marginally higher price? If you have a very large lot, can you produce two optimally sized lots by subdividing?

Each buyers has a limited price range he or she can work within. In general there are many more buyers in the lower-priced categories than in the upper. By subdividing, you are producing two or more affordable properties from one previously unaffordable one.

The shape of the lot is important, too. Property of a reasonable size but with a small street frontage does not lend itself well to subdividing. It leaves the newer lot sensitive to entrance and exit problems. This will have a substantial effect on the value of the rear lot. Odd-shaped lots such as L shapes and ones with sharp angles tend to waste space and are harder to sub-divide, too.

Subdividing takes time and money. Surveys are required and planning procedures can be lengthy. But the value of the parts can be significantly greater than that of the whole.

Although subdividing usually is the way to make money in real estate, there are many cases, particularly where uses have been changed from residential to commercial, where a larger lot is necessary if the parcel is to be buildable. Your home many not be on a large enough lot, but perhaps if you sold your house with the one next door it would make sense to a developer.

Tip 333: If your buyers are predominantly parents, see if you can get your house into a better school district.

School districts can have a large effect on the value of a home. Prestigious schools mean opportunities for children to "better themselves"—and give you a chance to do better selling your home.

In the San Francisco east bay area, for example, there are two communities, Oakland and Piedmont, side by side. Piedmont is a much more prestigious address, containing many estates and large homes. However, the Piedmont school district overlaps into part of Oakland. You might be able to get your home in-cluded in a school district if you can make a good case for it. If you are sure the home can't get into a better district, spend many hours researching the good private schools in the area.

Tip 334: Easements can add value.

Easements are legal agreements by which a property owner gives up some of the rights to use the land. Common easements are service easements, which allow the utility company to put gas lines under your property, and street-widening easements, which allow the city to take a little of your land should it ever decide to widen the roads.

A very common situation in urban and suburban areas is the common driveway. Typically the driveway is located on one lot, and the other home has an easement to use it.

Since an easement is a legal right, it has value when marketed properly. For example, if you live in a home with no parking spaces (common in many older cities) but you have a parking easement on the adjacent lot, that parking space is yours to sell and adds value to your home.

Tip 335: Turn a duplex into condominiums or TICs.

If you own a small multiunit building such as a duplex or triplex, you can add greatly to the value of the property by converting the units to separate ownership through either condominiumization or tenancy in common (TIC). Americans will pay a premium for home ownership. A rental duplex is worth less than one where the two units are owned by separate owners.

Condominium conversion laws are different in different cities and states. You will often find that an area that has restrictive laws on condo conversions has more lenient laws toward smaller buildings.

Tenancy in common is another form of ownership. It is usually used as a way to get around strict condo conversion laws. In a TIC, separate owners buy the entire building together in a partnership, but each gets his unit as his share of the partnership. Partners can then sell their shares to others when they decide to move.

Not every building makes for a good condominium conversion. Units that are good prospects tend to be larger, have higher quality of construction, and be in prime locations. If your home is a small multiunit building, rather than renting out the other portions, consider a conversion. It takes some time and legal expenses but the rewards can be very large.

Tip 336: Changes don't always make sense.

Remember, you want to make a change only if it adds value and is worth the time and effort. Many homes might qualify for the above changes, but the gain in value would be nominal and not worth the effort. Remember, you want to spend your time going after the biggest, easiest, and most profitable changes, not trying to see how many you can make.

CHAPTER THIRTY-ONE

Selling Condominiums and Co-ops

Selling a condo or co-op is similar to selling a home: you need to determine your market, and then market appropriately to that group. However, condominiums and co-ops also differ greatly from single-family detached homes. Since a condominiums or co-op works as a community, knowledge of and familiarity with the rules, amenities, and functioning of that community are essential to your success.

Tip 337: Understand the difference between condominiums and co-ops.

In some parts of the country, notably New York City, cooperatives have become an accepted form of residential ownership. While condominiums and cooperatives are not alike, they do share certain similarities.

Condos and co-ops differ in the way ownership is held. A co-op corporation holds title to the real estate, which consists of the land and improvements. The tenant-owners of the building become stockholders in this corporation. They are granted rights of occupancy through proprietary leases for specific apartments.

In a cooperative, the financing usually involves a blanket mortgage on the entire property. Each tenant-owner is responsible but not personally liable for his *pro rata* share. The owner of a condominium unit is personally liable. Taxes are handled in a similar manner.

Some specialized techniques are necessary to sell a condominium or co-op as compared with a single-family home.

Tip 338: Target your typical condominium buyer.

Who is a condominium buyer? Check with real estate agents in your area who deal with condos. Typically, condo buyers include the following:

- Retirement-age people. People in this group usually have money from selling a larger home but now want a low-maintenance, high-amenity setting.

- Young couples, usually without children, jumping on the equity ladder for the first time.

- Young or divorced people with good incomes who want the benefits of home ownership but like the conveniences of apartment living.

- Families who want to own a detached home but simply can't afford it at this time.

Read your condo declaration. Are there any age restrictions? You've noticed the lifestyle at the community. Who would your community most appeal to? If it's full of retirees, don't target young couples. People want to feel comfortable in their new home—and in their new community.

Don't assume that you can sell your condo to someone who is in the market for a house. Those people have often chosen houses for specific reasons. In a down market, there is usually sufficient price pressure to allow house hunters to find inexpensive homes without buying a condo.

Apartment complexes are a great source for prospects. Many don't realize that the mortgage on a condominium may not be much more than the rent they are currently paying. A good flyer with some hard facts will probably get you much more interest than simply listing with a real estate agent.

Tip 339: Market a community, not just your unit.

Condominium communities vary in size, price, and amenities. You will need information on all of the following in order to market it properly:

- Size of the community (number of people, not just number of units)
- Profile of people in the community
- Recreation and health facilities
- Parking and guest parking
- Security
- Assessment and inclusions
- Budget for management organization
- Insurance costs
- Sound-control features
- Mail delivery and laundry facilities
- How is the building secured? What type of system? do they have a guard?
- Available storage

Any one of these items can help differentiate your condominium from those in other communities in your area.

In addition to the fact sheet you would prepare for a home, there are a number of documents you should have ready for the prospective buyer of a condominium. You should have most of the following:

- A breakdown of the monthly maintenance charges
- A copy of the codes, covenants, and restrictions (CC&Rs)

- Assessments (or maintenance fees)
- Community profile

Be sure to have all the information above listed in your fact sheet. Make plenty of copies, since buyers are more likely to take fact sheets for condos than they are for homes.

Tip 340: Be sure the buyer understands that maintenance for the condo is similar to the maintenance for a home.

Many potential first-time condominium buyers view the maintenance charges as an add-on burden of expense. You need to show that, in reality, they would experience the same type of operating and maintenance costs in any form of home ownership. The difference here is that the costs are specified and spread over time. This way the buyer may be spending $100 per month toward maintenance, but he won't be hit with a one time $3,000 roof repair when he's short of cash.

Reduce the maintenance charge into separate items and then compare the list to the costs of running a typical home. You will usually find the costs comparable. If anything, because of the economies of scale, condominium maintenance costs are less than those of single-family homes. The extra money goes to pay for the amenities.

Tip 341: Sell the advantages of home ownership.

Since many condominium buyers are first-time buyers, you will need to provide some extra education about the advantages of home ownership. Everything you take for granted, from tax reasons to equity build-up, are new topics to most of these people. There is some fear, because home ownership is new to them.

Many people are wary of tax changes. In a down market, they are much more acutely aware that there are tax advantages and disadvantages for everything they do. Make sure they understand that condo ownership has very significant tax advantages over renting.

Tip 342: Sell the amenities.

Many people would love to belong to a health club or a country club but can't afford it. Buying into a condominium community allows the buyer who seeks these luxuries the chance to have convenient access to them at an affordable price. Few owners of single-family homes can afford to build a tennis court, swimming pool, and sauna on the premises.

Amenities don't include just the swimming pool. They include the conveniences of condominium living such as property management by professionals, security, lower cost, and freedom from the responsibility of maintaining a home. Even free parking can be considered a major amenity.

To most people, having a day to play tennis or read a book is more appealing than mowing the lawn or shoveling snow. Appeal to people's desire for the good life. Educate people to the positive qualities of the condominium lifestyle: low maintenance, lots of free time, good recreational facilities.

Tip 343: You are selling the condominium lifestyle, not just a single unit.

When people buy into a condominium community, the term *lifestyle* takes on a lot more importance than in buying a typical home. You are marketing not just your unit, but really the entire community.

Not everyone is selling a detached single-family home, and frankly, today not everybody wants one. Many of today's consumers are dollar rich and time poor.

Tip 344: Make friends with the resident manager.

The resident manager wields a lot of power. He or she needs to be a second salesperson for you. This person is someone that a prospective buyer is probably going to want to talk to, so educate him in the ways of marketing.

Sometimes the resident manager gets calls from people interested in living in the complex. He or she could send these inquiries to you to act on. Real estate agents with a buyer are also likely to call the manager. If you are friends with the manager and he or she knows that you are selling, you are more likely to get calls.

If many people in your community are selling, it is especially important to be friendly with the manager. It is a good idea to have the manager walk through your unit when it first goes on sale. Make sure to tell him or her what you have done to make your unit better than the others so that, when the manager is asked by real estate agents, your unit will stand out as special.

Tip 345: Get the word out to the other residents.

It is essential that the condo community know of your impending sale. Most are vitally interested in their neighbors. They may know of someone who hopes to move in.

Is signage permitted? Is there a very visible place you can post a sign? The sign does not necessarily have to be in the window of the actual unit for sale and usually should not be.

Tip 346: It takes two to properly show a condominium.

When presenting your condominium, whether it be at an open house or by appointment, you need to observe the same rules as would apply to marketing any home.

Get the key or lock combination of the recreational facilities of the complex. These amenities are a critical element in many condominium sales. Many buyers who are lukewarm on the unit will buy if the amenities excite them. Get the emotions going.

Before placing a sign, check for regulations regarding their size and display. Some associations require the sign to be of a particular size or color.

Leave a brochure at the front desk. The brochure should include a map of the complex, with the best route to reach the unit clearly marked. Note that the best route may not be the most direct. Rather, it might be the one that walks the buyer by the amenities or views first. The brochure should also include pertinent information about the unit itself, as you would do with any home.

For open houses, it is advisable to have two people hosting. One will remain in the unit, the other can escort interested prospects through the recreational facilities and common areas. In the worst case, if you are alone, and you have a hot prospect, walk him or her down to the recreational facilities and leave a note on the door that you will be back in 15 minutes.

Plan the timing of the open house to correspond with the image you want to project. If on Sunday afternoons the pool gets crowded with kids and is noisy, you may want to hold an evening open house or event when the recreational facilities are quieter.

Tip 347: Give the buyer a good first impression.

The curb appeal of your condo starts with the neighborhood, progresses to the building's front door, and continues eventually to your own. In this case, the building's front entrance is significantly more important than your own, but you have less control over it. The problem with most large buildings is they are more imposing than a house. Anything you can do to lessen that feeling will go a long way. You need to soften it and make the entrance welcoming.

If you are in a complex with a doorman, slip him a few dollars to greet your guests extra warmly the day of the showing. If you have appointments, call down their names to the doorman, so he can greet them properly. A caring smile and being greeted by name can go a long way toward making a good first impression on a potential buyer.

Tip 348: The common area of your condo or co-op is your "entry" in the buyer's eyes.

Unfortunately, the common areas are usually the first thing to go in a condominium complex. Homeowner's associations usually have a hard time spending money on upgrading an item when it is still functional. So, although the entry carpet looks a bit worn and makes a negative impression on buyers, it is unlikely you'll be able to get the association to replace it in time for your home sale.

The entry should be cleaned up and the carpets shampooed, and the place should look and feel in top shape. You need to lobby the association to do this. If it doesn't, ask the maintenance man to do it, or to just pay and have it done yourself. You need to make the place shine. Sensory impressions are critical. Smart management knows the effect an entrance has on residents and potential applicants. However, not all management is so alert.

How will they enter the unit? Just like the approach to a house, the approach to your condo is a key point. Knowing that security is one of the main reasons people buy condominium homes, you need to be able to answer questions concerning the unit's security. Is there a guard? Is there some sort of security system? Even better is to give buyers the feeling of security from the minute they walk through the door.

Tip 349: Renovate your condo to make it what people are looking for in attached housing.

Today's buyers are looking for exciting home design but with all the urban conveniences. When renovating your condominium, use the same rules as in a single-family home. Make it light, make it feel spacious, and make it so comfortable that the buyer wants to take off his shoes and stay awhile. For instance, if you are on the top floor, see if you can add a skylight.

In general, try to make your condo *not* feel like an attached home. If you are having major repairs done before a sale, consider adding amenities that you would add to a house. If there are other units for sale at the same time as yours, this will make yours seem more like an ideal home than the others.

PART IV

The Financial Angles

CHAPTER THIRTY-TWO

Financing Alternatives

Financing is a scary subject for most home sellers. The fear usually comes from feelings of insecurity because they don't understand how financing works. Financing is just using someone else's money in order to buy the home. When you use financing, you buy the use of someone else's money for a limited amount of time. Just like negotiating the price of a house or a car, the price of the money a buyer pays for is very important. Lower interest rates, better payment terms, and other options effectively lower the cost of money to a buyer or make it suit his lifestyle or payback ability better.

Financing is really not very complicated. There are basically three types covered in home transactions: conventional, government programs, and "creative" or other financing options.

Tip 350: No financing for the buyer means no sale for you.

You may wonder why a book like this would spend so much time emphasizing financing when it is the buyer, not the seller, who should be worried about this. In a down market, there are fewer buyers, and those buyers have a harder time getting a loan to buy your house. Understanding financing is not trivial, but it isn't all that difficult, either. If you know how to help a buyer get a loan and another seller doesn't, guess whose house will be sold and whose won't?

Unless you've got that elusive all-cash buyer, you are going to have to arrange some sort of financing or hope that the buyer is sophisticated enough to do it. After all the preparation you have done to get your house marketed, advertised, and seen, the last thing you want to do is have the sale fall short because of some fears or misunderstandings. In a down market, people are often even more scared of banks and their rules than in a normal market: don't let this get in the way of your sale.

The burden falls on you and your agent if you want to really sell your home. Learn financing to help the buyer and sell your home. The time you invest is, of course, applicable to other transactions that you will make in your life. It is likely that you are going to buy a house again within the next few years. What you learn now to help the buyer will help you when you are a buyer yourself.

> **Tip 351: Financing is a crucial element in all real estate transactions, especially in a down market.**

Financing a home purchase is one of the major hurdles to consummating a sale. Few people have a couple of hundred thousand dollars in their pockets to pay all cash. Financing is usually avoided by brokers until it must be faced, out of necessity. This is because most real estate salespeople are afraid of financing, too. This leaves most salespeople unable to supply the complexities and creativity that must be used to successfully complete a transaction in a down market.

Why should financing be more important in a down real estate market? As you have probably read in the newspapers, many banks now have large portfolios of "bad" or "questionable" mortgages: mortgages from people who might not be able to pay them back. If someone can't pay back a mortgage, the bank takes away that person's home and sells it. The bank takes what is still owed to it on the mortgage and gives the unlucky owner whatever is left from the sale price. Recourse on loans is described later in the book.

In a down market, foreclosure sales earn much less money than in a regular market. Banks start finding that they can't make back what they are owed on the mortgage because the price of the house has fallen so low that it doesn't cover the owed amount. If a bank has too many bad or questionable mortgages, it can easily go out of business (that is, be taken over by the government).

Thus, banks are now much more wary about financing home sales, especially to new buyers who don't have much of a track record. In such a situation, it is your job to help the buyer find financing so that you can sell your home as quickly as possible.

Tip 352: You must understand financing to get maximum price.

The old adage in real estate is location, location, location. A quick second to that is financing, financing, financing.

In order to sell your home, especially if you are not using a real estate agent, you need to understand financing. This is a subject ignored by most home sellers (and many real estate agents too!), but one that can make or break a sale and help get you the highest possible price for your property.

When talking financing, there are two main routes to travel: conventional financing and creative financing. As with anything in life, if you stick with the average way, you'll tend to get average results. Creative financing does not have to mean "no money down," although it might, and in many cases is just as safe as conventional financing.

Besides conventional loans open to everyone, the government has some special programs which apply to many Americans. These include VA and FHA loans. Your knowledge of these programs and a buyer's eligibility for them might make all the difference in qualifying a buyer to purchase your property.

How much house a buyer can afford depends largely on the financing chosen. New financing under fixed rate, adjustable rate, VA, or FHA mortgages may all have different down-payment and income criteria. Because most banks tie repayment of the loan to a certain percentage of your income, if you have a lower monthly payment (because of a longer term of the loan, for example, or a lower interest rate) than you can qualify for a larger loan amount. Affordable housing is one of this country's biggest problems. By playing with the loan terms and financing structure, you can create a house that becomes affordable to a buyer without dropping your price.

Tip 353: Understand the components of a mortgage.

Financing is made up of many separate elements. Any and all of these are negotiable and will add to or detract from a property's value. Whether the buyer is assuming your loan or getting a new loan or you are providing the financing, be aware of the way in which altering these elements can add to your home's value. There are many books which go into much more detail about mortgages and their fine points.

Interest rate

The rate a person pays on the loan is called its interest rate. This rate determines the total amount of money a person will end up paying over the course of the loan. Up until ten years ago, most rates were fixed, so you knew how much you were paying. Now you must consider some of the following to calculate how much interest will actually be paid over the term of the loan:

- What index is the rate tied to?
- How frequently can the loan rate be changed?
- Is there a prepayment fee?
- What are the points and other origination fees?

Amortization

This is the term that describes how you pay down the principal of the loan. Whether the payments go mostly toward principal or interest in the initial years will affect the total amount paid over the course of the loan. How your loan is amortized also affects the payment amount. If you have a 30-year fixed-rate loan, you will find that little of the principal is paid off in the first five years and the majority in the last five. If your loan was amortized differently, you might be able to pay it off faster. When carrying back a loan, how you amortize it will affect the amount paid to you.

Term
This is how long the loan is for. Standard residential loans are usually 30 or 15 years. Most seller second mortgages are five to seven years. The terms and the amortization periods do not always coincide. You might have a loan amortized over 30 years but due in five. This keeps the buyer's payments down but doesn't leave you until you are old and gray to collect.

Loan priority and subordination
If you were a lender relying on the security interest in the property, you'd be upset and surprised to learn, after the buyer had defaulted, that someone else now has a security interest superior to yours and that there is no money left for you. Mortgages usually develop priority in the order they are placed. If you carry back a second mortgage and the buyer later decides to refinance, he has to pay off your loan unless you are willing to place it behind the new loan. Subordination is this placing of one loan behind another.

Subordination is very valuable to the buyer and can be dangerous to the seller, as in the example above. However, offering to subordinate can enhance the value of your property by allowing a buyer to refinance when rates get lower without paying you off. If you put significant restrictions on the subordination terms, you can build in safety and have a marketable asset.

Assumability
Making a loan assumable adds value to it, as it allows the property to be sold or transferred even in times of high rates or tight money. With an assumable loan, you can offer attractive financing to buyers and make money with an assumption fee should the loan ever be transferred.

Recourse versus nonrecourse
Most loans on single-family homes are nonrecourse. That is, the property is the only security for the loan. All the buyer's other as-

sets are protected. For example, if Buyer A purchases a home for $150,000 with standard nonrecourse financing from Seller B, and later values fall and the property goes into default, Seller B will have to foreclose. If the property is now worth only $120,000 and it cost Seller B $10,000 in legal fees to get it back, he's now out $40,000. If the loan had been a recourse loan, he could get a deficiency judgement and collect against Buyer A's other assets. However, with a nonrecourse loan, he's got only the property.

If you are carrying back a significant part of the purchase price and the buyer has put down very little cash, go for a recourse loan. This will be your protection. Note that recourse loans are only as good as the buyer's assets.

All these components of loans are interchangeable and negotiable. For example, when dealing with a buyer and offering financing, you might be able to get the recourse loan if you lower your interest rate by a point and lengthen the term of the loan from five to seven years.

Tip 354: Real estate financing is flexible.

In this age of standardization, people are led to believe that the only way to buy a home is with a standard down payment and financing the balance. If a buyer wishes to put only 5% down, he or she is usually told that it will be impossible to find financing. If the buyer wishes to put 50% down, he or she is told he is throwing money away and not taking advantage of leverage and tax shelter opportunities. Unless the buyer puts 20% or 25% down, many real estate agents, buyers, and sellers feel uncomfortable. The reason for the discomfort is insecurity and a lack of knowledge. Don't be intimidated by a real estate agent without a flexible mind. Creativity is the key to negotiating a good deal.

The problem with standardization is it makes the value judgment that what is standard is good and what is not is bad, or at least suspect. You must overcome these attitudes first in your own mind and than in the minds of others. In a bad market, one can't afford to take the easiest way out. It is the creative mind that will succeed where others just throw up their hands in frustration.

Tip 355: Analyze the existing financing first, since it might be a selling point for your house.

Before looking at how to finance a sale, you should spend some time analyzing the loan currently on your property. Is it assumable? Does it have a good interest rate (in order to know this you need to learn the market)? How much can you refinance the loan for, and would that be an assumable loan to a new buyer? You may be able to provide better financing than the competition and thus make your home more saleable to marginal buyers.

Assuming a mortgage occurs when a formal agreement between the buyer and the lender is executed. This removes the seller's liability for the repayment of the loan. An assumption usually requires fee (1 point is common) and, very likely a change in interest rate.

If you have a fixed loan at 9% and current interest rates are 11%, a buyer will be able to save substantial amounts of money over the course of the loan by assuming, or taking over, your existing loan. You can often get a higher price because of these more favorable terms.

A buyer can usually save about 4% in loan origination fees by assuming an existing loan rather than originating a new one. On a $100,000 loan, you've just saved the buyer $4,000. Shouldn't some of that be added to the price?

Tip 356: Market the advantages of seller financing to the buyer.

There's no reason to enter into seller financing except to sell your home quickly or for a higher price. But unless the market understands what you are offering, you may be giving away your advantages. Some good reasons the buyer might want your financing are the following:

- He may be creditworthy but have only a limited amount of cash.

- The buyer has enough for a down payment but not for closing costs, too.

- The buyer can have special terms and provisions in the mortgage that would never appear in standard documents.

- The buyer might be allowed to include personal property in the purchase, such as using a boat as part of the down payment.

- The buyer can buy a property that does not meet the appraisal guidelines of most lenders.

Tip 357: You can be flexible with seller mortgages.

Seller financing allows you to negotiate other areas besides price. This flexibility creates the possibility for win-win situations between buyer and seller. Some major areas for flexibility are:

- Interest rate

- Term of the loan

- Collateral in addition to the property as security to the lender

- Whether there is a balloon payment or not

- Points, fees, and penalties

- Allowing personal property or services as part of the down payment or payment schedule

---

Tip 358: If your mortgage is not assumable, think about taking title "subject to."

Some loans have "due on sale" clauses and are not assumable. Check the fine print before advertising your loan as assumable. Even if it is not assumable, don't give up. You may still be able to restructure it to help out a buyer.

One way buyers have gotten around due on sale clauses is to purchase a property "subject to." By purchasing "subject to," the buyer continues to make the payments on the existing loan and hopes the lender will not find out.

When taking title "subject to" (assuming the loan without a formal agreement), nothing is done to notify the lender. However, the primary responsibility for the repayment of the loan still rests with the original borrower (the seller). If the property goes into default, the lender would foreclose. If sale of the property does not yield enough to cover the loan balance, the lender may get a deficiency judgment against the original borrower.

If the buyer has put down sufficient equity that it is unlikely he will walk away from the property, a "subject to" transaction is relatively safe for the seller and is often the only way to pass on good loan terms to a buyer. Don't rely on your real estate broker; use your attorney to put together the proper wording for a "subject to" agreement.

Tip 359: Before cutting your price, look at changing your terms.

Don't be scared by the headlines that say prices are falling. You have one job and one job only: to solve your prospective buyer's needs so that he can buy your house. Use financing as a problem solver.

There are a number of different areas where you can help. You can carry some of the financing or find a low-down-payment loan. If the buyer doesn't have much cash, look to FHA and VA loans as options when marketing your home.

If you provide seller financing, you can work with the buyer on the interest rate, the term of the loan, whether or not there will be a balloon payment, or any number of other options, without effecting the price.

Tip 360: Offer to prepay closing costs and financing costs to attract buyers.

Financing and closing costs can add up to 4% to the purchase price in cash. These days, fewer buyers have that extra cash. If you offer to pay their finance charges, you can increase your pool of qualified buyers.

Tip 361: Beware of penalties.

When a bank makes a loan, the borrower is making a promise to pay a specified sum of interest over the life of the loan. This interest is the bank's earnings. In order to discourage quick payoffs of loans and thus lose much of their anticipated income, some loans contain prepayment penalties.

Prepayment penalties can often be waived if the new loan is made by the same lender. The payoff penalty is often sizable, so it is advisable to contact the lender as soon as possible to discuss what options and policies will apply to the new buyer.

CHAPTER THIRTY-THREE

Types of Loans

> **Tip 362: Conventional loans are only your first line of attack.**

"Traditional" financing has been around only since the 1930s, when Franklin Delano Roosevelt decided that one way out of the depression was to make people feel confident taking out loans again. This is when the 30-year, self-amortizing loan was invented. Before that, it had been traditional for buyers to put down a significant down payment, sometimes in excess of 50%, to buy a home and then have only a short time, such as five years, to pay the loan off, with no assurance it would be renewed. When talking financing, many real estate agents act as if conventional financing were the eleventh commandment. Most of them are uncomfortable with anything they don't understand, and the average agent selling homes has not kept up with the latest changes in the financing market.

In conventional financing, the buyer comes up with a standard down payment (usually 20%) and a bank or savings and loan finances the balance. In a well-balanced market, where there are many buyers, this system works fine. In a market where sellers are cutthroat and competition is keen, this position must become the fallback position.

During the 1980s, many lenders went from being portfolio lenders (lenders which hold their own loans), to lenders who sell their loans on the secondary market. This has led to lenders becoming more and more restrictive in making unconventional loans. Before the inflation of the late 1970s, most lenders were portfolio lenders. They took in funds from the community and made loans. But when their 6%, 7% and 8% loans for 30 years almost bankrupted them during the inflationary 1970s, banks shifted to becoming loan processors rather than holders of loans.

The secondary market works as follows: A lender uses its own funds to make loans to borrowers. When it has accumulated a certain amount of loans, such as $5 or $10 million worth, it repackages them and sells them to investors such as the Federal National Mortgage Association (FNMA, also known as Fannie Mae). Because Fannie Mae has standardized guidelines for the loans it will buy, if a lender makes a loan that doesn't fit into these strict categories, it may be stuck holding the loan. This means a lender would be stuck holding a long-term loan, usually at a fixed interest rate, made with money borrowed at short-term rates. An excess of these loans can bankrupt a lender should short-term money rates climb.

Tip 363: Veteran's Administration loans are just as good in a down market as in an up market.

In 1942, Congress passed the Serviceman's Readjustment Act, commonly known as the GI Bill of Rights. One section of that legislation guaranteed home loans to eligible veterans. However, less than one third of those eligible for VA loans have used them since the program was founded in 1942. This means millions and millions of people are walking away from buying a home they might otherwise qualify for simply because *they don't know about this program or how it works*. This is where your knowledge can be helpful. Not only can a veteran and his or her spouse get a VA loan, but there are others who are eligible as well:

- Widows of veterans are eligible for VA loans if the veteran's death was caused by a service related injury or ailment and if the widow has not remarried.

- Any U.S. citizen who served in the armed forces of a country allied with the United States in World War II is eligible.

- A common-law spouse is equivalent to a spouse in the eyes of the VA. This means that her income can be used to qualify for a VA loan.

You don't need to fully understand how the programs work, but you do need to know if someone potentially qualifies. The first question you might ask a buyer is if he or she is a veteran or is eligible for a VA loan.

Some of the main advantages of a VA loan are these :

- No down payment. Up to a loan of $144,000 (1990), no down payment is required. For loans exceeding $144,000, a buyer may need up to 25% of the amount over $144,000. (Note: each lender has slightly different requirements.)

- Assumability. VA loans are assumable ($500 funding fee plus ½% assumption fee.) This means that when your buyer goes to sell, he or she will have an easier time qualifying the buyer.

- Rate. Loan rate are typically below those of conventional fixed-rate loans.

- Prepayment. VA loans have no prepayment penalty.

- Easier qualifying guidelines. Because of the way the VA looks at income, size of family, and so on, a buyer doesn't need to make as much money as he or she would with a conventional lender.

Tip 364: If the buyer doesn't qualify for VA but has a small downpayment, try an FHA loan instead.

The Federal Housing Administration (FHA), a division of the U.S. Department of Housing and Urban Development, provides mortgage insurance to private institutional lenders to facilitate home ownership. FHA loans currently account for 25% of all home mortgages, a significant amount by anyone's definition. The FHA works the same way as the VA. It does not write its own loans; it guarantees loans. This guarantee allows lenders to take risks that they otherwise wouldn't because instead of banking on you as a credit risk, they're banking on the U.S. government.

Typically, someone looking for an FHA loan might have some of the following characteristics:

- Needs a qualifying interest rate lower than the market rate

- Has a low down payment, usually 5%

- Desires a loan that is assumable and has no prepayment penalty

---

Tip 365: Hook up with a good mortgage broker.

If your buyer gets turned down for a conventional mortgage, it doesn't mean he or she is not creditworthy. Because so many loans these days are sold on the secondary market, if a buyer doesn't fall into very standardized categories, it is easy for a lender to turn him or her down. That's why so many alternative programs have sprung up.

The first step in selling your home conventionally is to know if your buyers are qualified. Many an hour has been wasted on well-intentioned buyers who just couldn't qualify for a loan. By locating a good mortgage broker you can get a handle on the various loan programs available to buyers.

A loan broker can also see how good your existing loan is in relation to these and whether it is assumable. He or she can also get buyers to start qualifying themselves quickly, so both you and they know what they can afford.

Working with a good mortgage broker can save you time, because the broker is familiar with the various programs of different lenders and can switch you around with relative ease. Many of the lenders that work with mortgage brokers will not accept loans directly from an individual borrower. Mortgage brokers also understand the complexities of finance and can guide your purchasers into what might otherwise be scary territory.

However, mortgage brokers work on commission, so you want to make sure the lender is paying the commission, not you. And many mortgage brokers don't have control over the lenders they work with although they may lead you to believe that they do.

Tip 366: If the buyer won't qualify, refinance and have the buyer assume the new loan.

A buyer may just miss qualifying for a new loan. One way to make the deal still possible is to refinance your mortgage and then have a new buyer assume it. The bank will qualify the new buyer, but usually it is a rubber-stamp approval. Even if you don't have a buyer ready, it always helps to have an attractive assumable loan on your property for a good percentage of the asking price.

Refinancing takes the pressure off of selling now if you are currently cash poor. By pulling cash out of your home, you give yourself a mental as well as a financial cushion from the current market conditions. An alternative to refinancing if you need the cash is to take out a home equity loan.

Tip 367: Use a buydown to help qualify the buyer.

This is a financing technique used by builders to qualify people who would otherwise not qualify for a loan. It falls under the category of creative financing but is put here because of its special applicability when used in conjunction with FHA or VA loans.

A buydown is an excellent marketing technique. For example, if interest rates are 11%, then you could arrange a temporary interest-rate buydown so that the buyer pays 8% the first year, 9% the second year, 10% the third year, and the full 11% from years four through 30. Although this costs you some of your profit, you can get a home sold to a buyer who would otherwise not qualify. Both the VA and the FHA will qualify a buyer on the first year's interest rate, so a buydown can allow you to have a larger pool of qualified buyers.

A buydown is also a great way to attract buyers during times of high interest rates. If rates are 12%, than you could offer a loan at 10% the first year, 11% the second, and finally the full rate in the third year. During times of high rates, low starting rates attract buyers.

Tip 368: Lenders have a full smorgasbord of mortgage plans.

Carrying a second mortgage isn't the only way to sell a home. It's usually best to let the bankers do the banking anyway. Buyers prefer sellers to carry the financing. Sellers rarely charge points and they don't even have to fill out those long and bothersome loan applications. So the buyer's natural tendency is to ask you to carry paper. You will probably have to do the searching for him to find an appropriate mortgage structure for his needs.

If your buyer has an irregular income or some other credit blemish, a large down payment will allow him to qualify. Although this book has mostly talked about low down payments, many people can afford larger ones. Banks conventionally will loan when a buyer puts down 20% of the purchase price. They are willing to loosen their terms if they see the buyer putting down more because they know their investment will be safe. If a buyer puts 25% down, his qualifying ratios don't matter anymore. Such buyers are known as "quick qualifiers."

Tip 369: Adjustable-rate loans usually allow for easier qualifying.

These have become as common as fixed-rate loans and can practically be termed traditional financing. A fixed-rate loan has a constant interest rate and equal monthly payments. Adjustable-rate mortgages (ARM) may have both interest rate and payment shifts, depending on the market. Lenders prefer ARMs because they shift some of the interest rate risk from the lender to the buyer.

In a negative amortization loan, your initial payments are low to make it easier to pay it back. They may be too low, however, to pay down the loan, especially ARMs which can have the payments go up at times when you are unable to pay them. This can be dangerous since you end up owing more, not less, as you pay off the loan.

Many ARMs do not have negative amortization. The advantage to ARMs is that they can be customized to amortize over shorter periods of time (such as 15 or 20 years), saving the buyer thousands of dollars in interest.

Because starting rates are usually several points lower on an adjustable-rate loan, the buyer is able to qualify more easily or to qualify for more house than he would be able to under a conventional fixed-rate mortgage. Adjustables are usually assumable, too, so it will be easier for your buyer to sell a few years down the road.

Tip 370: Graduated Payment Mortgages (GPMs) can help buyers who think they will be earning more in the future.

A graduated payment mortgage (GPM) is a great loan for young couples or others who can expect a significant rise in income over the life of the loan. A GPM lowers the buyer's payments during the early years of a loan when a buyer has a smaller income and raises them during the later years, when the buyer is supposedly earning more. In general, the increase in payments occurs during the first five years of the loan and then payments remain fixed. This can be accomplished by charging the buyer the full amount of the loan but requiring the buyer to pay only a small amount initially. The difference is added to the loan and paid off over time.

What this means for your buyer is that he can afford a larger house, or that his payments are smaller, leaving him more money to live on. Later, as his income rises, he can afford the larger payments. You win, and he wins.

Tip 371: If the buyer is going to stay in the house for ten or twenty years, look at Growth Equity Mortgages (GEMs).

Sometimes leverage isn't the only thing a buyer wants. Many buyers want to save on the interest they pay to lenders: thus the growing popularity of the bi-weekly mortgage. Another program that lenders offer is the Growth Equity Mortgage (GEM). The GEM is a fixed rate loan with annual payment increases of 3 to 7.5 percent, depending on the plan chosen. Why would someone want annual payment increases? It allows the buyer to pay off the loan in 13 to 15 years instead of the full 30.

Under the GEM, some lenders qualify buyers at a rate 2 or 3 percent below the initial rate, allowing them to purchase a larger home now. This program is especially good for those who expect their incomes to grow and for those who wish to make this home their final one.

CHAPTER THIRTY-FOUR

Creative Financing

Back in the early 1980s, when interest rates were 20%, home sellers had to resort to creative financing to sell their homes. Many were burned by fast-buck artists and "no money down" people. This has given creative financing a bad name. Yet it may be your ticket to getting the best price and terms for your home.

When Detroit had problems selling cars back in the mid-1980s, there was low-interest financing, while at the same time manufacturers raised their prices. What had formerly been a stagnant market suddenly became hot as buyers rushed to buy, taking advantage of the great financing. With the higher prices, though, they weren't getting nearly as good a deal as they thought. In the same vein, you can use financing to help you get top dollar for your home and a quick sale in a down market.

Creative financing is commonly used. It is simply having the seller receive something less than all cash for the house or the buyer having more than a single mortgage. The best definition of creative financing I've heard is that it is buyer and seller working together.

A word of caution, though. Some alternative and creative financing techniques put the seller more at risk than a conventional loan. So you must be extra careful in qualifying your purchaser as to his desire and ability to repay the loan.

Tip 372: Contracts for deed can help sell your house and possibly make you more money in the long run.

Under a contract for deed, the buyer makes a down payment to the seller and purchases the home without receiving title at the time of purchase. The seller receives payments from the buyer and keeps paying the lender on his original loan. The lender never discovers that you sold the house. This is an easy form of creative financing, but one filled with risks.

The contract for deed is similar in concept to the lease option. The main reason for using a contract for deed is to defeat a due on sale clause. Because title does not transfer with the contract, it is a little tougher for a lender to detect than an actual sale.

The major advantages of this type of deal are:

- Little or no down payment required. It's totally up to you what you need from the buyer. Bear in mind, though, that the less you receive from the buyer, the more incentive he has to walk away from the deal if things get tough for him.

- Because you retain title, you have the security of taking the property back easily if the buyer defaults.

- The buyer can get in with little expense because of the security the seller has.

- Homes with sale-contract terms tend to sell quickly.

- No appraisal.

- No closing costs.

- A quick sale. Closings are fast. In many cases a contract can be closed in a week or two. Contracts can be tricky, so get good professional help.

The disadvantages of this type of arrangement fall mostly on the buyer. The major disadvantage to the buyer is that the buyer is not the owner of record until all the terms of the contract are fulfilled. The buyer is risking buying a property without clear title. Anything that happens to the seller after the time of the "sale" but before all the conditions of the contract have been met can cloud the title.

The only disadvantage for the seller is in the potential for default. Although it is easy to get your property back, you don't really want to. By maximizing the down payment, you give the buyer incentive not to walk from the property. Buyers usually encounter a problem when the balloon payment comes due. It is up to you whether you want to foreclose or are willing to renegotiate terms, usually for a premium to you.

Because of the potential pitfalls, there should be an agreement between the parties as to what course of action should be taken should problems arise. Recording the contract for deed is one way of protection. However, it is possible this could bring the sale to the eyes of the lender. The buyer can also be protected if you give him a second lien on the property to cover the contract for deed. Because the contract for deed would not be recorded in this case, the lender would not be aware of any ownership transfer.

Tip 373: You can carry a second mortgage or other junior lien.

A second mortgage is created when a buyer doesn't have enough money to come up with the entire purchase price between his down payment and the loan from the lender. For example, if a buyer is purchasing a house for $150,000 and is assuming an existing loan of $90,000, there is a difference of $60,000 that must be found to reach the entire purchase price. Few buyers have this amount of cash, nor would they necessarily want to put it all into the house if they did. So let's say the buyer comes up with $35,000. The difference (the remaining $25,000) would be in the form of a second mortgage to the seller. The mortgage would normally be secured by the property, although it could be secured by something else the buyer owns.

Second mortgages usually have a shorter term than firsts, usually under 15 years. Most seller seconds are even shorter, such as 3, 5, or 10 years. If the blended interest rate of the two mortgages is attractive, you can get even more creative.

Second mortgages help facilitate the sale of your property by providing funds to the buyer that he could not get otherwise. Seconds are also a wonderful way to make up the difference be-

tween the remaining balance on a low-interest-rate first loan and
the price you want to get.

**Tip 374: Second mortgages are a good source of
high-yield investment funds.**

If you sold your home for all cash, what would you do with the
money? Many people would be investing it in bank CDs paying
7% or 8%. Others might gamble it in the stock market. If you
don't have a vehicle for your funds that will yield you more than
the 11% or 12% you can ask on your second mortgage, than carrying a second could be a great investment for you.

**Tip 375: If you are carrying a second, act like a
bank.**

You want to make sure your loan is going to be paid. Sure, you
could always foreclose on the property, but that can cost a lot of
money, and it isn't what you really want anyway. You want to sell
your home and collect the proceeds.

When taking back a second mortgage, imitate the pros. Banks
have developed procedures and policies over many years because they've been burned many times. Don't learn the hard
way; imitate the pros when financing a second on your property.
Some steps to take when carrying a second include these:

- Order a complete credit report. You want to make
  sure the buyer has a good history of paying his debts

- Analyze the buyer's ability to pay. What percentage
  of his income will be going to pay the mortgage and
  other debts?

There is no correct way to set terms or collect payments on your
second. You are the bank: you set the terms. Be flexible and create
a win-win situation.

Here are some terms that protect the seller:

- A due on sale clause. As you know, most lenders have these now. This protects you. If market rates go higher than your loan rate, you'd like to be paid off. This will never happen if your rate is better than the market. A new buyer will just want to keep your mortgage in place.

- Late penalties. All lenders charge late fees. You must too. Otherwise, how are you going to force your payments to be timely. Charge the maximum allowable by law. If the buyer is a timely payer, he won't have any objection to that.

- Prepayment penalties. It is rare that a seller puts a prepayment penalty into the mortgage and they are illegal in some areas. Yet this is just one area where amateurs get caught up in imitating amateurs instead of professional lenders. By putting in the penalty, you increase your investment yield if the buyer pays off early. And if you sell your loan, investors will love this option, too, making your loan more saleable.

Tip 376: A second mortgage doesn't mean you have to wait years for your money.

There are two typical ways of dealing with a second mortgage once it is created. One is to collect your payments for the term of the loan and then receive the balance at the end. But this can take three, five, seven or more years. The other common method is to sell your second at a discount for cash now.

The reason for discounting is to give an outside investor an incentive to purchase your mortgage. You may have created a five-year mortgage at 11% interest only, with a balloon payment at year 5. But you did that to sell your house. An outside investor might not think 11% was a good enough return considering the risk involved. These risks include the buyer getting sick, being unable to make payments, or willfully defaulting on the loan. Such risk might require 18% to an outsider. To get this, you charge less than the face value of the note. Now the cash flow, which is 11% of the face value, becomes 18% of the discounted value.

One way to get around taking a hit on the discount is to add some or all of it to the second mortgage. Sure, you are shifting the burden of the discount to the buyer, but because of the length of the mortgage and the financing terms, it usually translates into only a few more dollars per month. To do this, you must get the buyer to agree to a higher price. If you can show him how little it affects his terms, you might be able to have him cover the whole discount. Or you could split it.

Tip 377: Carry several mortgages, and discount only one for ready cash.

Instead of carrying a $25,000 second mortgage, why not carry a $10,000 second and a $15,000 third? It's legal, and it's safe as long as the equity is really there. The advantage to this method is that you can still sell the second on the secondary market at a discount, but now only a portion of your carryback is discounted. On the remainder you still receive monthly payments and eventually all the principal, too.

Why sell the second and not the third? Because a second mortgage is more readily salable and salable at a lower discount than a third mortgage.

Now, suppose that instead of that $15,000 third mortgage, you break it into a $6,000 third and a $9,000 fourth mortgage and you use the third mortgage as a commission payment. Most brokers object to carrying paper as a commission: they want cash. It's a shame, because many agents are actually poor money managers and a steady cash flow is one of the things they need most in a business that is feast or famine.

Tip 378: Be sure to give yourself some protection.

Getting your property back through foreclosure can be time-consuming and laborious. And there's no certainty that you'll get it back in good condition when you take possession. Best to guard against the risks now, so you lessen their chance of occurring.

- Don't sign any agreement that commits you to provide financing without your attorney first reviewing it. Don't trust standard forms.

- Make sure the terms you give the buyer are within the standards of the secondary-mortgage market. This will make it easier to resell the loan should you want to or have to. Ask a mortgage broker who deals in seconds what the current standards are. Also talk to mortgage brokers to find out what type of discount you would have to take in order to sell your loan.

- Run a credit check on the buyer. Make sure he has the desire to pay, even if his ability is stretched a little. A person with excellent credit makes the payments even if he has to suffer for a little while.

- Take out private mortgage insurance on your loan.

Tip 379: Be careful about the mortgages ahead of your seller mortgage.

You need to evaluate carefully what is underlying your mortgage. If you are carrying a second, and the buyer has a fixed-rate first ahead of your loan, you are fine. But beware of carrying a second behind a negatively amortizing adjustable rate mortgage. You might find your equity disappearing as the loan ahead of yours gets larger and larger each month.

Tip 380: A wraparound mortgage can make it much easier for a buyer to get a loan if you already have a good mortgage.

A wraparound or wrap mortgage, also known as an all-inclusive trust deed (AITD), is a creative method of financing property. Technically, only assumable loans can be legitimately wrapped within a new AITD. A wrap becomes profitable when the underlying loans are at a low, fixed rate of interest. This is because you intend to wrap the existing low interest rate loan with a new higher rate loan and earn the profit on the spread in interest rates.

This method of financing is also ideal when you have a large equity in the property. A wraparound is an excellent way to sell your home for a premium. You could run an add stressing a low down payment. Wraps are much easier to explain by showing an example:

> Suppose you own a home with $84,000 remaining on the first mortgage. This loan is assumable and carries an interest rate of 9%. Current rates are 12%. Your home is worth $140,000 today, and you want to sell. Although your low-interest-rate loan is desirable to a buyer, few people would want to put down $56,000 in cash to assume the $84,000 loan. For one thing, not many people have that much cash, and for another, it is rare that anyone puts 40% down on a house. He or she would rather buy a larger or nicer house.
>
> So you create a wraparound mortgage at 11%. The buyer puts down his 10% down payment of $14,000 and now has a loan of $126,000 at 11%. Each month that you receive the $1,200 payment, you continue to pay the amount due on your 9%, $84,000 loan, or $676. You pocket the extra $524 per month. The buyer wins, and you get a steady income. Once the underlying loan is paid off, you get the entire payment.

A wraparound loan has many advantages to the seller:

- Safety: Because you are making the payments, you know that the lenders are being paid. If the buyer misses a payment, you know instantly, not several months down the road when a bank notifies you that the buyer is in default.

- Yield: Because you set the payments on the wrap, you can increase your yield by increasing the spread between what you pay and what is paid to you.

- Price: Because of the advantageous terms (like low down payment), you create a vehicle that is very appealing to most buyers. This higher demand means you can ask a higher price. Also you save the buyer those expensive loan-origination fees.

Tip 381: You can imitate bank practices in your seller financing.

You can use some tricks banks have invented to help someone buy your home. Here are two:

Deferred-interest seller financing

You might wish to carry a second note from a buyer at no interest for a few years. You'll probably be able to get a higher price from a buyer with a gimmick like this, so essentially you *are* receiving interest in that form. Another variation is to defer part of the interest. You might set your note at 10%, perhaps receiving 8% in year 1 and deferring the remaining 2% until the loan is due. In year 2, you would get 9% and defer 1%. By doing this you can keep the mortgage payments closer to rent payments and let the buyer work his way up.

Graduated-payment seller financing

You can start the payments lower the first year and graduate them up in subsequent years to make it easier for the borrower to make payments. This is good only with a prepayment penalty on your note. Otherwise the buyer might sell quickly, and you would have been stuck with only the small initial interest payments.

Tip 382: Equity sharing is better than renting and can help a buyer get started.

Sometimes, despite doing everything right, you just can't seem to get the price you want for your house. Often, you know things will get better soon, but perhaps you're in a crunch because you already went out and bought another house or maybe you've been transferred and you just can't emotionally bear to let the house sit empty and unsold.

Equity sharing has been touted as the trend of the future. It's not. It's a way to solve two basic problems, the inability to rent your home for enough to cover your mortgage and to get the quality of tenant that would treat your home as an owner.

Problem 1: Negative cash flow.

Rents in many markets these days rarely cover the carrying costs of a single-family home, including taxes, insurance, and maintenance. Because equity sharing implies the resident receiving some of the appreciation, you can usually get above-market rents and not have to deal with maintenance.

Problem 2: Inability to rent.

Even though you may have a good property in a good neighborhood, you haven't been able to get the quality of tenant you would entrust your house with. You don't want to carry the mortgage payments on two houses. Equity sharing can fill the house with a qualified tenant.

Equity sharing allows you to carry a property that hasn't been selling without the hassles of renting:

- Management hassles: Few people like being called at 3am to fix a leaky faucet. You don't want to be in the landlord business.

- Vacancy problems: Many people would love to buy a house but simply can't afford it. By giving more people an opportunity, you find that your pool of potential residents is very large compared to the supply of available quality homes.

- Damage: Since the "tenant" is going to own a piece of the appreciation, he has every incentive to give the property full pride of ownership.

The resident also gets some advantages:

- No down payment: The down payment is the greatest obstacle for most would-be first time buyers. Equity sharing lets such a buyer get into an ownership position without having to have the money first.

- Tax deductions: Because these buyers are also owners, they can qualify for tax deductions that renters just can't get.

- Purchasing Power: Instead of saving for the down payment on a home in a lower-priced area, some people prefer to rent and use that money to spend on improving their lifestyle in a nicer neighborhood.

Tip 383: You need to educate potential buyers to the advantages of equity sharing.

Especially if you've already bought a new home and are stuck making two payments, you now can find an eager couple willing to carry the payments for a half-ownership in the house. Most people don't like paying above-market rents for this right. Show them that it's not them but the government that's paying the difference because of the tax benefits they'll receive.

Of the total payment of perhaps $1,000, perhaps $800 is for interest and property taxes, both of which are deductible. If they are paying $200 per month over market and you take $800 multiplied by their 28% tax bracket, they will get back $224 in tax savings: more than the extra $200 they think they're spending. Instead of losing $200 per month, they're actually making $24 per month by taking your offer.

Tip 384: Equity share can get you out of a bind quickly, especially if you've already bought a second house.

In order for this to be a good deal for you, too, you must eventually be paid. And you don't want to be old and gray when it happens. So put a time limit, say five years, on the deal. At that time, the buyer needs either to sell or to refinance the house to pay you off. Down markets rarely last five years, so the odds are good that the house will have appreciated by then. Even in the worst case, you've not lost a dime in the interim.

Tip 385: Lease options will increase your pool of buyers without incurring significant risk.

Lease option techniques are usually used by buyers who have little money now as a way to tie down a property and pay today's price in the future when the property is worth more. You can take advantage of this technique and it's something-for-nothing draw by offering your house for sale on a lease option.

By providing a lease option you dramatically open the pool of interested candidates. And, by increasing the supply of applicants, you can charge a premium rent on your home during the option period. Besides, the person optioning will give you an option payment (cash) for the right to tie up the property. This is cash that you can spend whether or not the buyer goes through with the option. Once again, it is a quick way out of a bind if you're currently making two mortgage payments. And, frankly, most lessees will end up purchasing once they are settled in rather than moving again—if the price is reasonable.

You can also use this "no or low money down" technique to get a higher price for your property. Let's say you have a house worth $100,000 using conventional financing. This would mean the buyer would have to come up with $20,000 plus closing costs and fees, or about $24,000. You can offer the house up for sale at $107,000, but needing only a $2000 option payment. There are a lot more people with $2000 in their hands than $24,000. Many of these people make good incomes, too. Once in your property, they have a strong incentive to buy, for full price, as they've now invested their option payment in addition to making higher monthly payments in order to make this work.

Many buyers want the option payment applied to the purchase price. And sometimes this can make or break a deal. The key to making this work is to set the monthly payments high enough to elicit a small positive cash flow. Thus, if you get $100 per month positive on the monthly payments by the optionees, after two years, you've collected $2,400 in addition to whatever interest it has earned in the bank. It's now a lot easier to apply that $2,000 option payment to the purchase price, knowing that they've paid it to you over the last two years, rather than walk away from the deal and losing their new "found" money.

Be sure to check the lessee's credit carefully, since these people may become your ultimate buyer. You are giving them possession of your home, and you need to be sure to get it back in the same condition if the deal is not consummated. Many real estate professionals discourage using lease options because so few of them become sales.

CHAPTER THIRTY-FIVE

Taxes

Selling your home for the best price in a down market is one challenge. Keeping the money afterward is another. No one likes to pay income taxes, but it's a fact of life. Yet, all too often, sellers never consider the consequences of their actions until April 15 rolls around. By then it is too late. The time to begin your tax planning is before you ever place the house on the market.

Tax laws allow you to pay less in taxes than you would otherwise, but only if your transaction is structured properly. Before formally putting your home on the market, a consultation with your tax preparer, attorney, or CPA could end up saving you thousands of dollars in federal, state, and local income taxes. This is money that you can either pocket or, if you want, cut from the price of the house to make it more attractive.

How you word your purchase agreement, the timing of the sale, your future home plans, and your age all affect the amount of taxes you will eventually pay. Once the home sale is complete, it is too late. All planning must be done before or while you are in the contract stage.

Tip 386: You must calculate your basis in order to know your potential taxable gain.

To figure out the profit you made on the sale of the house, first start with how much you paid for it. That figure is your tax "basis." To arrive at the adjusted-cost basis, add in the value of any capital improvements you've made to the house. Capital improvements are items that increase your property's value such as a new roof or an addition to the home.

Note that ordinary repairs do not count as capital improvements. Repairs are patching and painting, fixing the roof leak, and other routine maintenance items. Obviously, there can be some confusion as to what is an improvement and what is a repair. Contact a tax expert if you are unsure.

You do not have depreciation on a house unless you use it as income property (such as rental). If you have depreciation, you must see a tax advisor since the rules for depreciating property are complicated and change often.

As an example of how to calculate your adjusted basis, assume you bought your house for $120,000. You've made $15,000 of improvements. Your adjusted basis would be figured as follows:

Cost Basis	$120,000
Capital Improvements	$15,000
Adjusted Basis	$135,000

Tip 387: All costs of selling your house are tax deductible.

You can deduct the costs of selling your home from your sales price in determining your taxable gain. Repairs, which normally are not tax deductible, are deductible if they are made in order to prepare the property for sale. This is a great way to gain deductions while at the same time increasing the value of your home with smart renovations. To qualify as "preparing the property for sale," repairs must be made within 90 days of the signing of the sales contract.

Other deductible costs of sale include real estate commissions, title and escrow fees, attorney's fees, and transfer taxes, as in the following example:

Gross sales price	$195,000
Real estate commissions	$11,700
Documentary transfer tax	$215
Notary fees	$10
Document preparation	$50
Repairs needed for sale	$6,980
Adjusted sales price	$176,045

Now, figure the gain:

Adjusted sales price	$176,045
Adjusted Basis	$135,000
Gain	$41,045

Tip 388: Know the basic tax rules for selling your home to defer taxes.

The basic tax rule in home sales is as follows: If you sell your home at a profit and reinvest the proceeds in another house of equal or greater value within 24 months, you can defer paying tax on the profit. In other words, no tax on the sale now.

In addition to this basic rule, there are a few other guidelines for home selling which generally apply:

- If you sell your home at a loss, normally no tax is due.

- If you sell your home at a profit and don't buy another residence within 24 months, tax on your gain becomes due.

- If you are over 55 and you have lived in your home for at least five years, you may take a once-in-a-lifetime exclusion from federal tax of the first $125,000 of profit.

- If you sell your home at a profit and buy another home of lesser value within 24 months, you have to pay taxes on the gain, but it is less than if you bought nothing else.

Because tax laws are never simple and gain computations are not always straightforward, contact an expert before you assume you won't be paying any taxes.

Note that not everything can be deferred under these rules, only profit on your principal residence. If you have a home office and it takes up 10% of the area, than 10% of your taxable gain will have to be paid on the home office now. The rest can be deferred. Note that this applies only if you've been taking deductions for your home office, not just because a room that looks like one exists.

Another part of your home to which these rules might not apply is a part of it you rent out. Gains on the portion of your home that you rent out are taxable: the remainder, on the portion which is your principal residence, can be deferred.

As you can see, the tax consequences of selling a house are quite complicated. This book has not even touched on other issues such as deferred capital gains which can make a big difference in your decisions. In addition, tax laws change often and can be different for state and federal tax, depending on where you live. It is imperative that you get good tax advice before selling your house.

Tip 389: You want to avoid paying tax now if you wish to reinvest.

Although you will probably have to pay taxes eventually, deferral allows you to reinvest a larger amount in your next home, and thus have a smaller mortgage and less debt to pay off. If you pay taxes on the gain, you may lose up to 40% of it. The amount of additional taxes depends on your tax bracket. To see the actual effect, you should compute your tax liability with and without the sale of your home.

If you elect to defer payment of your taxes and you do not find another principal residence within two years, you are liable for both the tax and interest on the tax.

Tip 390: Waiting until you are 55 could save you thousands of dollars in taxes.

The tax law allows for one exclusion from paying tax when you sell your home. However, you must be over 55 to benefit from it. If you are currently nearing that age, waiting a few extra months could have a profound impact on your financial future.

Tip 391: Delay paying taxes with an installment sale.

For the most part, you don't have to pay tax on income until you receive it. One way to delay paying tax if you don't use the exclusion rule or roll it over into another personal residence is to stretch your receipt of payment over a couple of years. The major advantage of doing this to prevent a large tax bite in any one year and to keep you in a lower tax bracket.

Discuss with your tax advisor some possible scenarios for when you sell your house and what the different tax consequences might be.

Tip 392: Moving expenses can be tax deductible, too.

While you are right now concerned with selling your existing home, you might want to look ahead to see if your moving expenses can be tax deductible, too. The basic requirements to make moving deductible are these:

- The distance between the location of your new job and your old home must be at least thirty five miles more than the distance between your old job and your old home.

- Your move must be connected to your work at the new location.

There are some other requirements, too. But once you meet them, you can deduct your direct moving costs and some indirect ones, too, such as travel expenses and temporary living expenses while your new home is being readied. There are limits to the amounts that you may deduct, but the savings can total in the thousands.

CHAPTER THIRTY-SIX

It's Up to You

The Most Critical Sale You'll Ever Make

Selling your house in a down market can be frustrating. Long periods of time can go by when nothing seems to be happening. But the key is not to sit back and wait: take action. You need to constantly be asking two questions: "What else can I be doing to bring the home to my buyer?" and "What else can I do to insure I get a fair price for my house?" Make plans and then have the flexibility to respond to change and the market.

Control of your destiny is one key. Most people are willing to let others dictate their circumstances. Such a person lets the boss decide his or her pay rather than working to be worth the amount desired, lets parents and friends determine what career he or she should pursue, and let market conditions and a real estate agent's level of motivation dictate whether or not he or she can sell a house. You need to become action-oriented to produce results.

Be wary of using formulas. The suggestions in this book are a good start, but they are only suggestions. They are there to put you into a different mindset, to see a different way of selling your home in tough times. But every home is different. Use your creative imagination to conjure up the ideas that are appropriate to your market and circumstances.

There's no one here to carry you through the tough times. It is up to you to use your creativity, determination, and imagination to develop a marketing plan to sell your home and move on with your life. Some people get stuck with their homes on the market for three years, desperately waiting for an offer. Can you imagine putting your life on hold for three years? Use your mind, use your talent, but please, don't sit back and rot.

There are no panaceas. Markets get bad and property values go down. But even in the worst of markets, there are people selling homes and making money. Do your homework, put in the extra effort, and get out there. The little extra time and energy will reap you thousands of dollars in benefits and will save you months of agony and frustration.

Adjusting to Changes and Flexibility

A marketing plan is like a prescription; it is not a cure. Your goal is to keep the patient healthy. But sometimes, despite all your efforts, relapses or unexpected events occur. You need to manage your emotional state and keep yourself looking forward during these times.

Your ability to spot changing market conditions is crucial and a valuable skill to have. Interest-rate changes, banks dumping properties on the market, and bad newspaper articles will all affect you. The key is to adapt. Most people are using outdated strategies which are only partially effective when circumstances change.

If your home is not selling, review the value perception it creates in your prospects. Why aren't they buying? Why don't they sense the value you have created?

Is your property getting enough exposure? It is one matter to have no sales after 150 prospects have walked through the door, quite another when only three have.

The Secret of Success

It's really not a secret at all. Rather, it's a simple truism that has somehow escaped most sellers and professional agents. It's simply that you must be committed 100% to selling your house.

If you're not committed to try whatever it takes, than you might as well be satisfied with average results. Everyone who is selling "wants" to sell, but how many are really committed? If you were buying in your neighborhood and came across two houses that were equal in your mind, wouldn't you rather deal with the more committed seller?

It is the person who tries new things, who keeps his or her mind flexible and observant, who will get results. Most people are not really committed. Sure, they'll put in some energy initially, but when things get tough, they slacken off. That's when you need to keep up your enthusiasm and energy. A sale will often come just about the time you'd given up.

Yes, it will take more work. You need to put yourself out there, expose yourself to more people. Some of this will be uncomfortable. You may feel awkward. And most of it might not even work. But you must break through your fears. The way to keep on having a fear is to ignore it. The only way to overcome a fear is to act. Once you've tried something and seen it can't hurt you, the fear seems to vanish.

You must be committed and you must have persistence. Don't get discouraged. It may take some time, but eventually you'll hook up with the right buyer. Trying something for a week or two and then dropping it is not the professional way to market. People need time to be exposed to your house, and you need to continue making the consistent effort. If you follow this secret, you're 75% of the way to getting top dollar in a down market.

You Can Start Today

Don't say "If the market wasn't so bad, I'd try these ideas," or "There's so much here and most of it doesn't apply to my house." Say instead "What are the ten tips I can apply that *will* help me sell my house faster and for a better price?"

You must create compelling reasons for yourself. Why not try something new? Imagine how good it would feel to be able to sell your home quickly in a down market while other homes languish. Don't limit your beliefs. Too often we say things like, "I've already tried everything and nothing works." But it is rare that we've really tried everything (or, in fact, almost anything). Most people are afraid to step out of the norm and out of their ruts.

You have the tools to succeed. You have the knowledge, and you've done the preparation. Now it is simply a matter of putting it into action.

You have seen the importance of marketing, how tapping into buyers' emotions and values can excite them to buy your home.

7588

You know the importance of proper sales techniques.

You have seen how properly merchandising the home can appeal to the buyer's emotions.

And you've been introduced to how financing can accelerate a sale.

Your thinking is now different from that of the other sellers in your area. You will have an edge on those that are still waiting for things to get better. Will it all work right away? Maybe. Will it work eventually? It's up to you.